Praise for *Lincoln and McClellan*

"In this stimulating new book about the most puzzling personality of the Civil War and his uneasy relationship with Lincoln, Jack Waugh treats George B. McClellan with conspicuous fairness. Nevertheless, the general's glaring deficiencies, outsize ego, and petty tendency to blame others for his failures come through loud and clear, contrasting with the sure, steady, and patient demeanor of his long-suffering commander in chief."

—James McPherson, author of *Battle Cry of Freedom*

"Over the past quarter century, I have followed with great admiration Jack Waugh's rise to his current perch among the nation's preeminent Civil War historians. Each of his previous books, addressing monumental personalities associated with that searing national conflict, justifiably attracted legions of appreciative readers. But, in my opinion, *Lincoln and McClellan* represents the pinnacle of this gifted story-teller's career. It is surely his masterwork."

—Richard A. Baker, Historian Emeritus, United States Senate

"None spins a yarn more compellingly than John C. Waugh—particularly when it involves human conflict and its historical consequences. Now this gifted writer meets an irresistible subject and the result is a crackling good story about war, politics, and the clash of titanic personalities. Lincoln and McClellan come vividly to life in this book—and it is riveting to be in their company."

—Harold Holzer, author of *Lincoln: President-Elect*

"The Mathew Brady photograph pictures them facing-off after Antietam—the elongated Commander-in-Chief Lincoln confronting his short-statured commander of the Army of the Potomac, General McClellan. It is a vivid reminder of two leaders in conflict—one, self effacing but impatient, the other, self-important and arrogant. This story is told with great verve here by Jack Waugh. Wonderfully written, the author measures these leaders with a perception few possess. His effort illuminates why Lincoln was a great leader and McClellan a laggard. It is most welcome as we end Lincoln's bicentennial and begin the sesquicentennial of the Civil War."

—Frank J. Williams, founding chair of The Lincoln Forum and
a member of the U.S. Abraham Lincoln Bicentennial Commission

"John C. Waugh once again has melded an historian's skills with his experiences as a correspondent covering the Washington political scene, to give readers a tour de force. In a graceful narrative, Waugh unfolds the story of the clash of wills between President Lincoln as commander in chief and General McClellan. Because of his focus on the relationship of the commander in chief and a senior general, the book is relevant to readers today."

—Edwin Cole Bearss, author of *Fields of Honor* and
Chief Historian Emeritus, National Park

"With all the insight and verve that the history-reading public has come to expect from him, Jack Waugh has expertly brought to life on the printed page the interwoven stories of these two brilliant men and caught the essence of what prevented the success of their collaboration."

—Steven Woodworth, author of *Nothing but Victory*

"Drawing upon a wide range of personal accounts, Waugh has crafted the story of the Lincoln-McClellan relationship with an insight and an intimacy that few writers have ever achieved. A dramatic story, captivatingly told."

—James I. Robertson, Jr., author of *Stonewall Jackson:
The Man, The Soldier, The Legend*

LINCOLN AND MCCLELLAN

THE TROUBLED PARTNERSHIP BETWEEN A PRESIDENT AND HIS GENERAL

JOHN C. WAUGH

LINCOLN AND McCLELLAN
Copyright © John C. Waugh, 2010.

First published in 2010 by
PALGRAVE MACMILLAN®
in the United States—a division of St. Martin's Press LLC,
175 Fifth Avenue, New York, NY 10010.

Where this book is distributed in the UK, Europe and the rest of the world,
this is by Palgrave Macmillan, a division of Macmillan Publishers Limited,
registered in England, company number 785998, of Houndmills,
Basingstoke, Hampshire RG21 6XS.

Palgrave Macmillan is the global academic imprint of the above companies
and has companies and representatives throughout the world.

Palgrave® and Macmillan® are registered trademarks in the United States,
the United Kingdom, Europe and other countries.

ISBN: 978–0–230–61349–2

Library of Congress Cataloging-in-Publication Data

Waugh, John C.
    Lincoln and McClellan : the troubled partnership between a president
and his general / by John C. Waugh.
        p. cm.
    ISBN 978–0–230–61349–2
    1. Lincoln, Abraham, 1809–1865—Military leadership. 2. McClellan,
George Brinton, 1826–1885—Military leadership. 3. United States—
History—Civil War, 1861–1865—Campaigns. 4. Command of troops—
History—19th century. I. Title.

E457.2.W34 2010
973.7092—dc22   2010008452

A catalogue record of the book is available from the British Library.

Design by Newgen Imaging Systems (P) Ltd., Chennai, India.

First edition: May 2010

10 9 8 7 6 5 4 3 2 1

Printed in the United States of America.

For my four grandchildren,
Anna and Becky Waugh
and Wyatt and Henry Martin—
shaping a future with an appreciation of the past

CONTENTS

Photosection appears between pages 126 and 127

ACKNOWLEDGMENTS

N o book was ever written without a lot of people doing a lot of wonderful things behind the scenes. The writer may be out front, stage center, but offstage many helpful and loving supporters are making a writer's performance what it is. I am constantly aware and grateful for such help.

Some of it is always up close and personal—my wife, Kathleen D. Lively, who perennially, through ten books, has tolerated my long absences in the nineteenth century; my children, who don't have to wonder what their father is doing with his time; my grandchildren, to whom this book is dedicated, who thought me only good for loving; and my other admired relatives, who have always believed me somewhat eccentric in the first place.

I owe a good deal to a quartet a Palgrave. First in line for thanks is my editor, Alessandra Bastagli, who invested her interest and considerable skill and made this a much better book; her editorial assistant, Colleen Lawrie, so helpful with necessary details that go into getting a book out; Erica Warren, the production editor, who skillfully pulled it all together; and Debra Manette, a professional proofreader who added the polish.

My agent, Mitchell J. Hamilburg, and his now-retired associate, Joanie Kern, who have been backstage for every book I have written, were there again for this one. Special thanks to them for their always ready friendship, availability, help, and knack for interesting publishers in what I want to write.

I can't too often thank librarians and their libraries, and archivists and their archives—as essential for a writer of history as a spouse is to living. I am constantly trooping through the stacks at the three great university libraries in my part of the country, Texas Christian, Southern Methodist, and the University of Texas at Arlington, with occasional forays into the collections at Rice University in Houston and the University of Texas in Austin. I particularly want to thank Denise Arnett, the interlibrary loan librarian at the Arlington (Texas) Public Library, who so doggedly put into my hands obscure books that date back partway to the Gutenberg Bible. There is also always reason to appreciate Dr. John R. Sellers, the Civil War and Reconstruction specialist at the Manuscripts Division of the Library of Congress.

I also owe thanks to two people who understand what I clearly don't—computer technology: my son-in-law, Scott Martin, of Live on Page, who doubles as my computer guru; and Norma Pierce, of Civil War Traveler, who designed and maintains my website (www. johncwaugh.com), which she has so skillfully made award winning.

I have found in my work that fellow historians are invariably and selflessly helpful. I have on many occasions found myself being grateful in particular to that great Civil War historian Edwin Cole Bearss, a one-man truth squad, who has so often helped me avoid errors and mistakes of fact and to whom I am again grateful for keeping this book as accurate as I could make it. Any remaining gaffes are purely of my own doing.

It is also impossible to thank often enough the many readers, known and unknown, who read what I write and so often tell me how much they have enjoyed it. They are the X factor that drives the entire process.

For all of these wonderful stagehands, many thanks.

CAST OF CHARACTERS

Samuel L. M. Barlow: leading New York Democrat and close friend and confidant of McClellan

Orville Browning: U. S. senator from Illinois, a Lincoln confidant, who kept a meticulous account of their meetings in his daily diary

Catharinus P. Buckingham: Union brigadier general who delivered Lincoln's sacking order to McClellan

Ambrose Burnside: Union major general, McClellan's dear friend and successor as commander of the Army of the Potomac

Salmon Portland Chase: Lincoln's secretary of the treasury, a McClellan critic and short-time candidate for president in 1864 to unseat his boss

Andrew Curtin: Civil War governor of Pennsylvania, who was worried about Confederate invaders

Jefferson Davis: secretary of war under President Pierce and later president of the Confederate States of America

William Dennison: Civil War governor of Ohio, who won the race of governors to recruit McClellan at the beginning of the war

Stephen A. Douglas: U. S. Senator from Illinois, longtime Lincoln political rival admired by McClellan, but who died early in the war

William B. Franklin: Union major general and corps commander, an ardent McClellan ally

John Gibbon: Union brigadier general, former West Point classmate of McClellan who commanded a division in his army

Henry W. Halleck: Union major general succeeding McClellan as general in chief

John Hay: one of Lincoln's two young personal secretaries

Ambrose Powell Hill: Confederate lieutenant general, McClellan's close friend, who drove his division to rescue Lee's army at Antietam

Daniel Harvey Hill: Confederate major general in Lee's army, who held off McClellan for most of a day at South Mountain

Joseph Hooker: Union major general and corps commander, who opened the fighting for McClellan at Antietam

Thomas J. (Stonewall) Jackson: Confederate general, McClellan's West Point classmate and Lee's chief lieutenant

Joseph E. Johnston: Confederate general opposing McClellan on the Peninsula before being wounded at Fair Oaks

Robert E. Lee: Confederate general succeeding Johnston, driving McClellan in the Seven Days battles on the Peninsula and opposing him at Antietam

Abraham Lincoln: president of the United States

James Longstreet: Confederate lieutenant general in Lee's army, whom Lee affectionately called "my old war-horse"

George B. McClellan: general in chief of the Union Army succeeding Winfield Scott, and commander of the Army of the Potomac

Mary Ellen McClellan: McClellan's wife, called Nelly, his faithful confidante to whom he sent revealing messages

Irvin McDowell: major general, commander of McClellan's First Corps whose troops never made it to the Peninsula

Randolph B. Marcy: Union major general, McClellan's father-in-law and chief of staff

Montgomery Meigs: Union major general, quartermaster general of the Union army

John G. Nicolay: one of Lincoln's two young personal secretaries

Allan Pinkerton: private detective made chief of McClellan's Secret Service, wildly overestimating enemy strength

John Pope: Union major general, commander of the new Army of Virginia nd sharp McClellan critic

Fitz John Porter: Union major general, corps commander in McClellan's army and his close friend

William Howard Russell: British journalist skeptical of McClellan

Winfield Scott: general-in-chief of the Union Army before retiring November 1, 1861, and being succeeded by McClellan

William H. Seward: Lincoln's secretary of state

Edwin M. Stanton: Lincoln's hard-driving secretary of war, McClellan's erstwhile friend and ally who became his bitter enemy

J. E. B. Stuart: Lee's cavalry commander, celebrated for twice riding around McClellan's army

Benjamin F. Wade: U. S. senator from Ohio, leader of the McClellan-hating Radicals, and chairman of the Joint Committee on the Conduct of the War

Gideon Welles: Lincoln's secretary of the navy, who kept a detailed diary of men and events

A RAILCAR FOR DOUGLAS

When the war came, the president and the general were not strangers.

The new president, Abraham Lincoln, and his new major general, George Brinton McClellan, had known one another for four years before the war. McClellan had been a brilliant young officer in the Old Army, a star at West Point, a twice-brevetted hero of the U.S.–Mexican War, and the army's golden boy. But he had left the glory of military life in 1857 to become the superintendent of the Illinois Central Railroad. Lincoln was an Illinois lawyer and politician who was a sometime counsel to the line McClellan superintended.

At the end of 1857, McClellan was elevated to vice president of the line and, as such, thrown often in Lincoln's company. "More than once," McClellan later wrote, "I have been with [Lincoln] in out-of-the-way county seats where some important case was being tried, and, in the lack of sleeping accommodations, have spent the night in front of a stove listening to the unceasing flow of anecdotes from his lips."[1]

The anecdotes were often as rough-hewn as their teller. They smacked of "frontier freedom" and "would not always bear repetition in a drawing room."[2] And they rather rubbed McClellan the wrong way. "Lincoln's stories were seldom refined," McClellan remembered, and he was "never at a loss" for one. "I could never quite make up my mind how many of them he had really heard before, and how many he invented on the spur of the moment," but they were "always to the point."[3]

McClellan came to believe that Lincoln was "a rare bird."[4] His impression of the gangly, rough-timbered human tower from the Illinois frontier—six feet four inches high, a giant for his time—was mixed. He could see that Lincoln was an able lawyer, but he was hardly refined enough for McClellan's patrician taste shaped by a boyhood in the upper strata of Philadelphia society. McClellan had viewed Lincoln then, in the late 1850s, as he still viewed him four years later—as his social, intellectual, and moral inferior.[5]

Aside from his view of Lincoln as inferior to himself, McClellan had also seen him as too rare a bird to support politically.

Lincoln's main rival in Illinois politics for a quarter of a century had been Stephen A. Douglas, the "Little Giant," the U.S. senator from the state since 1847, and a Democrat. When Lincoln, a refugee from the shattered Whig Party, newly converted to the Republican, challenged Douglas for his Senate seat in what led to the celebrated "great debates" in 1858, McClellan left little doubt where he stood.

Douglas had been the godfather of the Illinois Central. The line owed its existence to the squat little Democrat, who had pushed the first land-grant railroad bill in history through Congress in 1850. Construction on the line began the next year and was completed in September 1856, only months before McClellan became its superintendent.

It was the first of the great land-grant railroads. Endowed with two and a half million acres of government land granted by Douglas's bill, it was, when completed, the longest rail line under one management in the world. Its 700 miles of track ran through prairie and wilderness the length of Illinois south to north, from Cairo, where the Ohio River emptied into the Mississippi, to Galena in the state's extreme northwest corner. A trunk line ran from Centralia to Chicago. The new railroad had opened to settlement the thousands of square miles of rich unplowed prairie through which it passed. Thousands of farms had followed its tracks and turned Illinois into an economic and political powerhouse.[6]

McClellan described Douglas, the benefactor of the line, as "a small, quick person, with a large head & a quick, bright eye."[7] And he liked and admired him. He particularly liked his politics, compared to those of the sometime attorney for his railroad, the frontier specimen for whom he had no special affinity.

In the campaign for the Senate seat that pitted those two political giants against one another in Illinois in 1858, McClellan early chose sides. In May 1857, he issued a pass to Douglas that let the senator travel the road anywhere, anytime, free of charge. He told Douglas, "Be kind enough to inform me what train you wish to go, that a suitable car may be placed at your disposal."[8]

When the Senate campaign opened, McClellan marshaled the resources of the Illinois Central behind the Little Giant's reelection bid. The senator rode the rails from campaign stop to campaign stop in McClellan's own plush personal railcar, bunting bedecked with flags flying, coupled to a platform car mounting a brass twelve-pounder, which boomed the great man's arrivals. In every town at every stop, this curious coupling on the rails was met by brass bands, jubilation, and pomp.[9] McClellan is said to have traveled often in the car with the senator and to at least one of his seven celebrated face-to-face debates with Lincoln.

And he did favors less visible for the Little Giant. Tipped off before election day that an Illinois Central special train had been chartered to carry Lincoln partisans into a county to vote illegally—not a unique practice in that time—McClellan told the road's superintendent: "I don't care how you accomplish it but that train must *not* reach its destination." Halfway there, the locomotive hauling the would-be voters broke down, stranding them past poll closing time.[10]

Now, four years later, the stars in crisis had worked to elect Lincoln president and raise McClellan to major general under him. In their rising and coming together again in Washington, in the summer of 1861, they had both been comets. And they were not strangers.

But nothing in their shared past was likely to matter now to either man. Both—Lincoln the president and McClellan his general—were intent in 1861 only on putting down a nation-threatening rebellion and saving the Union. They were in it together when and where it really mattered, whether they wanted to be or not—at the highest echelon, where the future of the young republic was at stake.

CHAPTER 1

PARALLEL BEGINNINGS

The Lincoln ancestral line, originating in the west of England, began migrating to Massachusetts in the first half of the seventeenth century. Some of it began drifting southwestward from there to New Jersey, to Pennsylvania, to Virginia—and then through the Cumberland Gap into Kentucky. There, on February 12, 1809, on a hardscrabble farm near a sinking spring on Nolen Creek in Harden County, Abraham Lincoln was born. His father was Thomas Lincoln, a struggling, illiterate farmer-carpenter. His mother was Nancy Hanks, carried into Kentucky in childhood, like her husband, through the Cumberland Gap from Virginia.

Their newborn son, named for Abraham, his grandfather on his father's side, was second in the line to a sister, Sarah, born two years before. The small family lived in a one-room log cabin until Lincoln was two years old, when Thomas moved them to another hardscrabble farm in Knob Creek valley ten miles northeast of Nolen Creek. There beside the Cumberland Road from Louisville to Nashville, the heaviest-traveled highway on the Kentucky frontier, Lincoln lived to age seven. Those were the first years he remembered.

Seeking a better venue in better soil, Thomas moved his family yet again, to the new state of Indiana, in late 1816. He settled them on a claim in Spencer County on Little Pigeon Creek in the southern quadrant of the state sixteen miles north of the Ohio River—on the "rough frontier line" where "the panther's scream, filled night with fear/And bears preyed on the swine."[1]

It was a hard, dangerous beginning. Thomas at first sheltered them in a "half-faced camp," a rough structure with no floor and open on one side.[2] And the first two years ended in a shattering sadness. In 1818, Lincoln's mother, Nancy, said to be "touched with the divine aptitudes of the fireside,"[3] came down with a deadly affliction gripping the frontier called the "milk sick," caught from cows that had fed on white snakeroot. Her death devastated the family. Lincoln's cousin Dennis Hanks, said, "Oh Lord, oh Lord, I'll never furget it, the mizry in that cabin in the woods when Nancy died."[4]

Thomas could stand the misery for only so long without a companion for himself and a mother for his children. In late 1819, he rode back to Kentucky to try his luck. He remembered Sarah Johnston, a woman he had known before, now a widow with three children of her own. Wasting no time or words, he said to her, "Well, *Miss* Johnson [*sic*], I have no wife & you have no husband. I came *a* purpose to mary you[,] I *knowed* you from a *gal* & you *knowed* me from a boy. I have no time to lose and if you are willing, let it be done Straight off."

Sarah is said to have said, "Tommy I know you well & have no objection to marrying you, but I cannot do it straight off as I owe some debts that must first be paid." Tom covered her debts that same day, and the next, December 2, 1819, they were married. They packed all she owned and her three children, ages nine, seven, and five, in a four-horse wagon and left for Indiana. There Sarah became an instant and beloved mother to her two new stepchildren.[5]

In his growing-up years in Indiana, Lincoln was developing into a strapping specimen, beginning his rise to his six-foot-four-inch height, and Thomas put an ax in his hands. Lincoln proved to be quick with it. Dennis Hanks would one day say, "You'd 'a' thought there was two men in the woods when he got into it with an ax."[6] But he was also said to be quick with a book when he could borrow one on the book-deprived frontier, an inclination his stepmother encouraged and applauded because she saw something special in her young stepson. She called him "diligent for Knowledge."[7] Dennis Hanks said, "Seems to me now I never seen Abe after he was twelve 'at he didn't have a book in his hand or in his pocket...constant and I may say stubborn reader." To Dennis, "it didn't seem natural, nohow, to see a feller read like that."[8]

This stubborn diligence for knowledge and for getting it on his own was the only way Lincoln would ever get it. There was little formal schooling on the frontier. First in Kentucky in the 1810s and then in Indiana in the 1820s, where work came first and education was catch-as-catch-can, Lincoln scratched out a bare minimum—less than a year—of organized education in blab schools. The teacher spoke a lesson and the students blabbed it back in unison. A teacher supposed to understand Latin was "looked on as a wizard."[9] It would be all the formal schooling he would ever have.

Lincoln was a seventeen-year-old swinging his ax and reading books on his father's Indiana farm when George Brinton McClellan was born on December 3, 1826, the third child and second son of George McClellan and Elizabeth Brinton McClellan, in the upper professional and social echelon of the Philadelphia gentry. The infant McClellan was baptized at St. Peter's Episcopal Church in Philadelphia, where he took his first and last names from his father and his middle name from his mother—an amalgam, the best from both.[10] While Lincoln's father was an unlettered—but skilled—carpenter, McClellan's father was a very literate and skilled Philadelphia physician, one of the most respected in the country, a pioneering surgeon said to be gifted with "skill and quickness of touch."[11] He graduated from Yale College in 1816 and studied medicine at the University of Pennsylvania, winning a doctorate in the spring of 1819, with a thesis on tying arteries. In his professional life as a practicing surgeon, he specialized in ophthalmology.[12]

McClellan's father was also a teacher, as distinguished an educator as he was a surgeon, a founder and guiding hand of the Jefferson Medical College in Philadelphia. There he taught anatomy and surgery, and his lectures, one observer recalled, "were models of terse statement and lucid analysis." Another said of him, "He taught, executed, and communicated in a day more than others did in a week—his weeks were months of ordinary men. . . . He consequently distanced his contemporaries, and, as a youth, was found among his seniors and the master-spirits of his profession."[13]

The father's quickness was not just in surgery—he owned a string of fast trotters, which he ran on the racetracks in Philadelphia. While courtly and charming, he was also quick to embrace an opinion and tenacious and uncompromising in holding to it. He had a lightning disposition to go with his quick scalpel and his fast trotters.[14] These were qualities likely to be handed down in a son's genes.

McClellan's gifted, warmhearted mother, who had married his father in 1820, was deep-rooted in the Pennsylvania ethos, descended from its original Quaker settlers.[15] His ancestral line on his father's side snaked from the McClellans of Scotland, where one of his distant forebears fought with Braveheart, the Scottish rebel William Wallace, in the thirteenth century. Three brothers in the McClellan line immigrated to America in the early eighteenth century. One of these, McClellan's grandfather Samuel, fought in the French and Indian Wars and on Bunker Hill in the Revolution, and rose to be a brigadier general in the Connecticut militia.[16] The beat of the military drum also pounded loudly in the young McClellan's genes.

When McClellan was only four years old, in the spring of 1830, Lincoln had reached maturity, and his father again had moving on his mind. Tom had heard that the prospects were good and the soil was rich in Illinois. So they moved again, a family grown to thirteen since all but Lincoln had married and had children of their own. With Lincoln driving one of three ox-drawn wagons, they crossed the Wabash in the spring of 1830 and settled on land overlooking the Sangamon River near Decatur in central Illinois.

His duty done, Lincoln struck out on his own in 1831, to the small new frontier village of New Salem, northwest of Springfield. There, taking odd jobs, he launched on a program to better himself and carve out some kind of a future.

Young George McClellan, far more privileged by birth, was growing up and getting the best education Philadelphia offered. At age five, he was attending what was called an infant school. The next four years he was enrolled in a private school, and at age ten he studied with a private tutor, "a one-eyed German Jew by the name of Schiffer," who grounded the young scholar in the classics. In 1838, at the age of eleven, able to converse in both Latin and French, he was enrolled in a preparatory academy of the University of Pennsylvania, and at age thirteen he matriculated to the university itself. By age fifteen, he had completed a classical education.[17] In learning he was a rocket, as quick with mathematics, literature, and language as his father was with a scalpel.

As he was growing up, McClellan thought to become a lawyer, a chosen profession for gifted, precocious, and ambitious young men of his time. But he was hearing that pounding of the drum in his genes.

In 1842, instead of going into the law, he went to West Point. He was legally too young for the academy—not yet sixteen—but he went anyhow. And West Point, knowing an exception when it saw one, waived the rule and enrolled him anyhow.

In Illinois, Lincoln got into politics. He became a Whig in what was a Democratic state, and in 1832 he ran for the state legislature from New Salem in a short and failed campaign. He ran again in 1834, and this time was elected. By 1836, in his second term, he had become a leader of his party in the state assembly.

By the early summer of 1842, when McClellan was climbing for the first time from the boat landing on the Hudson River up to the plain at West Point, Lincoln had become a lawyer, self-taught. He had moved to Springfield, the new state capital, in 1836 to practice his new profession. Still on the rise in politics, he was reelected to the legislature for two more terms. By 1840, he had become a leader of his party statewide.

For the next four years, while McClellan and his classmates studied to become engineers and officers in the army, Lincoln immersed himself ever deeper in politics as he continued to shape a career in the law. It was not thought inconceivable that he would one day step up to a higher elective office. He had a certain bipartisan appeal, partly because of his gift for telling a story. Recognizing that talent, the Democrats, his political enemies, persuaded him in the summer of 1842 to help them entertain the Democratic ex-president, Martin Van Buren, who was traveling through Illinois. Lincoln had worked hard to help defeat the "Little Magician" in the 1840 presidential election, won by the Whig William Henry Harrison. Now Lincoln was spending an evening swapping stories with his old political target.[18]

McClellan, in his first days at West Point in that same summer, found himself in one of the most beautiful settings in America. Savage, majestic cliffs plunged dramatically from the plain to the dark-running river, overhung by "woods climbing above woods, to the clouds and stretching to the horizon."[19] It was a setting in which nature had worked a masterpiece.

None of this mattered to McClellan. He was feeling homesick and abandoned—"as much alone," he wrote home, "as if in a boat in the middle of the Atlantic." Not a soul, he grieved, "cares for, or thinks of me. Not one here would lift a finger to help me; I am entirely dependent on myself—must think for myself—direct myself, & take the blame of all my mistakes, without anyone to give me a word of advice."[20]

But that would pass. His classmates were not seeing him as he was at first seeing himself. Everyone was a conditional cadet those first weeks and months at the academy—pending passing a fundamental physical, a small battery of entry tests, and turning in worthy early performances on the drill field and at the blackboard. One of McClellan's fellow conditionals, Dabney Herndon Maury, a Virginian almost too old for West Point as McClellan was too young, met the teenage Philadelphian and thought him "such a little bred and born gentleman, only fifteen years and seven months, while I—God save the Mark—was twenty."[21]

As McClellan had been a rocket in his early learning years in Philadelphia, he soon proved also a rocket at West Point. The first day in class, Maury found himself seated next to the precocious teenager, purely by the logic of the alphabet. That juxtaposition would not last long. The next week McClellan left for the section at the head of the class, Maury complained, "while I remained *tutisimus in medio* [securely in the middle] four blessed years." Maury was "very sorry to lose Mac from my side, especially during recitations, for he used to tell me things, and was a great help."[22]

McClellan would entrench himself at the top of the class or next to it throughout his four years at West Point, glorying in what he was becoming. He was becoming passionately taken with military engineering and military tactics—the two pursuits West Point at that time was mainly about.

The only classmate at West Point who regularly shaded McClellan in class ranking was Charles Seaforth Stewart, whose middle name owed to his having been born at sea—in the middle of the Pacific—the sole son of a navy chaplain and missionary. Stewart had an even more high-powered educational grounding before West Point than McClellan; he had been seasoned at a crack preparatory school in New Jersey. He would best McClellan in the end, finishing first, with McClellan second and not happy about it. McClellan had wanted to place first, intended to, and vowed he would. It was a disappointment, the only thing in his West Point experience he could justifiably complain about.

Stewart said of McClellan, "He was a noble, generous-hearted, clear-headed enthusiastic, able fellow. There was not a mean thought in him. He was well educated, and, when he chose to be, brilliant. In every point so far as I can recall, he was true and honorable, and our personal relations were always very pleasant as cadets."[23]

But class ranking had little to do with intangibles. And in those, McClellan finished in solid first place. "A pleasanter pupil," one of his instructors said of him, "was never called to the blackboard."[24] It was an assessment widely shared by his classmates. They all thought him "prepossessing," yet with all that he "bore every evidence of gentle nature and high culture, and his countenance was as charming as his demeanor was modest and winning."[25] They had little doubt who their real star was. It was not the cadet born at sea but the young one born to the gentry in Philadelphia. One classmate spoke for all when he thought McClellan "the ablest man in the class.... We expected him to make a great record in the army, and if opportunity presented, we predicted real military fame for him."[26]

McClellan graduated in the class of 1846 with fifty-eight classmates, a melting pot of young men from all of the twenty-six states in the Union and from "every degree of provincialism."[27] It included a countrified cadet from the hills of western Virginia, Thomas Jonathan Jackson, who had started at the foot of the class but had clawed his way up to a respectable seventeenth of the fifty-nine by graduation time.

Jackson and McClellan, though classmates, had not been particular friends. Generally, however, McClellan, with his patrician ways, preferred Southerners to Northerners. "I am sorry to say," he wrote home, "that the manners, feelings & opinions of the Southerners are far, far preferable to those of the majority of the Northerners at this place. I may be mistaken, but I like them better."[28] The Union-shattering issue of slavery, hovering on the horizon, did not yet stir these young men's emotions. There was as yet no clear line North and South drawn on the plain at West Point.

In May 1846, double happiness, however, came on the plain for McClellan and his classmates. They were about to graduate, and war had come to oblige their new soldierhood. That month President James K. Polk requested, and Congress dutifully declared, war on Mexico. "Hip! Hip! Hurrah!" McClellan wrote home. "War at last sure enough! Aint it glorious!" Having graduated, he figured he would now doubtless be going direct to the Halls of the Montezumas to fight "the crowd—musquitoes & Mexicans &c."[29] Life was good.

The members of this biggest-ever graduating class had longed all spring for a war to go to, star in, become heroes in, and win promotion in. There was not much thought about dying in it. Action was as ardently desired as graduation itself. "Nothing is heard but promotion, glory and laurels," one of McClellan's classmates wrote home.[30]

McClellan did not go immediately to the seat of war in Mexico, as he ardently hoped. His getting there was roundabout and delayed. He had been handpicked to be one of three officers—the junior of the three—to command, organize, train, and then take to Mexico a special company of sappers, miners, and pontooners—an engineering outfit, the first of its kind in the American army. It was to be constituted at West Point. Thus McClellan's first step to war and to Mexico went only as far as across the plain.

But it was only delay to war, not denial. By the end of September, the three officers had recruited and whipped the company—which would become known as "the pick and shovel brigade"[31]—into shape and had it on a ship on its way from New York City to Brazos de Santiago at the mouth of the Rio Grande, in Mexico.

It was neither war nor glory that McClellan found first. It was "musquitoes." Under their attack, he came down with malaria. It was touch and go for a time—he nearly died. However, being of sturdy body and rugged constitution, he was nursed back to health within a month by his West Point roommate, Jimmy Stuart, a South Carolinian who had arrived in Mexico with the Mounted Rifles. West Point continued to bless its own.

Recovered, McClellan was soon having the time of his life. "You never saw a merry set as we are," he joyously wrote home. "[N]o care, no trouble—we criticize the Generals—laugh & swear at the mustangs & volunteers." A regular officer, he assured his mother, "has no fixed habits—"it is immaterial to him whether he gets up at 2 A.M., or 9—or whether he don't go to bed at all. When on a march we get up at 2 or 3, when we halt, we *snooze* it, til 8 or 9—when we have cigars we smoke them, when we have none, we go without—when we have brandy, we drink it, when we have not, we make it up by laughing at our predicament—that is the way we live."[32]

As with many of the other thirty of his classmates bound for the various theaters of the war, McClellan and his company were eventually folded into General-in-Chief Winfield Scott's army in its stirring march from Veracruz to Mexico City. It was a conquest built on history, along the same National Road Hernando Cortés had followed in his subjugation of Mexico 325 years before.

McClellan was one of Scott's engineers, often working side by side with another engineer, a Virginian, Captain Robert E. Lee, who carved out a heroic reputation in the war primarily for his sagacious and daring reconnoitering of enemy positions. And McClellan fashioned a heroic reputation of his own. At the fighting at Contreras on the outskirts of Mexico City, two horses were shot from under him as he was placing into position the battery of Tom Jackson, his West Point classmate, now an artillery lieutenant.

When the war ended, McClellan had been twice brevetted—to captain—for gallantry under fire, and had survived in spite of the heroics and the shot-from-under horses. When Scott rode into Mexico City on September 14, 1847, a conqueror of the Montezumas worthy of Cortés, McClellan was there, and sighing with relief. "Here we are—the deed is done," he said, "I am glad no one can say 'poor Mac' over me."[33]

He returned to West Point with his pick-and-shovel company, alive and riding high on heroism and accomplishment, with his two brevet promotions and ever more enhanced self-esteem. There was no longer a war, but the future in the army for this young officer looked more than promising.

There were no such heroics for Abraham Lincoln over the Mexican War, and no promise from it. Quite the opposite. As McClellan and his classmates were graduating from West Point, Lincoln, who had continued his steady rise in politics in Illinois, was running successfully for the U.S. Congress. As a member from 1847 to 1849, he had vigorously denounced the war McClellan was fighting, charging President Polk with waging it unprovoked against a weaker nation on the most questionable of grounds. It was the prevailing Whig position.

On January 12, 1848, in a speech on the House floor, Lincoln charged the president with having waged an unnecessary and unconstitutional war based on "the sheerest deception" from "beginning to end."[34] He introduced a failed resolution challenging the "spot" where Polk claimed the war was started by Mexico. This attack from an obscure frontier Whig freshman congressman did not trouble Polk all that much, but it did not sit well with Lincoln's constituency. It is not a wise and popular thing to oppose a war your country is waging.

The feeling against him at home was not likely to catapult him into a second term. He therefore did not even try for reelection but retired a one-term congressman with an unremarkable record and a tarnished reputation.

When McClellan returned home a hero from the war, Lincoln returned home a nonhero. In effect turned out of office, his future political prospects were dim and uncertain.

CHAPTER 2

BETWEEN TWO WARS

As the decade of the 1850s opened, the slaveholding South and the antislavery North were at one another's throats. The issue then, as in a face-off thirty years before, was over whether slaves and slavery would be allowed in a vast swatch of new-won territory.

In 1820, the battleground had been over admitting slaves into the huge Louisiana Purchase territory north of the state of Louisiana— the South demanding that right and threatening secession without it, the North denying it. The fierce threat of disunion then by Southerners was deflected only by a hard-won compromise that drew a line through the territory at 36 minutes, 30 degrees latitude, with slavery expansion permitted in the territories south of it and prohibited in the territories north of it.

Now another huge swatch, of land, newly wrested from Mexico in the U.S.-Mexican War and stretching across the Southwest through the New Mexico and Arizona territories to California, was raising the same issue yet again: to what extent, if any, would slavery be admitted into this new territory. Southerners again demanded an unrestricted right to take slaves into it, when and where they pleased; Northerners again heatedly resisted. Secession was again threatened by the South, more fiercely than before.

A second compromise, hammered out on the floor of the U.S. Senate over nine months in 1850, much of it during a sweltering, debate-riddled Washington summer, again deflected the anger—for a time.

Tempers cooled to a livable level, the cry of disunion died down, but the rumble remained.

Politically hampered by his opposition to the Mexican War, out of office and not planning to run for reelection, Lincoln returned to his law practice in Illinois in 1849. There he spent the next half decade in virtual political exile, traveling as a lawyer over the sprawling Eighth Judicial Circuit six months of each of those five years, gaining prestige in the law but figuring any bright future in politics was nonexistent.

Lawyers riding the circuit—taking the law, court and all, to county seats where lawyers were rare but cases were not—traveled through fourteen counties in central Illinois from the Illinois River eastward to the Indiana line. The circuit encompassed nearly a fifth of the area of the state—11,000 square miles, across "desolate and solitary prairies, devious roads or no roads at all." It was twenty to nearly seventy miles between county seats, and there were few rails to ride on the Illinois prairie in the early 1850s. So the lawyers—as many as twenty-five or thirty at a time—and their traveling judge covered them by buggy or by horseback. Lincoln rode from county seat to county seat in "a rattle-trap buggy" pulled by a rawboned horse named "Old Buck," at a clip of four to five miles an hour.[1]

This "ambulatory bar" was something of a traveling road show. When it hit a county courthouse, the town turned out. The circuit-riding judge held court for three days to a week and tried the cases the local clients brought. On the Eighth Circuit laughter and wit came with the justice—largely because of Lincoln and his stories, told in the evenings after court adjourned for the day.[2]

Lincoln was not a case-reading, precedent-citing lawyer. "Practically," his law partner, William H. Herndon, believed, "he knew nothing of the rules of evidence, of pleading or practice, as laid down in the text-books, and seemed to care nothing about them." But he had "a keen sense of justice, and struggled for it, throwing aside forms, methods, and rules, until it appeared pure as a ray of light flashing through a fog-bank." When he did have to learn or investigate a subject, Herndon said, "he was thorough and indefatigable in his search. He not only went to the root of the question, but dug up the root, and separated and analyzed every fibre of it." But he never crammed on any question until he had a case in which the question was involved. "He thought slowly and acted slowly," Herndon said; "he must have time to analyze all the facts in a case and wind them into a connected story."[3]

And often in a courtroom he would weave a story suited to the case. This made him "a jury lawyer," who "played on the human heart as a master on an instrument," said his fellow lawyer and friend James S. Ewing.[4] Another lawyer who was a stranger to Lincoln and his ways told Usher F. Linder, who often practiced on the circuit with Lincoln, that his storytelling was a waste of time. "Don't lay that flattering unction to your soul," Linder answered. "Lincoln is like Tansey's horse, he breaks to win."[5]

Lawyering on the circuit—winning some, losing some—suited Lincoln's instincts, talents, and style. His personality, character, appearance—his entire persona and aspect—fit its rough-and-tumble fabric.

"Imagine," wrote Henry C. Whitney, a lawyer who often traveled with Lincoln on the circuit, "a loose-jointed, carelessly attired, homely man, with a vacant, mischievous look and mien, awkwardly halting along in the suburbs of the little prairie village, in the midst of a crowd of wild, Western lawyers, he towering above the rest, taking in the whole landscape, with an apparent vacuity of stare, but with deep penetration and occult vision." That was Lincoln, whose lawyering was at full throttle but whose political hopes lay dormant.[6]

Just as Lincoln's political star had seemingly set, McClellan's military star began rising. For three years following his return from the Mexican War, he was reassigned to West Point with his engineer company. It was a slow start up the ladder, and a relatively unhappy time. Though gifted with a charming personality, he was inclined to bristle under superiors he believed inferior to himself and with whom he openly differed. He could not get along with the superintendent of the academy, who was something of a martinet. McClellan grew restive, lobbying unrelentingly for reassignment, wearing thin the patience of the chief of engineers, Joseph G. Totten, with complaints about how he was being treated and requests for different duty.[7]

This inability to get along with those in authority was emerging as a dominant trait of this brilliant young officer. Like his father, now deceased, McClellan was quick to come to a concrete opinion, adamant in holding to it, and warlike in defending it against all contrary opinion and evidence.

After three years of duty at West Point, McClellan's wishes to move on were finally gratified. He was ordered to the Pea Patch, an island in the Delaware River south of Philadelphia, for temporary engineering work on the construction of Fort Delaware. There followed a few months in the national capital preparing a bayonet manual he had written at West Point for publication.

Then, turning his eyes to the setting sun, he lobbied for an assignment in the far West, so much of it still so unexplored and unknown. Gratified also in this, he was assigned second in command of an expedition to track the source of the Red River. There he found a superior officer, Captain Randolph B. Marcy, whom he could get along with. It was a happy assignment for McClellan, but by its nature also a passing one.

In July 1852, the Red River expedition ended, and McClellan was ordered to Texas as an aide to the department commander, who was inspecting posts on the frontier. In the fall of the year he was put to work surveying rivers and harbors on the Texas coast.

His reputation was rapidly ascending. Isaac I. Stevens, a one-time army engineer, now governor of Washington territory, had taken note of it. Congress had authorized the War Department, under its new secretary, Jefferson Davis of Mississippi, to conduct surveys to explore the most money-wise and geologically friendly route for a transcontinental railroad from the Mississippi River to the Pacific. Stevens was charged with conducting a survey of likely routes for a line from St. Paul to Puget Sound. It was to be the most ambitious exploration yet undertaken by the army. He needed an officer of McClellan's talents to command the survey of the northernmost of the routes under consideration— between the 47th and 49th parallels, inland from the Pacific coast over the uncharted Cascade Range.

Stevens told McClellan that "the expedition will be altogether the most complete that has ever set out in this country."[8] It excited McClellan's imagination and squared with his ambitions. He accepted the assignment immediately. For three months in 1853, he commanded a party looking for a likely pass for a railroad through the mountains in the Cascades between the Columbia River and the Canadian line. Opting on the side of caution, he found no route that he thought feasible. Another, bolder expedition sent out later found two promising passes through the mountains that he had not.

It was a rare failure for McClellan. As was his way, he would not see it as in any way his fault, and was furious with Stevens. "I have done my last service under civilians & politicians," McClellan raged in his journal, "I will not consent to serve any longer under Gov. S. unless he promises in no way to interfere—merely to give the general orders & never to say one word as to the means or time of executing them."[9] The two men were alienated.

McClellan was in no way, however, alienated from the secretary of war. Davis, himself a West Pointer, had also taken note of the young officer from Philadelphia and had made him his protégé. McClellan charmed the Davises, both the secretary and his wife, Varina. She said of him, "Captain McClellan was quite young, and looked younger than he really was from an inveterate habit of blushing when suddenly addressed; his modesty, his gentle manner, and the appositeness of the few remarks he made, gave us a most favorable impression of him."[10]

From Davis's bounty in 1855 first came McClellan's promotion to captain and orders to the newly organized First Cavalry Regiment on the frontier. He would never ride with the regiment, however, for on the heels of that appointment came the choicest favor the secretary could bestow on a young officer: assignment to an elite three-member commission to Europe, where the Crimean War was raging, to study the art of war and the European organization of armies.

The commission reeked with prestige. Its other two members were steeped in experience, both graduates of West Point before McClellan was born: Major Richard Delafield, first in his class in 1818, a fortifications expert and superintendent of the academy during the first two years that McClellan was a cadet; and Major Alfred Mordecai, first in the class of 1823, an ordinance specialist.

Both of these veteran officers nearly lapped the twenty-eight-year-old McClellan in years. But brash and self-confident as well as young, McClellan early became dismissive of their prestige, their seniority, their expertise, and their talents. He wrote the wife of Randolph Marcy: "Of my two friends one [Mordecai] gives me much trouble—he is a confirmed old fogie—raising objections...humming and hawing at everything—he may once have been a very good officer—but he is altogether too old and worthless now—the lord deliver me from all such hereafter." To his brother John McClellan he wrote, "But the d---d old fogies!! I hope that I may never be tied to two corpses again—it is a hell upon earth—but thank heaven can't last forever."[11]

It lasted a year, and McClellan returned home steeped in the European way of waging war, and with a knack for strategic analysis.

The report he wrote from this assignment won him yet more praise and prestige. So did the idea for a saddle he introduced into the American army, patterned on a Hungarian model used by the Prussian cavalry and easy on the hindquarters. The McClellan saddle would become standard in the American army in 1859. The young officer was, among other talents, an innovator, something of the beau ideal of what a young officer ought to be. Only thirty-one years old, he was riding the highest of reputations. It was at this high tide, at the crest of his army career, that he decided to leave it.[12]

Knowing McClellan was about to resign from the army and was looking for a position in the business world worthy of his talents and reputation, Abram S. Hewitt, a director and executive board member of the new-laid Illinois Central Railroad, urged the line to snap him up. "He is an A-1 man and I wanted to get him before," Hewitt wrote his associates. "He is a gentleman of lengthened education, and for mental and physical endurance has no rival in the army...in my judgment the best man to be secured in the country."[13]

In January 1857, McClellan was hired as chief engineer of the line—at a salary of $3,000 a year, a sharp spike upward over the less than $1,500 he was making as a captain in the army—and the promise of its accelerating soon to a whopping $5,000, far above average, with the prospect of early further promotion.[14]

McClellan's army friends were puzzled. One of them, J. K. Duncan, wrote him: "We are wondering here what induced you to take off the harness. A Young Captain, cock-full of big war science, the Secretary for a patron, and the chance of dying gloriously among the Siwash on the frontier, were supposed to be glory enough to reconcile anyone to inspecting horse blankets through the short period of our human existence, three score and ten."[15]

McClellan was soon riding as high on the railroad as he had been in the army. Within the year he was promoted to vice president, running the line in Illinois. With the perks of high position came the private railcar, outfitted for prestige and comfort, with bed and sofa.

For the first four years of the new decade, as McClellan was making big tracks in the West and big strides in reputation, Lincoln had continued practicing law in partial political eclipse. Then something dramatic happened. In early 1854, Stephen A. Douglas, his old Illinois rival, powered through the U.S. Senate and into law the Kansas-Nebraska

Act. It was intended to make way for the country's conquest of the West over yet-to-be laid intercontinental rail lines. One of its provisions abolished the most critical "line" laid down across the slavery controversy—the divide across the Louisiana Purchase territory in 1820, reconfirmed in 1850, that confined slavery south of 36′ 30°. Douglas's new law permitted slavery to spread anywhere into any territory, North or South, if the people there desired it. Whether a territory would become free or slave was entirely up to its citizens. This doctrine was called "popular sovereignty," and whether slavery was voted up or down did not matter as long as it was the will of the people.

The permissive new law awoke the fitfully sleeping North–South anger over slavery, unchained a dormant demon, and catapulted Abraham Lincoln back onto the political stage. Lincoln said the abolishment of the politically sacred line that had confined slavery in the territories for more than three decades "aroused him as he had never been before."

Lincoln had not been idle in exile. As he rode the circuit, he had closely studied this incendiary issue that seemed threatening to shatter the Union. He had read widely and thought deeply on it. Although he had stepped away from active politics in the half decade since leaving Congress, he had continued to be the man his party in Illinois thought of for important occasions. When the Whig president Zachary Taylor died in 1850 and the great Whig senator Henry Clay in 1852, Lincoln had been called to speak their elegies. He had also campaigned sporadically for Winfield Scott, when that general had run unsuccessfully as the Whig candidate for president in 1852.

Lincoln had also quietly been honing not only his grip on the slavery issue but his analytical powers, reading and mastering the six books of Euclid. He was reading Shakespeare and other poets, adding an edge to his eloquence.

When Douglas put popular sovereignty at the forefront of his slavery strategy, Lincoln railed against it. He charged that it ignored the moral issue—that slavery is wrong. Lincoln believed nothing could be done about slavery in the states where it already existed but that it must not be permitted to spread into the territories. Only by containing the "peculiar institution," as slavery was then called, would it ever find its way to ultimate extinction. Its ultimate extinction was what Lincoln was seeking, and he believed it would never happen under Douglas's popular sovereignty doctrine. Indeed, slavery would be set in concrete "alike lawful in *all* the States, *old* as well as *new*—*North* as well as *South*."[16]

When the Kansas-Nebraska bill passed into law, Lincoln began building a strong argument against it and against the spread of slavery into the territories under any conditions. Drawing on all of his years of preparation as he had traveled the circuit, he honed his argument. What he was saying and how he was saying it were so powerful that the enemies of the bill turned to him as their spokesman. He had no legal standing. He was not an officeholder. He had no particular mandate to confront Douglas. Yet he just seemed, by the strength of his argument, to be the one to do it. On August 26, the Scott County Whig convention was in session in the courthouse in Winchester. Lincoln attended. He had "got up a speech on the Kansas-Nebraska bill," one friend noted, "which he has never made before and he has come down here to 'try it on the dog' before he delivers it to larger audiences." Called to the podium, Lincoln tried it on the dog standing in front of the judge's seat. The pro-Lincoln newspaper the *Illinois Journal* called it "ably and eloquently" done, a "masterly effort...replete with unanswerable arguments."[17]

As Douglas rode the rails from Washington to Chicago, past his own burning effigies, to defend his new law in Illinois in 1854, Lincoln, armed and ready, stepped forward to meet him. On October 3, Douglas spoke in the Hall of Representatives in Springfield. Lincoln, listening in the audience, rose and announced that he would answer the senator the next day. He did so, and continued to do so wherever Douglas spoke. This marked Lincoln's return to the political stage. And because of what he was saying and the fact that he was boldly and successfully challenging one of the preeminent and most powerful stump speakers in the country, he was attracting attention. As he continued to speak out on the issue, refining and sharpening his argument, his prestige in politics quickened to match McClellan's in the army and on the railroad.

Despite McClellan's success and soaring prestige, working on the railroad was not completely satisfying to him. It did not have the same romance and self-gratification of his army years. As he ran the line and rode the rails in his private railcar, he hankered to return to the call of the trumpet and the pounding of the drum. He even considered for a passing time joining friends from the Old Army in the ill-fated filibustering campaign in Nicaragua.

He wrote his old Red River expedition commander and continuing friend, Randolph Marcy, who was in the army putting down the Mormon uprising in Utah: "I still hope to reenter the service if we ever have another war, but I believe that I have seen enough of peace service."[18]

He wrote Mrs. Marcy, now also a close and continuing friend, "If affairs [in Utah] take a turn at all serious, I have determined to give up my present position with all its advantages of high pay, etc., and reenter the service, at least until the trouble is over—I cannot bear the idea of my old friends being in campaign without me."[19]

He wrote his friend Samuel L. M. Barlow in New York, "The plain truth of the matter is that the war horse can't stand quietly by, when he hears the sound of the trumpet.... Railroading is all very well—my position is satisfactory enough—but I like the old business better.... Life is too short to waste bickering about cross ties and contracts—I cannot learn to love it."[20]

Nothing, however, came of all this. Instead, McClellan moved even higher in the calling he could not learn to love. Leaving the Illinois Central in September 1860 to become president of the Ohio & Mississippi River Railroad headquartered in Cincinnati, he was proving very talented at bickering over cross ties and contracts.

What he could learn to love—and desperately did—was Captain and Mrs. Marcy's daughter. On the Red River, Marcy had talked glowingly of his eldest daughter, the beautiful Mary Ellen—called Nelly. When McClellan finally met her, he saw that she fully lived up to expectations. He was smitten. He knew immediately that he must have her; she must become his wife. It did not seem to be a problem. Her parents adored him; therefore, she must adore him also. When he proposed, however, she refused him. It was a devastating blow to McClellan's self-esteem, but in no way did it dampen his passion for her.

Miss Marcy was a devastator of suitors—"stubborn-chaste against all suit," as Shakespeare would say.[21] She had been proposed to by more than just McClellan—indeed, by an army of suitors, some more than once—and had refused them all, save one. That one, ironically, was one of McClellan's dearest friends and one-time classmate at West Point, the Virginian Ambrose Powell Hill. She did love Hill, and in the spring of 1856, dismissing all her other suitors including McClellan, she had accepted his ring and they had become engaged.

Virtually the last thing the Marcys wanted for their beautiful, talented, and seductive daughter was a soldier for a husband, and particularly that one. Though a soldier himself—perhaps because of it—Marcy abhorred the idea of her marrying one, specifically the one she had picked out, and having to waste away her life, her charm, and her beauty on some remote frontier outpost. The only soldier Marcy knew whom he might relent and permit her to wed was an ex-soldier—the charming, and incidentally, socially qualified, George McClellan.

The Marcys invoked parental privilege over Mary Ellen, demanding she break off her engagement to Hill. Mrs. Marcy played hardball. She had learned that in a youthful indiscretion in his West Point years, Hill had contracted gonorrhea, along with its side effects—severe pelvic pain, fever, and difficulty urinating, which had led to prostatitis.[22] She let that be known. Under this intense parental pressure, Nelly eventually gave in and very reluctantly returned Hill's ring. This, however, did not automatically open the door for McClellan. She still did not love him. In despair, McClellan began a flanking movement around her maddening lack of affection. He instead courted the Marcys, particularly Mrs. Marcy, as a likely pathway into Nelly's heart. For the rest of the decade of the 1850s, he pursued this dream of wedded bliss with this aggravating beauty without stint and without much hope.

It was not that Nelly disliked McClellan or disapproved of him; she simply did not love him. But bit by bit, communicating his heart's desire on a regular basis to Mrs. Marcy, he finally gained direct access to Nelly herself. They began exchanging letters. And gradually the glacier melted. Finally, in early 1859, sensing that a change had come over her heart, he proposed again. This time she accepted, and they were engaged on October 25, 1859. She had decided after all that she did love this relentless suitor. They were married in New York City on May 22, 1860, in a lavish wedding that was the social event of the season.

When Mary Ellen did marry, she married totally. McClellan soon found that she would give him unconditional, unquestioning love and support. And he would lean on her, writing her daily— sometimes more than once a day—when they were apart. She became his rock, his sounding board, his partner, his intimate correspondent, his comfort in everything. In his letters he poured out to her, his most sympathetic ally, his most private thoughts about war, men, life, God, and destiny. It would be with her that he would "share all my thoughts."[23] It was a good thing for him; with nearly everyone else not in his circle of affection, he was inclined to share very little of the real McClellan.

CHAPTER 3

CATCHING
THE BRASS RING

In November 1842, eighteen years before McClellan married Mary Ellen Marcy in New York City, Lincoln had married Mary Todd, a cultured Kentucky belle living with a sister in Springfield, Illinois. His path to wedlock had been no less agonizing than McClellan's. He had courted two other women before Mary, and neither had worked out. And his courtship with Mary had been stormy. Engaged to her in 1840, he broke it off, not convinced he really loved her. But two years later they were reconciled and reunited, and then united in marriage.

As McClellan's marriage had forged a close bonding, Lincoln's was also a union designed to prosper. Mary Todd was driven by ambition rivaling Lincoln's own. It had become both a workable marriage and a strong political partnership. They had together produced four children, all boys. One of them, the second born, had died in early childhood.

Five days before George McClellan married Mary Ellen, Abraham Lincoln was nominated for president of the United States by the Republican Party in Chicago. Since he had reemerged to confront Douglas in 1854, the crisis of the times had carried him—against all odds, it seemed—to the pinnacle of the new party and made him its nominee. And six months later, in the election in November 1860, the electorate, or a plurality of it, had made him president.

When he returned from Congress in 1849, Lincoln had thought himself politically dead. "How hard—oh, how more than hard," he told his law partner, William H. Herndon, "it is to die and leave one's country no better for the life of him that lived and died her child!"[1] He had believed that was his fate.

But the slavery issue had spectacularly reignited his political career. Riding a rising reputation from his repeated confrontations with Douglas, in which he more than held his own, Lincoln had made a run for the U.S. Senate from Illinois in 1856 and lost. But he had continued to speak out against slavery in the territories, still challenging Douglas, who had become one of the most powerful politicians in the country, a strong Democratic contender for the presidency.

All of Lincoln's political life he had been an ardent Whig, the party's leader in Illinois. But his party had crashed and shattered on the hard rock of the slavery issue in the mid-1850s, and Lincoln for a time had been left rudderless. In 1856, needing new moorings, he had switched to the newly emerging Republican Party, which had been reconfigured into a union of Whigs, antislavery men, Free-Soilers opposing the extension of slavery in the territories, and foes of the Kansas-Nebraska Act—anti-Nebraska men from all shades of political allegiance. These diverse parts had formed themselves into the new political power challenging the pro-Nebraska arm of the Democratic Party, led by Douglas.

In 1858, when Douglas's U.S. Senate seat had come up for filling or refilling, the Republican Party turned almost by reflex to Lincoln, who had established himself as the most potent, able, and articulate voice in their party and as perhaps the only man who could unseat the powerful Little Giant. The Illinois State Republican convention met in Springfield in June 1858 and resolved that he was its "first and only choice."[2] Lincoln delivered another powerful speech, in which he said, "A house divided against itself cannot stand."[3] It became a stunningly controversial utterance but set the tone for what followed.

What followed were the celebrated face-to-face debates of 1858, in which Lincoln and Douglas hammered one another on the issue of slavery in the territories seven times, three hours each debate, from the same platform in seven different Illinois towns. The campaign had been something of a forlorn hope for Lincoln from the start. Although in the election the Republicans edged the Democrats in the popular vote, the Democrats controlled the state legislature, and at the time

U. S. senators were not selected by direct popular vote but by legisla-
tures. Douglas retained his seat.

But from the campaign Lincoln emerged with a yet more highly
burnished national political reputation. He continued to speak in
Illinois and neighboring western states and, in February 1860, delivered a speech of such power in Cooper Union Hall in New York City
that he became a serious presidential contender. A month before the
national Republican convention in Chicago, Illinois Republicans met
in Decatur, named him their favorite-son candidate, and sent a delega-
tion and a team of his political friends and fellow lawyers to Chicago
to see him nominated. He was considered a dark horse, but in the
maneuvering in caucus rooms and on the floor of the convention none
of the better known, more favored candidates could muster enough
votes, and Lincoln was nominated on the third ballot.

In the election campaign he once again faced Douglas, the nominee of the main wing of the Democratic Party, which had split into
warring northern and southern parts. Capitalizing on that schism in
the Democracy, Lincoln won a plurality vote and was elected. On
March 4, 1861, he was inaugurated in Washington even as seven Deep
South states had seceded in protest of his election and formed a government in rebellion.

Within a month of his inauguration, the new Confederacy, composed of the seven seceded states, fired on the Federal garrison at Fort
Sumter in Charleston harbor. It was armed rebellion, and Lincoln
called on the still-faithful states for 75,000 militia to put it down. Four
Southern border states seceded in protest, joining the Confederacy. It
was to be a war between sections.

The newly married George McClellan had seen the war coming, seen
it so clearly that when he left the Illinois Central Railroad in Chicago
to head the Ohio & Mississippi Rivers line in Cincinnati in August
1860, he had hedged his bets.

"So strongly was I convinced that war would ensue," he later wrote,
"that when, in the autumn of 1860, I leased a house in Cincinnati for
the term of three years, I insisted upon a clause in the lease releasing me
from the obligation in the event of war."[4]

When the war did come, it was obvious that this former army star
would be called to high command. He wrote his friend, Major Fitz
John Porter, "I throw to one side all questions as to past political parties

etc—the Govt is in danger, our flag insulted & we must stand by it."[5] The calls came soon, and urgently. Three states, the three with the largest military obligations under Lincoln's call for 75,000 militia—New York, Pennsylvania, and Ohio—all wanted McClellan to command their volunteer forces. His preference was Pennsylvania, his native state, and he set out in that direction after the firing on Fort Sumter to hurry the appointment.

As he was stopping over in Columbus, Ohio, that state's enterprising governor, William Dennison, invited him to the capitol and made his pitch. Dennison explained the situation to McClellan: the call from Lincoln to raise thirteen regiments—some 10,000 troops, one of every seven militiamen called for by the president. Organizing this mob would require the sure hand of extraordinary leadership. Dennison believed McClellan held such a hand, and offered him command of Ohio's volunteer army. McClellan instantly accepted, without further thought.[6]

Pennsylvania and New York would have to find some other commander. McClellan's employers at the railroad would simply have to understand: This was war. Even Nelly would have to be told of his decision later, but she would support him whatever he decided. That same day, Governor Dennison rammed a special bill through the state legislature clearing the path for McClellan. By nightfall, the former young captain of the regular army was rocketed to major general of volunteers over all Ohio troops.

McClellan sprang into action. He began immediately restocking a virtually depleted, outdated armory and whipping an untrained rabble of raw volunteers into something that could fight. He laid out a training camp seventeen miles east of Cincinnati and named it Camp Dennison. Within weeks, he had shaped a respectable fighting command on his hard anvil of discipline.

Watching McClellan at work, the powers in Washington were impressed. Within a month, Lincoln elevated McClellan to command of the entire department of the Ohio, including Ohio, Indiana, Illinois, western Pennsylvania, western Virginia, and Missouri—much of the region west of the Alleghenies. He was promoted to major general in the regular army, and instantly catapulted through five permanent ranks, ahead of every other officer in the army except the general-in-chief, the venerable but physically rickety Winfield Scott himself.

The first place McClellan took his new command to fight was into western Virginia, in the late spring and early summer of 1861. The two-fifths of Virginia west of the Alleghenies were pro-Union. In April, following Lincoln's call for 75,000 militia, the state's western mountain section, in effect, seceded from the parent. To try to wrest its errant part back in line, the Confederacy had rushed in troops. McClellan sent his army to counter the Confederates and followed it there, he wrote Nelly, to "a continuous ovation all along the road. At every station we stopped crowds had assembled to see the 'Young General.' Gray-headed old men & women; mothers holding up their children to take my hand, girls, boys, all sorts, cheering and crying, God bless you! I never went thro' such a scene in my life & never expect to go thro' such another one." He heard them say, " 'He is our own general'; 'Look at him, how young he is'; 'He will thrash them'; 'He'll do,' &c, &c ad infinitum."[7]

Western Virginia became a battleground—the first of the war. There McClellan's army fought and won four small skirmishes—at Philippi, Laurel Hill, Rich Mountain, and Corricks Ford—that by mid-July had driven back the Confederates and secured much of that part of the state for the Union. McClellan had won it with superior numbers— some two to one—and with a successful flanking movement at Rich Mountain.

In Washington, however, things were not going well. Driven by an urgent Northern compulsion to crush the rebellion immediately in one blow and drive on to the Confederate capital in Richmond, a too-hasty battle had been fought on July 21, 1861. A green Federal army attacked a green rebel army across a little stream called Bull Run on the plains of Manassas, only a score of miles southwest of Washington. The attack was repulsed, and the Union army under Brigadier General Irvin McDowell staggered back into the national capital in disarray through a driving rainstorm. The shocked nation was plunged into despair.

The sole slivers of light in the dark clouds were the four small victories in western Virginia, won by the charismatic young McClellan. They were only skirmishes—"petty Union victories," Lincoln's two personal secretaries, John G. Nicolay and John Hay, later wrote—but they "came to the longing hope of the North, hitherto vexed by delay and disappointment, as a great joy."[8]

Following his victories and showing a knack for the theatrical, McClellan telegraphed stirring, triumphant reports to Washington over wires he had trailed behind him into western Virginia. His stirring words electrified the victory-hungry North. "How like the sound of the silver trumpets of Judah," wrote Sophia Hawthorne, the wife of the noted New England man of letters, "I conceive an adoring army following the lead of such a ringing of true steel." He was being called "the young Napoleon" and seen as the great hope to save the Union.[9]

All of these telegraphed bugle blasts from his fields of victory somewhat puzzled McClellan's friends. They could agree there was a ringing of true steel about him, but they found the silver trumpets of Judah rather contradicted the McClellan they knew.

One wrote that his "personal intercourse with those about him was so kindly, his bearing so modest that his dispatches, proclamations, and correspondence are a psychological study, more puzzling to those who knew him well than to strangers. Their turgid rhetoric and exaggerated pretense did not seem natural to him. In them he seemed to be composing for stage effect, something to be spoken in character by a quite different person from the sensible and genial man we knew in daily life and conversation."[10]

But Washington, no more than the country at large, could resist such blaring of silver trumpets or ringing of true steel. The call to him from Lincoln came through General Scott the day after the disaster at Bull Run. "Circumstances," Scott wired McClellan, "make your presence here necessary. Charge [Brigadier General William S.] Rosecrans or some other general with your present department and come hither without delay."[11]

The news that McClellan had been ordered to Washington to save the Union was "hailed with satisfaction throughout the loyal states," one observer reported. "Good news! good news!" a bank cashier in Indiana joyfully shouted. "General McClellan has been ordered to Washington to take command of the army. There will be no more Bull Runs."

"You think, then," asked another, "that General McClellan is going to save the nation?"

"Certainly I do. He is to do for the people of the United States what Moses did for the children of Israel. I have not a particle of doubt that he has been raised up for this very purpose."[12]

McClellan turned his command over to Rosecrans and on July 23 caught a train through Wheeling, Pittsburgh, Philadelphia, and Baltimore to Washington. Word of his coming preceded him, and crowds turned out to cheer as he passed along the tracks, with what he called another "continuous ovation."[13] In Pittsburgh, he was mobbed by admirers. In Philadelphia, where he stopped over for a night at his brother's home, a large clamoring crowd congregated outside. He arrived in Washington in the late afternoon of July 26.[14]

He was swelling with pride, writing in a letter to Nelly: "Who would have thought when we were married, that I should so soon be called upon to save my country? I learn that before I came on they said in Richmond, that there was only one man they feared & that was McClellan."[15] He was believing his press notices.

The McClellan who pulled into the Baltimore and Ohio Railroad station to universal acclaim on July 26 brought with him an array of acquired traits, characteristics, and tenaciously held opinions, personal and military. These personal hallmarks would define him in this first year of the war—and define his relationship with Lincoln, the rough frontier lawyer he had known on the Illinois Central, whom he did not especially like or respect and who was now his commander in chief.

CHAPTER 4

THE REAL McCLELLAN

George McClellan's arrival in Washington in July 1861 was "like the advent of a beneficent Prince."[1] He looked and sounded Napoleonic and glory-bound, answering the call of destiny. He carried the hope of the Union with a confident air, a model of strict, ramrod-straight military bearing. Some said of McClellan that he was "the only man ever born who can strut sitting down."[2]

The general exuded charm, but it was in no sense unalloyed. His bearing suggested strut, and so did his attitude. McClellan said of himself that he had a "naturally defiant disposition."[3] Like his father, McClellan had no taste for personal compromise. He was trigger-ready to take all disputes as far as appeal could take them, until he either got his way or getting his way was hopeless or pointless. He would nitpick relentlessly in defense of his presumed rights.

McClellan had very little stomach for criticism, tending to view arguments contrary to his own as challenges to his personal integrity. "I don't care much for anybody's opinion," he wrote his brother John, "as long as I am in the right."[4] And in the right he generally assumed himself to be. When he reached an opinion, and it became cemented in his mind as right, it was rarely subject to change.

In the past, McClellan had shown repeatedly that he tended to be impatient under another's command, critical of superiors, somewhat haughty, irritated with their interference, and often irritating them with officious unsolicited suggestions or complaints. McClellan exhibited, however, a mitigating humbleness when contemplating the Creator.

Here was a superior he had no quarrel with but strictly deferred to. His strong belief in a guiding God was buttressed by the undeviating faith of his young wife, Nelly, whom he called "the little Presbyterian."[5]

McClellan's upbringing in Philadelphia's elite had shaped his character, steeped him in gentility, self-restraint, a strict sense of etiquette, dignity, good taste, personal morality, and social responsibility. These were the trappings of polite culture and personal refinement that he had accumulated early in life. They were present in him still, and were bound to last. He was convinced of his own moral, cultural, and intellectual superiority and tended to look down on those he believed fell short of these ideals.[6]

But McClellan had a knack for making and keeping friends. As many of his fellow cadets had seen at West Point, he possessed an inherent personal charm coupled to unusual intelligence and competence. He inspired admiration and adulation. And for nearly everyone in the North in the summer of 1861, he was a symbol of confidence and hope.

Politically, as a product of the conservative Philadelphia elite, his upbringing had been firmly anchored in Whig philosophy—an allegiance shared by Lincoln. His father was an ardent Whig, a personal friend of the two greatest Whigs of his time, Henry Clay of Kentucky and Daniel Webster of Massachusetts. His father's idolatry of those two giants lived on in McClellan. In the Red River expedition early in the 1850s, he had named the highest mountain in the Wichita chain after the great Webster. The big bay horse he wrapped his legs around was named Dan Webster.

McClellan's take on slavery was that it ought to be handled with reason, moderation, and mutual forbearance. He favored gradual emancipation and compensation to slaveholders—measures Lincoln had also long favored. This did not mean McClellan had an affection or affinity for blacks. He believed them inherently inferior, in no way equal to whites. His belief about slavery and the slave was typical of most white Northerners of his time.

McClellan believed that instead of reason, moderation, and forbearance, the Union had too long been divided by irrational passion, extremism, and self-serving politics. In particular, he deplored the moral absolutism, divisiveness, and impassioned rhetoric of the abolitionists. When the Whig Party collapsed, McClellan, like Lincoln, was left politically rudderless. While Lincoln jumped the sinking ship to the new Republican Party, McClellan, put off by the growing power of abolition-driven Free-Soilers in Lincoln's new party, bolted in the opposite direction—into the Democratic camp, which he believed more faithfully mirrored his sense of restraint and social order. He became "a strong Democrat of the Stephen A. Douglas school."[7]

McClellan, however, shared many of Lincoln's beliefs about the war, beliefs both men had come to from long-held Whig backgrounds. Both believed that the overweening objective of the war was to preserve the Union, not free the slaves; that the military policy should aim at a quick restoration of the Union; and that slavery should not be permitted to complicate that goal. Both thought slavery wrong, and both wished to see it placed on the course of ultimate extinction. Lincoln had often said so; McClellan believed so, if less ardently. He wrote Nelly in 1861, "When I think of some of the features of slavery I cannot help shuddering. . . . It is horrible, & when the day of adjustment comes, I will, if successful, throw my sword into the scale to force an improvement in the condition of those poor blacks."

But not just then, not before restoring the Union and getting the country back to the way it used to be. And in no way would he fight for abolitionists. "I will never be an abolitionist," he assured Nelly, "but I do think that some of the rights of humanity ought to be secured to the negroes—there should be no power to separate families & the right of marriage ought to be secured to them."[8]

Before the war, Lincoln and McClellan were sharply divided on the issue of slavery in the territories. Lincoln believed it must be disallowed at all costs, on moral grounds. McClellan embraced Douglas's "popular sovereignty" policy: Forget morality; slavery should be permitted in any territory—voted up or down—as the majority in the territory wished.[9]

But more important than how the two men agreed or disagreed was McClellan's personal view of the president. He still saw Lincoln as lacking personal refinement and the desirable trappings of "polite culture," a jokester, with the lack of discipline necessary for reasoned action in these desperate times, prone to cave in to political pressure and not do the right thing.[10]

There was a major hitch in McClellan's view of politics and politicians in general. He ardently believed that war should be left strictly to professionals—such as he—that politicians could not understand it and should not be permitted to run it.[11] In the Old Army, he had once compared Congress in session to animal performances in a beer garden.[12] This mind-set applied from top to bottom, from the president on down—perhaps to Lincoln especially.

This antipathy to practicing politicians was a deep-seated belief nurtured in the days of the Mexican War when he saw the starkly partisan president James K. Polk making war decisions based not on military necessity but on politics. McClellan presumed that any politicians who questioned him or his actions now, even a president, were bound to be driven by ignorance, narrow-minded partisanship, or selfishness.[13]

Just as his personal character, politics, and view of politicians were fixed, so was McClellan's military character.

It was generally believed that no young officer in the army had a better grip or was better grounded in military organization, strategy, and tactics—on the science of war. He had studied it diligently, widely, and deeply in the literature and firsthand in the Crimea. However, he had not been deeply tested in command. Despite his aura of promise and authority, he, like all of the subalterns catapulted overnight to general rank when the war came, had never commanded men on the monumental scale that this war demanded.

The famed but skeptical Irish reporter with the *London Times,* William Howard Russell, came to America to see this new war begin, and called McClellan " 'the little corporal' of unfought fields."[14] But McClellan had commanded enough—in his rail-line explorations in the Cascades and in his campaign in western Virginia—to suggest the kind of commander of large armies that he might be. It was a mixed picture.

In his explorations in the mountain West, McClellan had fallen short of brilliance.

Some saw his victories in western Virginia, which were so lavishly lauded and had rocketed him to Washington, as not worth all the hoopla and adulation. They had not conclusively proved his qualifications for bold battlefield command. Although McClellan had been in overall command in western Virginia, he had not been personally present at any of the four skirmishes in the mountains.

The most important of his victories, routing the Confederates on Rich Mountain, had broken the back of Confederate power in western Virginia. But it was waged and won by his lieutenant, Brigadier General William S. Rosecrans, while McClellan was two miles down the mountain. And when McClellan heard the distant firing, he misinterpreted it and failed to attack the Confederate camp in the rear or divert the enemy in his front, as agreed. One of his soldiers, watching him, later wrote, "With indecision stamped on every line of his countenance," McClellan did nothing.[15] He recoiled into his native caution when things were not going as he expected.

What can be pieced together about McClellan in the way of a military profile suggests both strength and weakness. He had shown a genius for organization and a quick grasp of detail. He had shown an ability to whip raw troops quickly into shape. He had a brilliant, well-balanced mind and a gift for strategic analysis. He was a demon for work. He would be prudent but perhaps overcautious. He would not likely believe in chance or act rashly or aggressively. He had a bent for magnifying difficulties in his front and therefore falling a shade short in execution.[16]

It could be expected on a larger stage that he would be deliberate in making plans and cautious in executing them. He would be circumspect and not inclined to rush into battle. He was likely to make certain everything was in order and the odds heavily in his favor before risking a fight and committing his soldiers to battle. As he wrote Nelly in early July before the battle on Rich Mountain, "I shall feel my way & be very cautious, for I recognize the fact that everything requires success in my first operations."[17]

In his Crimean report, McClellan had written, "One of the clearest rules of war [is] to undertake no important operation without full and reliable information as to the obstacles to be overcome and the means of resistance in the hands of the enemy."[18]

His mind-set suggested he would opt for maneuver in his new command rather than head-on assault. From western Virginia he had assured Scott on June 5, through the assistant adjutant general, "No prospect of a brilliant victory shall induce me to depart from my intention of gaining success by maneuvering rather than by fighting; I will not throw these men of mine into the teeth of artillery & intrenchments, if it is possible to avoid it.... I am trying to follow a lesson long ago learned from him [Scott]—i.e.—not to move until I know that everything is ready, & then move with the utmost rapidity & energy."[19]

McClellan admired the writings of the eighteenth-century French marshal Maurice Comte de Saxe, a "quintessential" apostle of limited war. In his campaigns in Flanders and the Netherlands in the mid-1700s, Saxe had moved methodically, with caution, along river-ways, ever protective of his logistics. He preferred maneuver to giving battle, avoiding rash attack, and fighting defensively behind fortifications whenever possible. And he admired siege operations.[20] All of this had struck McClellan as a sensible way of waging war.

He would be likely to wage this war he was now in with the same disciplined Saxe approach, based on thorough preparation, avoiding failure at all cost. One of his admirers believed that "[e]ver present with him was this horror of slaughter that could be saved by some better way. He always wanted the 'largest battalions'—to have more men, so that *less* men should *perish*."[21]

At last in Washington, McClellan, age thirty-four, had brought all of these personal, political, and military beliefs, traits, and convictions along in his baggage. He rode in with them, pedestaled on high in public esteem—the "young Napoleon" come to save the Union and expected to perform Napoleonic magic on the battlefield.

It was a case of high expectations riding on very young shoulders.

CHAPTER 5

MAN ON HORSEBACK

O n July 26, the day McClellan arrived in Washington, he reported immediately to Lincoln. The physical contrast between these two men when they met in the White House was striking. The bearded Lincoln towered over McClellan, his elongated frame free of excess body fat. As he rose from a chair to greet his new general, as was likely, the operation must have been picturesque, rather like the parts of a telescope extending. One visitor watching the president rise had thought that the unwinding "was never coming to an end."[1] When unwound and stepping to greet McClellan, Lincoln likely resembled, as yet another said, "the offspring of a happy marriage between a derrick and a windmill."[2]

As Lincoln brought a unique vision to the eye, McClellan more closely fit the norm. The ever-observant Irish journalist William Howard Russell, who was observing McClellan closely, described him as "a very squarely built, thick-throated, broad-chested man, under middle height, with slightly bowed legs, a tendency to *embonpoint*. His head, covered with a closely cut crop of dark auburn hair, is well set on his shoulders. His features are regular and prepossessing—the brow small, contracted, and furrowed; the eyes deep and anxious looking. A short, thick reddish moustache conceals his mouth; the rest of his face is clean-shaven."[3]

The next day, McClellan assumed command of a force encompassing Irvin McDowell's Department of Northeastern Virginia and Joseph K. F. Mansfield's Department of Washington—no more than

50,000 men. It was the new Military Division of the Potomac, the major command in the East, which within the month McClellan would rechristen the "Army of the Potomac." He was also in command of Union hopes and hearts from top to bottom. There were isolated sinks of envy, carping, nitpicking, skepticism, and discontent, but it was buried under an avalanche of adulation.

"McClellan . . . is 'the man on horseback' just now, and the Americans must ride in his saddle, or in anything he likes," wrote Russell, one of the few skeptics among the living. "Every one . . . is willing to do as he bids," he wrote, "the President confides in him, and 'Georges' him; the press fawn upon him, the people trust him."[4]

The noted satirist James Russell Lowell wrote: "There is nothing more touching than the sight of a nation in search of its great man, nothing more beautiful than its readiness to accept a hero on trust." No commander, he wrote, "ever had more . . . paid-up capital of fortune, this fame in advance, this success before succeeding, than General McClellan."[5]

McClellan was somewhat in awe of himself. "I find myself in a new & strange position here," he wrote Nelly, with whom he shared his most personal thoughts. "Presdt, Cabinet, Genl Scott & all deferring to me—by some strange operation of magic I seem to have become *the* power of the land. I almost think that were I to win some small success now I could become Dictator or anything else that might please me but nothing of that kind would please me—*therefore* I *won't* be Dictator. Admirable self denial!"[6]

Within the week after arriving, McClellan went up the Hill to Congress to push for a bill increasing the number of his aides. He was "quite overwhelmed by the congratulations I received & the respect with which I was treated. I suppose half a dozen of the oldest made the remark I am becoming so much used to. 'Why how young you look—yet an old soldier!!' It seems to strike everybody that I am very young. They give me my way in everything, full swing & unbounded confidence. All tell me that I am held responsible for the fate of the Nation & that all its resources shall be placed at my disposal." When he later stood in the congressional library overlooking the capital city, a crowd gathered just to stare at him.[7]

Lincoln's two personal secretaries, John Nicolay and John Hay, later wrote, "In every one, from the President of the United States to the humblest orderly who waited at his door, he inspired a remarkable affection and regard." McClellan was "given a peculiar warmth," they believed, "by his unusually winning personal characteristics. In consequence he was courted and caressed as few men in our history have been."[8]

McClellan was beginning to be impressed with the sobering challenge and responsibility of it all. "It is an immense task that I have on my hands," he confessed to Nelly. "Oh! How sincerely I pray to God that I may be endowed with the wisdom & courage necessary to accomplish the work." With that help from on high, he told her, he believed he could do it.[9]

He began immediately laying pipe to that end. On August 2, he wrote Lincoln a memorandum outlining big plans requiring a big army and big money. The idea, he told the president, was to "crush the rebellion at one blow, terminate the war in one campaign," crush it "at its very heart." He had in mind displaying "such an overwhelming strength, as will convince all our antagonists...of the utter impossibility of resistance"—to convince the South it was in a war it could not win.

His idea was to get the war over as soon as possible, make it short, decisive, and certain. While crushing enemy power to resist, he would also pursue "a rigidly protective policy as to private property [including slaves] and unarmed persons, and a lenient course as to common soldiers." In short, in crushing the rebellion, he wished not to also crush hopes "for the permanent restoration of peaceful Union."

This single great battle, of course, would be waged in the East, by an army under his command. "The rebels," he wrote Lincoln, "have chosen Virginia as their battle-field—and it seems proper for us to make the first great struggle there." But at the same time, he would wish to see "movements on other points, both by land and water"—on the Mississippi, in Missouri, through Kentucky and Tennessee. All other operations, however, would be secondary, and in support of this one massive blow dealt by him in Virginia.

It would not be cheap, he told the president, and we must think big. For his army alone, he told Lincoln he would need 273,000 troops, fully equipped, a unity of action with a strong naval force, and abundant reserves ready to "supply any losses that may occur."[10]

It was a big order. But if anyone was equipped to do it, it was this precocious West Pointer with his gift for organization, his administrative smarts, and his confident know-how. Though so young, he seemed to know what he was about. And he was wasting no time putting the necessary parts together.

McClellan was inheriting a wrecked army of 50,000 mostly raw volunteer infantry, fewer than 1,000 cavalry, and 650 artillerymen with
9 skeleton field artillery batteries of some 30 guns. It was an army
at loose ends, still reeling from its rout at Bull Run.[11] He called it
"a perfect pandemonium"—virtually "no army to command; a mere
collection of regiments cowering on the banks of the Potomac, some
perfectly raw, others dispirited by the recent defeat."[12] No one disputed
that. One newspaper reporter called what McClellan was inheriting
"rather a mob than an army."[13]

McClellan's job was to reconfigure this imperfect, scattered nucleus,
lick it into shape, organize it into an instrument he could fight with,
secure Washington from attack, and generally rescue order from
chaos. It was, William Howard Russell conceded, "a task of Herculean
magnitude."[14]

McClellan figured he could do it. "I see already the main causes of
our recent failure," he wrote Nelly the day after he arrived. "I am sure
that I can remedy these & I am confident that I can lead these armies
of men to victory once more. I start tomorrow very early on a tour
through the lines on the other side of the river." Then, he believed, he
would "be able to make up my mind as to the state of things."[15]

The sight of McClellan riding the lines around Washington was high
drama. He sat his saddle with grace and authority—and tall in it,
because, as one journalist wrote, "he was commenced for a tall man
and built for one, as far down as his hips."[16] The body below was less
impressive. But on horseback no one suspected. In a saddle atop Dan
Webster, he was the towering beau ideal of a general—as he had been
the beau ideal of a young subaltern. "He sat upon his handsome horse,"
one soldier said, "like a born centaur."[17]

Dan Webster was a good match—the beau ideal of a war horse, a
large, powerful bay seventeen hands high. He appeared able, without
fatigue, loss of equanimity or dignity, to trot all day long at a gait that
forced other horses to gallop to keep pace. McClellan's aides called him
"that Devil Dan."[18]

Astride Devil Dan, McClellan caused a stir in his army from the
start. He materialized constantly among the men, riding everywhere,
seeing everything. "Not a camp did I not examine," he later wrote,
"not a picket line that I did not visit and cross....There was no part
of the ground near Washington that I did not know thoroughly."[19]

He told Nelly, "I *must* ride much every day for my army covers much space, & unfortunately I have no one on my staff to whom I can entrust the safety of affairs—it is necessary for me to see as much as I can every day & more than that let the men see me & gain confidence in me."[20]

Russell was impressed with this passion "to make himself known to the men personally, to familiarize them with his appearance, to gain the acquaintance of the officers." The journalist believed it to be McClellan's studied strategy to "spend nearly every day in the camps, riding out at nine o'clock, examining the various regiments as he goes along, not returning till long after nightfall . . . having incessant inspections and reviews," and issuing all orders with a bugle blast. "These little excursions," Russell wrote, "are not the most agreeable affairs in the world; for McClellan delights in working down staff and escort, dashing from the Chain Bridge to Alexandria, and visiting all the posts, riding as hard as he can, and not returning till past midnight."[21]

Seeing him, the men took him into their hearts, calling him "Little Mac" and cheering at a high decibel level when he galloped among them. He would acknowledge their cheers, snatching off his cap and twirling it above his head. Often he would stop to chat casually with a squad or a company of soldiers, promising them "Boys, every foot of ground taken by us hereafter will be held."[22]

The great New England man of letters Nathaniel Hawthorne watched this spectacle in a visit to Washington and described how McClellan "rode off, followed by his cavalcade, and was lost to sight among the troops. They received him with loud shouts, by the eager uproar of which—now near, now in the centre, now on the outskirts of the division, and now sweeping back towards us in a great volume of sound—we could trace his progress through the ranks."

This show won Hawthorne's own heart. "If he is a coward, or a traitor, or a humbug, or anything less than a brave, true, and able man, that mass of intelligent soldiers, whose lives and honor he had in charge, were utterly deceived, and so was this present writer; for they believed in him, and so did I; and had I stood in the ranks, I should have shouted with the lustiest of them."[23]

But even as McClellan rode through the camps, omnipresent, basking in the love of his soldiers, clouds were gathering—both in the general's head and in his headquarters.

CHAPTER 6

THE NUMBERS GAME

McClellan was a micromanager. A man of great faith in his own ability, he had little faith in the ability of either those above or below him. In his campaign in western Virginia earlier in the summer, he became convinced that he must supervise every aspect of every operation of his army if he were to succeed.

"In heaven's name," McClellan had fumed in a dispatch to Washington from Beverly on July 19, "give me some General Officers who understand their profession. I give orders & find some who cannot execute them unless I stand by them. Unless I command every picket & lead every column I cannot be sure of success."[1]

The general complained to Nelly, "I have not a Brig Genl worth his salt—[Thomas A.] Morris is a timid old woman—Rosecranz a silly fussy goose—[Newton] Schleich knows nothing."[2] To compensate for their deficiencies, he had appointed his father-in-law and onetime commanding officer, now a brigadier general—Randolph Marcy—inspector general of his army and later his chief of staff.

This first year of the war, there was a shortage of officers who had been sufficiently trained and tried. Too few West Pointers were available—many of the best of them had bolted to the Confederacy—and McClellan had little trust in untried citizen officers. Distrusting as he was, he leaned toward secrecy in his thought, management, and planning.

But in Washington, micromanaging, riding every day, keeping details and intentions to himself, McClellan was accomplishing much.

His genius for organization was apparent and paying off. While forging a growing army, soon to become the largest on the planet, he was also shoring up Washington's defenses, beefing up the fortifications ringing the capital. By the end of 1861, work would be mostly completed on forty-eight forts and batteries. Nearly 480 guns would be frowning out from these fortifications, manned by 7,200 artillerists.[3]

McClellan clearly believed that the fate of the Union rested solely in his hands. People were telling him so. He was telling Nelly, "I receive letter after letter—have conversation after conversation calling on me to save the nation.... Pray for me, darling, that I may be able to accomplish my task—the greatest, perhaps, that any poor weak mortal ever had to do.... God grant that I may bring this war to an end & be permitted to spend the rest of my days quietly with you."[4]

The weight of this enormous responsibility further fueled his distrust, his secrecy—and his innate caution. One of the letters offering him advice said, "Your military reputation is at stake in the next battle. You should, therefore, move cautiously, slowly—surely." This was not something McClellan needed to be told; he had no intention of doing otherwise. His study of the military organization, strategy, and tactics of the European armies in the Crimea had buttressed his belief that an army must be organized to the point of virtually unattainable perfection before it risked battle.[5]

Preparation to that indefinite point was going to take time, and McClellan would not be rushed. After the general's first month in Washington, William Howard Russell was reporting what he and others were beginning to notice. "For my own part," Russell wrote, "I confess that General McClellan does not appear to be a man of action, or, at least, a man who intends to act as speedily as the crisis demands." As yet, Russell was thinking, he has "certainly done nothing in the field to show he is like Napoleon."[6]

Within ten days of McClellan's arrival in Washington, things had begun to go wrong. Paranoia had set in. He began hallucinating about numbers, seeing a Confederate Goliath across the Potomac.

Believing questionable intelligence, McClellan began to think he faced on his front a rebel juggernaut at least 100,000 strong, well trained, well led—and twice his size. It was massed at Manassas Junction and Centreville, commanded by accomplished generals whom he had served with in Mexico: Joseph E. Johnston and P. G. T. Beauregard. And he believed they were about to attack. He wrote Nelly on August 8: "I have hardly slept one moment for the last three nights, knowing well that the enemy intend some movement & fully recognizing our own weakness. If Beauregard does not attack tonight I shall look upon it as a dispensation of Providence—he *ought* to do it."[7]

That same day, virtually in a panic, he wrote the old general-in-chief, Winfield Scott, that he had information from various sources that a Confederate force far outnumbering his own was about to attack, that Washington was insecure and in imminent danger. "I am induced to believe," he told Scott, "that the enemy has at least 100,000 men in front of us. Were I in Beauregard's place, with that force at my disposal, I would attack the positions on the other side of the Potomac, and at the same time cross the river above the city in force." He told Scott that his own army was "entirely insufficient for the emergency," that he must be reinforced immediately at whatever cost to other operations. "I urge," he wrote, "that nothing be left undone to bring up our force for the defence of this city to 100,000 men, before attending to any other point."[8]

The Confederate numbers would continue to multiply in his mind. By mid-August, he would have it topping 150,000, dwarfing his insufficient 55,000.[9]

Scott was not buying any of this. "Relying on our numbers, our forts, and the Potomac River, I am confident in the opposite opinion," the old general wrote the secretary of war, Simon Cameron. He was convinced that Washington was not "insecure" and in "imminent danger," as McClellan claimed. Scott wrote, "I have not the slightest apprehension for the safety of the Government here."[10]

General Joseph E. Johnston, in overall Confederate command in the East, in effect agreed with Scott. Assessing his own strength about the same time McClellan was wildly inflating it, Johnston was counting but 41,000 of all Confederate arms capable of fighting. Carefully observing Federal activities from his own lines, he saw McClellan's force on the other side of the river steadily increasing. To his way of thinking, there was no way he could mount a successful direct assault on Washington. The better course would be to attack the Federals elsewhere in Union territory. To do that, he would need 50,000 to 60,000 effective seasoned soldiers—a crack force—which he did not have. The best strategy, he believed, was to dig in around Manassas and Centreville, stay strictly on the defensive, and await a move by the enemy.[11] So both sides were standing, as John Nicolay put it, "Waiting for something to turn up, which in its own good time will no doubt come."[12]

Knowing nothing of the true state of Confederate affairs, McClellan only saw a stubborn, antiquated old general-in-chief questioning his numbers. And he had that low threshold of tolerance for opinions counter to his own. In his view, the Confederates were a monstrously large enemy in his front, and the big enemy in his rear had now become his superior, General Scott.

Up to this point, the two men had gotten on reasonably well. Scott had been in McClellan's life since boyhood. The old general had been one of his father's Whig friends, and he had attended McClellan's wedding. Like every other man in the army, McClellan had been awed and inspired by Scott's masterminding of the war against Mexico from Veracruz to Mexico City. Soon after McClellan arrived in Washington, the two men had attended an official White House function together, arm in arm. McClellan wrote Nelly, "It made me feel a little strangely last evening, when I went to the Presdt's with the old General leaning on me—the old Veteran & his young successor; I could see that many marked the contrast."

But now it was war between the two of them. In a letter to Nelly on August 8, McClellan asked how they think "that I can save this country when stopped by Genl Scott—I do not know whether he is a *dotard* or a *traitor!* I can't tell which. He *cannot* or *will* not comprehend the condition in which we are placed & is entirely unequal to the emergency. If he cannot be taken out of my path I will not retain my position, but will resign & let the admn take care of itself...that confounded old genl always comes in the way—he is a perfect imbecile. He understands nothing, appreciates nothing & is ever in my way."

A week later, he wrote her, "Genl Scott is the most dangerous antagonist I have—either he or I must leave here—our ideas are so widely different that it is impossible for us to work together much longer."

The next day, his anger and frustration had expanded to embrace the president as well. "I am here in a terrible place—the enemy have from 3 to 4 times my force—the Presdt is an idiot, the old General in his dotage—they cannot or will not see the true state of affairs."[13]

Lincoln as president impressed him even less than when he first knew him in Illinois as a lawyer. "The Presdt," he wrote Nelly, "is nothing more than a well meaning baboon." He had taken to calling Lincoln what Edwin M. Stanton, a prominent Washington lawyer and fellow Democrat, was calling him, "the original gorrilla." McClellan said of Lincoln: "What a specimen to be at the head of our affairs now."[14]

By the end of August, McClellan's army had grown and the crisis in his front had eased. He wrote Nelly, "Friend Beauregard has allowed the chance to escape him. I have now some 65,000 effective men—will have 75,000 by end of week. Last week he certainly had double our force. I feel sure that the dangerous moment has passed." A week later, although his mind was still relatively at rest, his thinking was cautious. He wrote her, "I do not think they will dare to attack—we are now ready for them altho' I would much like another week to complete my arrangements."[15]

If his mind and the problem in his front had lessened, the problem in his rear had not. His enemies in the administration were expanding in his mind to include, besides Lincoln and Scott, virtually the entire cabinet. In early October, he wrote Nelly, "There are some of the greatest geese in the Cabinet I have ever seen—enough to tax the patience of Job." He wrote: "I can't tell you how disgusted I am becoming with these wretched politicians—they are a most despicable set of men & I think [Secretary of State Henry] Seward is the meanest of them all—a meddling, officious, incompetent little puppy—he has done more than any other man to bring all this misery upon the country & is one of the least competent to get us out of the scrape." He believed Secretary of the Navy Gideon Welles "weaker than the most garrulous old woman you were ever annoyed by." Attorney General Edward Bates was in his mind "a good inoffensive old man—so it goes."[16]

And it only got worse as the days passed. "I have a set of scamps to deal with—unscrupulous & false—," he wrote Nelly at the end of October, "if possible they will throw whatever blame there is on my shoulders, & I do not intend to be sacrificed by such people. It is perfectly sickening to have to work with such people & to see the fate of the nation in such hands."

But there was still Providence to fall back on. He wrote Nelly, "I still trust that the all wise creator does not intend our destruction, & that in his own good time he will free the nation from the imbeciles who curse it & will restore us to his favor."[17]

As McClellan was railing against the "imbeciles" and "incapables" above him, the country and the Congress were becoming disillusioned with him. As Russell had suggested, their young Napoleon seemed not to have a stomach for fighting. "The newspapers begin to accuse me of want of energy," he complained to Nelly. But, he assured her, "I have left nothing undone to make this army what it ought to be & that the necessity for delay has not been my fault."[18]

On October 21, a little unintended clash at Ball's Bluff, a high rise above the Potomac forty miles upstream from Washington outside of Leesburg, Virginia, turned into an ineptly executed disaster. In it, one of Lincoln's closest friends and political allies from his Illinois years, the Union commander Edward Baker, a senator and a colonel who was inexperienced in the art of war, was slain.

Baker became an instant martyr, Lincoln wept for his old friend, and McClellan scrambled to avoid blame. Indeed, the disaster had happened without his knowledge and direction, and he was telling Nelly "I am in no manner responsible for it."[19]

This trait from earlier in his military career—shifting the blame elsewhere when things went wrong or he was found wanting—surfaced again. In the wake of the Ball's Bluff disaster and rising public and political clamor for an early advance, McClellan was telling Nelly that his movements "are not within my own control...I am thwarted & deceived by these incapables at every turn. I am doing all I can to get ready to move before winter sets in—but it now begins to look as if we are condemned to a winter of inactivity. If it is so the fault will not be mine....I have one great comfort in all this—that is that I did not seek this position, as you well know...." It had been "thrust upon me. I was called to it." He had still, however, that one constant hope: "I still trust that God will support me & bear me out—he could not have placed me here for nothing."[20]

Although he now considered Washington safe, McClellan was in no way disabused of the imagined power of the Confederates. The rebel host had continued to grow ever more formidable in his mind. Yet he had little in the way of accurate, firm knowledge. Virtually no meaningful reconnaissance was being carried out, and what existed was "wretchedly inefficient." Not only was McClellan's reckoning of enemy strength wrong; he also had no notion of Confederate intentions.[21]

CHAPTER 7

UNDER SIEGE

M cClellan's early inflated estimates of the size of Confederate strength rested mainly on random reports, rumors, guess-work, and his own imagination. He needed help to authen-ticate what he earnestly believed, and he knew how to get it. He had met Allan Pinkerton, a private detective from Chicago, in his Illinois days on the railroad in the late 1850s, and Pinkerton had done work for him on railroad security. McClellan had been so impressed that when he came to Washington in August 1861 he brought Pinkerton with him to head a Secret Service and intelligence operation. By October Pinkerton was producing his own estimates of enemy strength.[1]

Pinkerton was a Chartist refugee from Scotland with a cloak-and-dagger mentality. He had been a sheriff's deputy in Chicago before he became the first detective in that city's newly formed police force, where he won an instant reputation breaking a counterfeiting ring. In 1850, he founded one of the first private detective agencies in the country, particularly noted for helping escaping slaves and pro-tecting the mail from robbers. He had since built himself a national reputation.[2]

However, Pinkerton was not trained in calculating military num-bers and knew little of war or warfare, or how to gauge enemy strength. And he began sending out agents as untrained as he to gather estimates. He began delivering numbers—pulled in large part from escaped slaves, and short on critical analysis—even more inflated than McClellan's. The general, willing to accept yet higher numbers of imagined Confederate strength that confirmed his own calculations, readily accepted Pinkerton's figures.[3]

Scott, the general-in-chief, still believed none of it. What he did believe, however, was that it was time for him to retire, to get out of an aggravating situation. He had become antiquated, overweight, and virtually immobile. McClellan had been promising Radical senators in Congress a rapid advance on the enemy if they would help rid him of the old man.[4]

McClellan believed Scott "was no longer himself when the war broke out," that "the weight of years and great bodily suffering pressed heavily upon him, and really rendered him incapable of performing the duties of his station . . . simply an obstacle, and a very serious one, in the way of active work."[5]

Scott would not disagree entirely with that assessment. The old general—known to soldiers as "Old Fuss and Feathers" for his love of protocol and resplendent military dress—had been trying to retire ever since McClellan produced his inflated numbers of Confederate strength in early August. He was now in his mid-seventies, not only feeling creaky and old but rather agreeing that he was in the way. Virtually a national institution, a hero since the War of 1812, the military genius who had conquered Mexico in the U.S.–Mexican War, the preeminent American soldier for nearly half a century, he was now unable to get his considerable six-foot-five-inch, 300-pound bulk atop a horse or walk more than a few paces at a time.

"In short," Scott wrote the secretary of war on August 9, "being broken down by many particular hurts, besides the general infirmities of age—I feel that I have become an incumbrance to the Army as well as to myself, and that I ought, giving way to a younger commander, to seek the palliatives of physical pain and exhaustion."[6]

It angered and pained Scott that McClellan was bypassing him, not consulting him, not meeting with him, veering flagrantly from the proper military channels.[7] McClellan was doing all of this purposefully. Since Scott "objected to all I proposed," and didn't give in, he later confessed, "I quietly went to work in my own way." Scott had practically lost control of affairs from the moment McClellan had arrived in Washington. To him it was an insufferable position. He asked Lincoln to permit him to retire, but the president, admiring of his experience and intelligence, was loath to let him go.[8]

Scott was to endure more than another month of McClellan working in his own way before writing another letter to the secretary of
war, complaining that McClellan prided himself "in treating me with
uniform neglect, running into disobedience of orders." He cited specific instances, and told the secretary "I shall definitively retire from
the Army."[9] He did so, with Lincoln's acquiescence this time, on the
last day of October 1861.

McClellan was quietly gratified. When he was informed of the old
general's intention, he wrote Nelly, "I feel a sense of relief at the prospect of having my own way untrammelled, but I cannot discover in my
own heart one symptom of gratified vanity or ambition."[10]

On November 1, Lincoln elevated McClellan to general-in-chief,
replacing Scott in command of the entire Union army. "You will,
therefore, assume this enlarged duty at once," Lincoln wrote, "confer-
ring with me so far as necessary."[11] That same day, in a general order,
McClellan notified the army of his ascendancy and praised Scott's long
and distinguished service to the country. "While we regret his loss,"
McClellan wrote, "there is one thing we cannot regret—the bright
example he has left for our emulation."[12]

When Scott went to catch the train that would take him to New
York and away from all this frustration, McClellan rose at four o'clock
in the morning and rode out through "pitch dark & pouring rain"
with most of his staff and a squadron of cavalry to see him off. Scott
was cordial and polite; McClellan was moved. He wrote Nelly, "The
sight of this morning was a lesson to me which I hope not soon to
forget. I saw there the end of a long, active & ambitious life—the end
of the career of the first soldier of his nation—it was a feeble old man
scarce able to walk—hardly any one there to see him off but his successor. Should I ever become vainglorious & ambitious remind me of
that spectacle."[13]

The evening Lincoln promoted McClellan he visited the general's
quarters. McClellan read the president his general order to his army
about Scott's resignation. Lincoln thanked him and said, "I should be
perfectly satisfied if I thought that this vast increase of responsibility
would not embarrass you."

"It is a great relief, sir," McClellan assured him. "I feel as if several
tons were taken from my shoulders today. I am now in contact with
you, and the Secretary. I am not embarrassed by the intervention."

"Well," Lincoln replied, "Draw on me for all the sense I have, and all the information. In addition to your present command, the supreme command of the army will entail a vast labor upon you."

"I can do it all," McClellan said.[14]

McClellan now believed what Scott had believed, that Washington was safe from immediate attack. He was still convinced, however, buttressed by Pinkerton's estimates, that the Confederates in his front were vastly superior in strength and discipline to his own army. But despite the supposed discrepancy in numbers, he could now, theoretically, be the aggressor. His mind-set, however, was not in that direction. He was still not ready and he did not intend to act until he was, despite the rising clamor for him to do so.

McClellan believed, this late in the year, six months into the war, that he could do one of two things: go into winter quarters or assume the offensive. The latter did not seem to him an option. It would have to be mounted against Confederates at an imagined 150,000 strong, and with a force "greatly inferior in numbers to the army I regard as desirable and necessary." What he thought desirable and necessary would be a total effective force of some 200,000 men and something just short of 500 cannon. He estimated that he now had some 130,000 effectives but only some 76,000 available for an offensive, and he was still 200 guns short.

The new general-in-chief would not fight; he would continue to prepare. So all would continue to be quiet along the Potomac, and that was no longer generally considered a desirable condition but a curse. If there was quiet on the Potomac, there was very little silence from the people in the North. The public outcry was "On to Richmond!" which the influential *New York Tribune* was running daily at its masthead.[15]

On November 8, McClellan wrote his New York friend, Samuel L. M. Barlow: "My intention is simply this—I will pay no attention to popular clamor—quietly, & quickly as possible, make this Army strong enough & effective enough to give me a reasonable certainty that, if I am able to handle the form, I will win the first battle"—the one big one. But, he promised Barlow, when he was ready to strike the blow, "it will be heavy, rapid, & decisive."

Another thing, McClellan wrote Barlow: "Help me to dodge the nigger—we want nothing to do with him. I am fighting to preserve the integrity of the Union & the power of the Govt—on no other issue." He believed emphatically that abolitionism must not be allowed to intrude on this central goal. The slavery issue, in his mind, must remain "incidental & subsidiary."[16]

This attitude was not likely to endear him to abolitionist senators, the so-called Radicals in Congress, who were at first so enamored of McClellan and were now, particularly since Ball's Bluff, disillusioned and impatient. For them, the end of slavery was not in the least incidental and subsidiary.

McClellan had assured the senators that if they would help rid him of Scott, he would advance on the enemy. But in the days since Scott departed, with the year rapidly running out, there was still no sign of movement—still no sign of "On to Richmond." Lincoln was under intense political pressure. The people were restless for the general to take the army to the field and engage the enemy. Washington was uneasy, sensitive to the feeling in the country. Radical members of Congress were becoming increasingly critical not only of McClellan but of the administration. Indeed, Lincoln was himself growing anxious, beginning to doubt the general.

"Providence, with favoring sky and earth," a New York congressman reported Lincoln saying, "seemed to beckon the army on, but General McClellan, he supposed, knew his business and had his reasons for disregarding these hints of Providence."[17]

Instead, McClellan was holding huge, impressive parades and reviews of his growing Army of the Potomac, which, by late November, had ballooned to an aggregate strength of more than 168,000 troops. For three months, the government had been feeding more than a regiment a day into the mix. It was now the biggest army on the globe, and McClellan had been whipping it into world-class shape.[18]

The grandest of these showy reviews, before an awed 30,000 spectators, was on November 20—some 65,000 men, seven divisions marching, fifteen batteries of artillery booming salutes. John Nicolay called it "the largest and most magnificent military review ever held on this continent," and *Harper's Weekly* called it "brilliant beyond description." But it further highlighted the stark fact that this great army was not being led into battle. One Washingtonian observed, "It cannot be disguised that there is springing up again both in Congress & the Country a good deal of restlessness & impatience, at the apparent inactivity of the immense army we have in the field."[19]

Where his growing army of critics saw mindless, maddening delay in these showy parades and reviews, McClellan saw military method. It was part of his organizational management style. He used these reviews to "accustom regiments to move together and see each other, to give the troops an idea of their own strength, to infuse *esprit de corps* and mutual emulation, and to acquaint myself with the capacity of the general officers."[20] In his mind, the reviews were doing much to make his army what he wanted it to become—that "a certain amount of the pomp and circumstance of war was potent in producing soldierly spirit and bearing among the men."[21]

As McClellan continued to hold fast to his own timetable, the Republican Radicals in Congress continued to fidget. They were becoming lethally unhappy. One of the most radical and lethal-minded, Senator Benjamin F. Wade of Ohio, complained, "I begin to despair of ever putting down this rebellion through the instrumentality of this administration. They are blundering, cowardly, and inefficient." As for McClellan, "He seems to have adopted the maxim of the old woman...that 'all boys should learn to swim well before they went into the water'...I don't know what is to come of all this imbecility."

Senator Zachariah Chandler of Michigan, once a McClellan admirer, was now writing, "I am greatly disenchanted with Genl McClelland. He seems to be devoting himself to parades and military shows instead of clearing the country of rebels."[22]

Republicans all, they had begun to suspect that McClellan's politics—offensively Democratic, they believed—was figuring in the delay, and they became suspicious of his motives. In many of their minds, his being a Democrat was worse than the inactivity itself. They deplored commanders who held political views contrary to their own, who had sympathy for Southerners or favored a policy of conciliation with the rebels. To their way of thinking, anybody who wanted to be carefully prepared before going into battle was either a coward or not man enough to do the job, which was to wage immediate, hard-handed, destructive war against the slave power.[23] McClellan appeared to them to be in the clutches of all these unfortunate backsliding traits.

In early December 1861, a handful of Radical congressmen decided to act, to take a direct role in dealing with the rebellion. They created a tool that they could wield against this delaying and Democratic apostasy—a Joint Committee on the Conduct of the War. Chandler was one of the seven members—three from the Senate, four from the House—appointed to it. Wade, its chairman, frankly admitted its intention was to "frighten" the administration—and the reticent McClellan—"into a fight."[24]

"We must run some risk," Wade said. "We can not keep such an army as this without doing something; we must get money for the army, and to get that we must do something, and do it as soon as it can be done, we must run a little hazard."[25] The joint committee would begin holding hearings, conducting them in Star Chamber fashion.

Under this siege from an increasingly unfriendly Congress and cabinet and a restless public, McClellan pleaded with Lincoln, "Dont let them hurry me, is all I ask." Lincoln replied, "You shall have your own way in the matter I assure you."[26] But the assurance was a one-way street. McClellan was not taking the president, the one man who could do him good, into his confidence.

One evening in mid-November, not two weeks after Lincoln had elevated McClellan to command of all the armies, the president, Seward, and John Hay had called on McClellan in his quarters on Lafayette Square. The general's servant informed them McClellan was at a wedding but would soon return. They waited. After about half an hour, McClellan did return. His servant informed the general that the president was waiting to see him, and McClellan, paying him no mind, passed the door where the three waited and went up the stairs. They waited another half hour and sent the servant to remind the general that they were there. The answer came down that the general had gone to bed.

As they left, Hay railed against "this unparallelled insolence of epaulettes." The president said it was better at this time not to be making points of etiquette and personal dignity.[27] The general might be getting his rest, but he was undermining his relationship with this one man, more than any other, whom he desperately needed on his side.

McClellan opened up enough on December 10 to tell Lincoln that he was contemplating a different strategy than a head-on overland advance against the Confederates in his front. He told Lincoln, "I have now my mind actively turned towards another plan of campaign that I do not think at all anticipated by the enemy nor by many of our own people."[28] It would involve shifting the base of operations southward on the Chesapeake to the James, York, or Rappahannock rivers—a turning movement. But he did not give Lincoln any details and had not mentioned it since. And the Radicals with their Committee on the

Conduct of the War were now looking angrily, impatiently over both their shoulders.

Lincoln could shield McClellan only so much and for so long. Feeling betrayed by men and events, McClellan withdrew further into the less attractive corners of his character. He became ever more over-whelmed, more distrustful, more paranoid, more secretive and uncom-municative, more cautious.[29] Philippe, Comte de Paris, an observer from French royalty serving on McClellan's staff, had noticed that the disaster at Ball's Bluff had dramatically heightened the general's con-stitutional caution. He was to write: "It was the first time that he had put his hand to the tiller, and the cumbrous vessel had not obeyed the helm as the pilot had expected." [30] From that day, the Comte de Paris believed, "a fatal hesitation took possession of McClellan."[31]

One of the first witnesses the new committee called was McClellan himself. But on December 20, three days before he was to appear, he came down with a fierce case of typhoid. It was bad timing all around. The public clamor to act was at its peak, his headquarters were para-lyzed without him, his army was abruptly brought to a standstill, the administration and all of Washington were suddenly at loose ends.

And nobody was more distraught over this than Abraham Lincoln.

CHAPTER 8

PRESIDENTIAL ANGST

As the year 1862 opened, Lincoln was clearly seeing what Benjamin F. Wade and the Radicals were seeing, what the public was seeing: Nothing was happening. The general was down with typhoid. The army was paralyzed without him. There was no telling when anything might be done.

The quiet along the Potomac and in the West too—along the Mississippi—worried Lincoln. Nothing good was happening anywhere. Little had happened since McClellan had become general-in-chief two months before and told Lincoln, "I can do it all."[1] An incipient impatience was growing even in this patient president's mind. He is said to have described McClellan and his army about this time as "an admirable engineer, but he seems to have a special talent for a stationary engine."[2]

As McClellan continued to lie in his sickbed through the early days of the new year, Lincoln wandered into Quartermaster General Montgomery Meigs's office on January 10 and sat dejectedly before the open fire.

"General," he asked Meigs, "what shall I do? The people are impatient. [Secretary of the Treasury Salmon Portland] Chase has no money and he tells me he can raise no more; the General of the Army has typhoid fever. The bottom is out of the tub. What shall I do?"

The able quartermaster general listened sympathetically and suggested Lincoln consult some of McClellan's other generals, since the general-in-chief was indisposed. Ask them what they thought he ought to do.[3]

Lincoln immediately did so, summoning two of McClellan's generals, Irvin McDowell and William B. Franklin, to a meeting in the White House at eight o'clock in the evening on January 10. McDowell arrived first and found Lincoln alone. Joining them soon were Franklin, Seward, Chase, and an assistant secretary of war.

Lincoln told the two generals that he was "greatly disturbed at the state of affairs" and since McClellan was sick and inaccessible, he needed to speak with someone. He told them that he wished their opinion on how to commence operations with the Army of the Potomac—soon. The president told them that if something was not done, "the bottom would be out of the whole affair." He suggested that if General McClellan did not want to use the army, he "would like to *borrow it,* provided he could see how it could be made to do something." After some discussion, in which both generals confessed ignorance of the army's actual condition, Lincoln said he wished them to consult with one another, get more information, and meet with him again the following evening.

McDowell and Franklin met the next morning at the Treasury Building and agreed that the first thing to be done was to clear out the Confederates from in front of Washington. They agreed that the assault on the rebels ought to be mounted from the army's present base rather than attempting it from a change of base, as McClellan was apparently contemplating. Uncomfortable in what they were involved in with Lincoln, unknown to McClellan, they wondered uneasily whether they should acquaint the ailing general with what the president was asking of them. But they concluded that was Lincoln's decision, not theirs.

The two generals fortified themselves with further information on the condition of ordnance, subsistence, and numbers of the army and met with the president again. The same men from the night before were there, joined this time by Postmaster General Montgomery Blair. The group was divided on whether operations should be from the present base or from a base on the lower Chesapeake. Lincoln ordered the two generals to consult with General Meigs about transporting an army by water and to meet again the next day at three o'clock. The generals met with Meigs the next morning, January 12, and he agreed with them that the operation should be from the present base, with the entire army concentrated to that end. A change of base, Meigs argued, would take too long—four to six weeks. They all met again with the president that afternoon.[4]

Meanwhile, lying in his bed, McClellan learned that a council of war was being held behind his back. He "mustered strength enough on Sunday morning [January 12] to be driven to the White House," where, he later reported, "my unexpected appearance caused very much the effect of a shell in a powder magazine. It was clear from the manner of those I met there that there was something of which they were ashamed." There he told Lincoln "in a general and casual way" what his new campaign plans were. The president invited him to appear the following day at a larger meeting with members of the cabinet, Franklin, McDowell, and Meigs. That done, Lincoln cut short the meeting on the twelfth.[5]

At eleven o'clock on January 13, the meeting convened. McClellan was there, a sullen presence. When Franklin and McDowell had concluded their report and recommendation, McDowell spoke somewhat apologetically of the awkward position they were in. McClellan replied coldly, "You are entitled to have any opinion you please." Otherwise he was saying nothing, offering nothing.[6]

Meigs moved his chair next to McClellan's. "The President evidently expects you to speak," Meigs whispered. "Can you not promise some movement towards Manassas? You are strong."

"I cannot move on them with as great a force as they have," McClellan snapped.

"Why, you have near 200,000 men, how many have they?"

"Not less than 175,000 according to my advices."

Meigs was taken aback. "Do you think so?" He nevertheless thought McClellan ought to say something. "The President expects something from you."

"If I tell him my plans they will be in the New York Herald tomorrow morning," McClellan rasped. "He can't keep a secret, he will tell them to Tadd [Lincoln's nine-year old son, Tad]."

"That is a pity," Meigs sympathized, "but he is the President—the Commander-in-Chief; he has a right to know; it is not respectful to sit mute when he so clearly requires you to speak. He is superior to all."[7]

The president asked generally what and when anything could be done, saying much the same thing he had said in his first meeting with Franklin and McDowell. McClellan finally replied that the case was so clear a blind man could see it, and spoke of the difficulty of knowing what force he could count on for any movement. Chase then asked McClellan a direct question: What did he intend doing with his army, and when did he intend to do it?

After a long pause, McClellan said he was very unwilling to divulge his plans, always believing that in military matters, the fewer persons who knew them the better, and that he would tell them only if he was ordered to do so. He said, in effect, that no general commanding an army would willingly submit his plans to the judgment of such an assembly, in which some were incompetent to form a valuable opinion and others were incapable of keeping a secret. Anything made known to them would soon spread and become known to the enemy.

Lincoln did not order McClellan to divulge his plans. But he did ask whether the general had a time fixed in his own mind when a movement could be commenced. McClellan said he had—but he was not revealing it. Satisfied, Lincoln then said, "I will adjourn this meeting."[8]

Seeing in all this only a conspiracy behind his back, McClellan had not done himself any favors at this meeting. But Lincoln, despite growing reservations, still had enough confidence in the general and was content, now that McClellan was out of bed, to turn the affairs of the army back to him.[9]

As it turned out, it was not Tad who would leak his plans to the *New York Herald* but McClellan himself. The day after he had refused to discuss his war strategy in the meeting with Lincoln, the cabinet members, and his subordinate generals—on grounds that anything he said would end up the next day in the *Herald*—McClellan granted a three-hour exclusive interview to Malcolm Ives, a *Herald* correspondent.

"What I declined communicating to them," he told Ives, "I am now going to convey through you to Mr. Bennett [James Gordon Bennett, founder, publisher, and editor of the *Herald*] . . . *all* the knowledge I possess myself, with no reserve"—all that he had in mind as the commanding general. He did so, in an astonishing leak of official military planning, confident that Bennett would use the information wisely and not reveal where he got it. McClellan shared with Ives the most current reports from the armies in the western theater, from operations currently afoot on the North Carolina coast, and from other operations under way or contemplated. He told Ives how all this fit into his own plans for a war-ending offensive against Richmond. "They must be beaten and they shall be beaten in Virginia," he told Ives, "and then I will knock them to pieces at New Orleans." He would continue briefing Ives on a regular basis, partly to plant stories "to help me throw dust in the eyes of the enemy."[10]

Behind this leaking operation was Edwin McMasters Stanton, a lawyer and the attorney general in the closing months of the feckless James Buchanan administration. He had suggested that McClellan tell all to Ives and had arranged the meeting.[11]

No one in the country was a harsher or more satiric critic of Lincoln than Stanton—going back to 1855, when Lincoln had been retained as a consulting lawyer in an important patent case that Stanton, a high-powered Pittsburgh lawyer, was involved in. Sophisticated, abrupt, rude, and haughty, Stanton had spurned Lincoln as a hick from the sticks and refused to serve with him, consult with him, or otherwise participate with him in the case, which the Lincoln-Stanton side ultimately won. Stanton had looked at this gawky, drawling, storytelling frontier lawyer and reportedly called him a "giraffe." But amazingly, half a decade later, the giraffe had been elected president. Stanton was now calling him the "original gorilla," the epithet that McClellan had borrowed.[12]

After arriving in Washington, McClellan often consulted with the sympathetic Stanton, a Democrat. On occasion, as he had became increasingly beleaguered, the general "concealed" himself "at Stanton's to dodge all enemies in shape of 'browsing' Presdt, etc."[13]

Stanton, this human haven from browsing presidents, was five foot five inches in height, broad shouldered, and fifty, with a long gray-flecked brown beard and severe but lively eyes that peered through narrow spectacles. He was peppery, generally irritable, and often looked as if he had not slept well. The common wisdom was that he was no respecter of persons, precedents, formulas, or red tape, and was capable of dealing heavy blows with great coolness and celerity. He was blessed with an unflagging talent for saying no.[14]

Despite his prejudices and a cantankerous no-saying nature, Stanton was an incredibly competent and able man, of unstinting passion and energy. And there was no question of his utterly unselfish and driven devotion to the Union. For these reasons, even more incredibly, Lincoln, a forgiving man, on January 13—the very day of the conference with McClellan, the cabinet members, and the generals—named this Lincoln-bashing, acid-tongued, perpetual motion machine as his new secretary of war. "I have made up my mind," Lincoln said, "to sit down on all my pride, it may be a portion of my self aspect, and appoint him to the place."[15] Stanton was to replace Simon Cameron, a political appointee from Pennsylvania who had been as inept as Stanton was likely to be adroit.

McClellan was heartened by this turn of events. Having this ally in the job most relevant to his own, he thought, would be a vast improvement. However, Stanton was anything but predictable. He was fiery and passionate and irascible, a human volcano ever on the edge of eruption, "inclined," one officer in frequent contact with him said, "to make all around him nervous."[16]

John Hay is reported to have begged John Nicolay never to send him to Stanton to ask a favor, that "I would rather make a tour of a smallpox hospital."[17] Lincoln, however, believed his new secretary of war was simply "terribly in earnest; and he does not always use the most conciliatory language," that his "bark is a great deal worse than his bite."[18] The president said, "There's Seward is an Episcopalian, Chase is an Episcopalian, Bates is an Episcopalian, and Stanton swears enough to be one."[19]

But, as with most such men, Stanton had gentler side—a weakness for people in distress, women and the aged in particular. Hidden beneath his gruff exterior was something of a compassionate interior. It cropped up every now and then.[20]

Despite his friendship with McClellan, Stanton had a Radical's mind-set about the war. He wanted the army to fight, to advance immediately, to roll back and destroy the hated slave power. He was not going to have any more truck with McClellan's delay than Wade and his Joint Committee on the Conduct of the War. Within a month of taking office, Stanton threw in with the Radicals, sharing their impatience, intolerance, and frustration with McClellan's continued inaction.[21]

In late January, Lincoln, with this new hard-driving secretary of war, and still looking to prod McClellan to some kind of action, took to writing war orders himself. On January 27, he wrote General War Order No. 1. In it he called for a simultaneous movement of all Union land and naval forces for February 22. Four days later, he issued Special War Order No.1, which specifically ordered the Army of the Potomac on that day to launch an expedition overland to seize and occupy a point on the railroad southwest of Manassas Junction.[22]

Instead, McClellan was now actively laying groundwork for his campaign not "at all anticipated by the enemy nor by many of our own people"—which he had hinted at to Lincoln in early December but had offered no details.[23] His plan, instead of moving overland against the concentrated Confederate strength, was to a move down the Chesapeake, landing a vast force at Urbanna near the mouth of the Rappahannock River, and from there rapidly marching the fifty miles to Richmond—the end run around the Confederates massed at Manassas and Centerville, a massive turning movement. It looked to him to be a shorter, safer road to Richmond than the overland route.[24]

McClellan had ordered his chief engineer, John Barnard, to study the logistical problem of shifting a 100,000-man army to that line—toward the James, York, or Rappahannock rivers. Barnard returned, leery of the scheme; it looked to him impractical, if not imprudent.[25] But that had not derailed McClellan's intentions. He was pushing the plan forward anyhow.

Lincoln's attention and preferences, however, were firmly fixed on the overland strategy. His war orders were based on an advance aimed at the Confederate entrenchments at Centreville and Manassas. On February 3, he wrote McClellan, "You and I have distinct, and different plans for a movement of the Army of the Potomac—yours to be down the Chesapeake, up the Rappahannock to Urbana, and across land to the terminus of the Railroad on the York River—mine to move directly to a point on the Railroad southwest of Manassas." He then asked McClellan to justify his plan.

Lincoln asked:

1st. Does not your plan involve a greatly larger expenditure of *time,* and *money* than mine?

2nd. Wherein is a victory *more certain* by your plan than mine?

3rd. Wherein is a victory *more valuable* by your plan than mine?

4th. In fact, would it not be *less* valuable, in this, that it would break no great line of the enemy's communications, while mine would?

5th. In case of disaster, would not a safe retreat be more difficult by your plan than mine.

Lincoln proposed a deal. He told McClellan if he could satisfactorily answer these five questions, "I shall gladly yield my plan to yours.[26]

CHAPTER 9

PLANNING FOR ARMAGEDDON

O n the same day Lincoln was asking these pointed questions—February 3—McClellan was sending the president a twenty-two-page defense of his plan, which in effect answered them.

McClellan first reviewed what he had accomplished since coming to Washington. He had found no army to command after Bull Run, only a collection of disorganized regiments "cowering on the banks of the Potomac...undisciplined, undrilled & dispirited," and the capital without defenses, "almost in a condition to have been taken by a dash of a single regiment of cavalry."

The capital was now "secure against attack," he reminded Lincoln, the enemy "confined to the positions they occupied before 21 July." He wrote: "I have now under my command a well drilled & reliable Army to which the destinies of the country may be confidently committed. This Army is young, & untried in battle, but it is animated by the highest spirit, & is capable of great deeds. That so much has been accomplished, & such an Army created in so short a time from nothing will hereafter be regarded as one of the highest glories of the Administration & the nation."

Lincoln was unlikely to quarrel with any of that. McClellan's accomplishment in raising and training a huge army and securing Washington had been extraordinary.

However, as big and ready as the army was for glory and as fully able to repel an enemy, attacking an entrenched position "long since selected, studied, & fortified"—and against such towering, if imagined and overestimated, numbers, was another matter. And any attack, in McClellan's thinking, had to be quick, deadly, successful, and complete. He told the president, "our true policy" was to be "fully preparing ourselves & then seeking for the most decisive results—I do not wish to waste life in useless battles, but prefer to strike at the heart."

Neither could Lincoln quarrel with that.

So there are two ways to go about it, McClellan suggested: "a direct attack upon the enemy's entrenched positions at Centreville, Manassas etc, or…a movement to turn one or both flanks of those positions, or a combination of two plans." In McClellan's mind, undertaking both at the same time was out of the question: The relative strength of the two armies, his and the Confederate's, did not justify that.

He argued that of the two realistic options, his, the turning movement on the lower Chesapeake, "affords the shortest possible land routes to Richmond, & strikes directly at the heart of the enemy's power in the East."

The roads in that region, unlike those on Washington's front (then deep in winter mud and difficult of navigation), were "passable at all seasons of the year." The country on his preferred route was "more favorable for offensive operations than that in front of Washington (which is *very* unfavorable)—much more level—more cleared land—the woods less dense—soil more sandy—the spring some two or three weeks earlier."

A flanking movement in force by his plan, McClellan argued, "obliges the enemy to abandon his entrenched position at Manassas, in order to hasten to cover Richmond and Norfolk." This movement, if successful, "gives us the Capital, the communications, the supplies of the rebels. Norfolk [the former federal naval base Gosport, on the Elizabeth River just upstream from Norfolk, now in Confederate hands] would fall; all the waters of the Chesapeake would be ours; all Virginia would be in our power; & the enemy forced to abandon Tennessee & North Carolina."

The point of landing for this end-around operation, promising "the most brilliant results," McClellan believed, would be at Urbanna on the lower Rappahannock. Should circumstances render that impracticable—"the worst coming to the worst—we can take Fort

Monroe as a base, & operate with complete security, altho' with less celerity & brilliancy of results, up the Peninsula."

This movement, empowered by the force he hoped to assemble there—a 140,000-man army—McClellan argued, "will not at all expose the city of Washington to danger." It would leave the city "quite safe."

His way, he told Lincoln, although involving a thirty-day delay up front, in the end promises "a decisive victory which will probably end the war" and will be "far cheaper than to gain a battle tomorrow that produces no final results, & may require years of warfare & expenditure to follow up."

Such, McClellan argued, "is precisely the difference between the two plans"—the president's and his. A battle gained at Manassas, he wrote, "will result merely in the possession of the field of combat." And even that is not guaranteed. "On the Manassas line the rebels can, if well enough disciplined (& we have every reason to suppose that to be the case) dispute our advance, over bad roads, from position to position. . . . It is by no means certain that we can beat them at Manassas."

On the other line, his line, he argued, "I regard success as certain by all the chances of war. We demoralize the enemy, by forcing him to abandon his prepared position for one which we have chosen, in which all is in our favor, & where success must produce immense results. My judgment as a General is clearly in favor of this project."

McClellan argued throughout his memo that this operation, twinned to simultaneous movements in the West, which he had been vigorously advocating and planning for as general-in-chief, would be devastating for the rebels and very likely end the rebellion.

"I will stake my life, my reputation on the result," he said; "—more than that, I will stake upon it the success of our cause." However, "I hope but little from the attack on Manassas—my judgment is against it."[1]

McClellan's argument was long yet trenchant. It was buttressed throughout with detail of the movements and circumstances likely to follow the landing at Urbanna on the road to Richmond. If not entirely convinced, Lincoln was mollified. McClellan had made his point.

However, the president's most palpable fear, despite McClellan's assurances, was that by the general's plan the capital would be left wide open, vulnerable, and easy prey to the great Confederate horde McClellan claimed lay waiting on Washington's doorstep. The numbers were flying. Pinkerton had put the Confederate strength at more than 100,000. McClellan was holding to his own estimate of 150,000. A third report, on February 21, from the Comte de Paris of his own staff had estimated Confederate strength on the Potomac at 70,000, but with another 12,000 to 18,000 under Major General Thomas J. (Stonewall) Jackson in the Shenandoah Valley.[2]

Whatever the numbers or Lincoln's reservations, McClellan continued preparing for his turning movement. The president did not formally suspend his orders for an advance overland nor willingly yield his preference, but he did not halt the general's preparations.

A daughter, May, had been born to the McClellans in October 1861. Nelly and the baby were now in Washington with the general, in a house he had taken for them at H Street and Madison Place. McClellan was ecstatic. "The baby is splendid," he boasted to his mother-in-law; she "laughs inordinately & so loudly that it is almost a nuisance—converses intelligently in 3 languages."[3]

In a tragic counterpoint to McClellan's joy, Lincoln's son Willie, age eleven, caught fever and, on February 20, died in the White House. Now a father himself, McClellan shared the president's agony. He wrote Lincoln a note of condolence on February 22, the day the president had ordered for an advance on all fronts.

"I have not felt authorized to intrude upon you personally in the midst of the deep distress I know you feel in the sad calamity that has befallen you & your family," the general wrote Lincoln, "yet I cannot refrain from expressing to you the sincere & deep sympathy I feel for you. You have been a kind true friend to me in the midst of the great cares & difficulties by which we have been surrounded during the past few months—your confidence has upheld me when I should otherwise have felt weak. I wish now only to assure you & your family that I have felt the deepest sympathy in your affliction."

He told the president, "I am pushing to prompt completion the measures of which we have spoken, & I beg that you will not allow military affairs to give you one moment's trouble—but that you will rest assured that nothing shall be left undone to follow up the successes that have been such an auspicious commencement of our new campaign."[4]

For some time in late 1861 and early 1862, as part of the general discontent that McClellan was not taking his biggest army on the planet to fight the enemy, was the nagging hold the Confederates had on the

Potomac above and below Washington. Clamor was afoot to break its grip and open the Baltimore and Ohio Railroad's direct link to the Ohio Valley.

McClellan was, in fact, working on the problem. His plan was to position a bridge of canal boats linking the Maryland side of the Potomac with Virginia at Harpers Ferry, which his troops could cross to occupy Winchester and Strasburg and secure his line of supply. The project became an embarrassing cropper when McClellan's engineers failed to measure the width of the locks beforehand; they turned out six inches too narrow for the boats to pass through, and too slight a discrepancy for the naked eye to detect. The entire operation fell apart for the lack of a tape measure. It was being said by wags in Washington that the canal expedition had died of lockjaw.

Stanton, McClellan's onetime ally, now a Judas, stormed into the White House on the evening of February 27 shouting, "it is a d---d fizzle!" It meant in Stanton's mind that McClellan "doesn't intend to do anything." Even Lincoln's considerable patience was jolted. The president called in Randolph Marcy, McClellan's father-in-law and the general's trusted right hand, and angrily demanded, "Why in the [blank] nation, Gen. Marcy, couldn't the Gen. have known whether a boat would go through that lock, before he spent a million dollars getting them there? I am no engineer: but it seems to me that if I wished to know whether a boat would go through a hole, or a lock, common sense would teach me to go and measure it. I am almost despairing at these results. Everything seems to fail. The general impression is daily gaining ground that the Gen. does not intend to do anything. . . . I am grievously disappointed and almost in despair."[5]

Feeling that this message ought to be delivered directly to McClellan, on March 8, Lincoln called him to the White House—"to talk plainly" about the canal fiasco and the mood in the country. (Since the evening of the "insolence of epaulettes" affair when Lincoln had been kept cooling his heels in vain in McClellan's waiting room, the president had required the general to come to him for meetings.)

Lincoln's patience was fraying. He told a Pennsylvania congressman, "One thing I can say, that the army will move, either under General McClellan or some other man and that very soon."[6]

Despite his shaken confidence in the general, Lincoln had been gamely defending him, trying to protect him from Radical and public anger as best he could, trying to give him the time he coveted.

The president, however, was less certain than ever that, in the highly charged political atmosphere, he could protect him much longer, unless McClellan acted boldly against the Confederates to put down the clamor—and, more important, silence ugly charges now rising of treason and disloyalty.

In the meeting with McClellan on March 8, Lincoln advised the general of these charges. McClellan was outraged at the suggestion that he was a traitor. He shot to his feet, demanding a retraction, saying he "could permit no one to couple the word treason with my name."[7] Lincoln assured him that neither he nor his cabinet believed in any way that McClellan was anything but loyal, but talk of treason was clearly in the air. McClellan, who had called a meeting of his generals for later that day to acquaint them with the flanking strategy down the Chesapeake, angrily told Lincoln he would put the plan to them for a vote so that the president could decide for himself "whether I was a traitor or not."[8]

When the generals met that day, they were asked by McClellan, to their surprise and without discussion, to vote on whether the army should change its base of operations from Washington to the lower Chesapeake. Eight of the twelve favored the Urbanna plan. Four, including McClellan's chief engineer, John Barnard, and his three senior generals—Edwin Sumner, Irvin McDowell, and Samuel Heintzelman—did not.[9]

Eight was enough. The Urbanna plan would proceed. But that same day, as the generals were meeting and voting, Lincoln issued General War Orders Nos. 2 and 3 without consulting McClellan. The president's frayed patience was showing. Exercising his power as commander in chief, he was stepping in, intent on getting something moving. He and Stanton were at one with these moves, both believing them necessary. The first order created four army corps to be commanded by the four most senior of the generals under McClellan—McDowell, Sumner, Heintzelman, and Erasmus D. Keyes. Under this order, the defenses of Washington would be left in the hands of Brigadier General James Wadsworth, the military governor of the District of Columbia.[10]

This was obnoxiously offensive to McClellan. He had expected to name his own corps commanders and only after putting them through a trial of fire to see who qualified. The four named were not among his favorites, nor were they his strongest supporters. And he despised and distrusted Wadsworth, a political general. It was a slap in the face, similar to a vote of no confidence.

Lincoln's second order clearly laid down the requirement for the safety of Washington. "No change of base of operations of the Army of the Potomac," it ordered, "shall be made without leaving in, and about Washington, such a force as, in the opinion of the General-in-chief, and the commanders of all the Army corps, shall leave said City entirely secure." It ordered the movement to the new base to begin as early as March 18. It also ordered that the army and navy cooperate to clear enemy water batteries and other obstructions around Washington before the movement down the Chesapeake.[11]

This second order raised no serious objections from McClellan. He was confident of Washington's safety. The important point won was that, with these orders, the administration had committed itself to his plan, abandoning the overland strategy favored by Lincoln.

March 8 had been a busy day, but the next day was even busier, In the morning, while McClellan was meeting with Lincoln and Stanton, word arrived that the Confederates had pulled out of their positions at Centreville in front of Washington and from the water batteries deployed on the Virginia side of the Potomac downstream from Alexandria—taking leave lock, stock, and barrel.

Confederate General Joseph E. Johnston, reading intelligence coming from across the Potomac, had become convinced that McClellan was up to something, readying an early movement of some sort. So he began pulling his army back on March 8, stealthily and secretly, to a less exposed position behind the line of the Rappahannock. This movement came as a total surprise to McClellan.[12]

As if that were not shocking enough, equally astonishing news had just come from Hampton Roads in the waters around Fort Monroe on the Peninsula. The former Union man-of-war USS *Merrimac,* captured by the Confederates when they seized Norfolk, had been rechristened the CSS *Virginia,* refitted, sheathed in iron, and equipped with a ramming prow. In this monstrous configuration, it had sailed among the wooden-hulled Union fleet anchored in the Roads on March 8, wreaking havoc and disaster. It sank one Union warship, ran another aground, and failed to destroy a third only because of an ebbing tide before retiring. What might happen when the monster emerged again was a terrifying prospect.

The problem was mitigated and the waters were pacified the next day, March 9, when a newly minted Union ironclad, USS *Monitor,* steamed into the Roads and met the *Virginia* as she sailed out again. In one of the world's epic sea battles, the two ironclads fought for five hours to a standstill. The born-again *Virginia* limped back into its lair at Gosport. For now, at least, the Roads was secure.

McClellan's Urbanna strategy, however, was in disarray. It had required that the Confederate army remain entrenched in place before Washington so it could be flanked. That situation no longer held. Landing his great force at Urbanna was no longer an option. The flanking expedition would have to go deeper, to Fort Monroe and Newport News, and mount its campaign for Richmond up the York and James rivers on the Peninsula—the fallback plan.

A cautious probe McClellan sent out immediately into the abandoned works at Centreville brought more bad news. In the entrenchments, which the general believed to be so formidable, were batteries of pine logs camouflaged to resemble gun muzzles. When the public in the North learned of this, they derisively called them "Quaker Guns." McClellan's credibility took another serious body blow.

And now came yet another punch to his battered solar plexus. On March 11, Lincoln drafted yet another war order. This one relieved McClellan as general-in-chief of all the armies on grounds that he had taken the field as the major general in personal command of the Army of the Potomac, and that was responsibility enough.[13]

From the field, where he was surveying the abandoned Confederate positions, McClellan wrote his beloved Nelly, "I regret that the rascals are after me again. I had been foolish enough to hope that when I went into the field they would give me some rest, but it seems otherwise—perhaps I should have expected it. If I can get out of this scrape you will never catch me in the power of such a set again." He told her he did not expect the virulence to diminish, only to increase.[14]

Indeed, that appeared to be likely. Nathaniel Hawthorne, in Washington at the time, observed, "[T]he outcry opened against General McClellan, since the enemy's retreat from Manassas is really terrible, and almost universal; because it is found that we might have taken their fortifications with perfect ease six months ago, they being defended chiefly by wooden guns." Angry Senate Radicals brought a resolution to the floor calling for McClellan's dismissal. It was blocked, however, by a parliamentary maneuver.[15]

To a dispassionate observer, it would appear that McClellan had brought much of this on himself. His arrogant distrust of politicians in general and those above him in particular, including the president, and his repeated delays had in effect squandered much of his personal capital in Washington and in the country. Perhaps most seriously it had further eroded Lincoln's faith in him.

However, it had not yet destroyed that faith. Lincoln had no intention of abandoning the general just yet. In part, this was simply that McClellan was still the president's best, perhaps only, option. There was no ready alternative, and McClellan had come to him confidently recommended with a solid reputation. Following a conversation with the president, Illinois Senator Orville Browning, who kept a meticulous daily diary, wrote that Lincoln had been assured by all the leading military men that McClellan "possessed a very high order of military talent." Lincoln told Browning that he did not think they could all be mistaken. Yet he "was not fully satisfied with [McClellan's] conduct of the war—that he was not sufficiently energetic and aggressive in his measures." But, Lincoln added, "he had studied [McClellan] and taken his measure as well as he could—that he thought he had the capacity to make arrangements properly for a great conflict." Lincoln told Browning he "had given [McClellan] peremptory orders to move now, and he must do it."[16]

A friend of McClellan's wrote Barlow in New York that "Lincoln has declared so emphatically that he will not back down on Mac that the hounds in and out of Congress have ceased their yelpings," if "only for a time."[17]

The time, meanwhile, had at last come for McClellan's onslaught against the Confederate flank, for his first move toward Richmond—to that one great war-ending battle he had always contemplated, planned for, and delayed for.

CHAPTER 10

TROUBLED MINDS

T he army that McClellan began embarking in late March for the
Peninsula 200 miles away was the largest ever assembled on the
North American continent. The challenge of getting it there
was gargantuan. It was to be, one awed European observer noted, "the
stride of a giant."[1]

At Perryville, Alexandria, and Washington, Assistant Secretary of
War John Tucker collected 113 steamers, 188 schooners, and 88 barges
and boarded 121,500 men, 14,592 animals, 1,150 wagons, 44 batteries,
and 74 ambulances. With them he crammed aboard pontoon bridges,
telegraph equipment, and the enormous quantity of equipage and supplies a force of such magnitude demanded.[2]

Anne Frobel, refugeeing in Fairfax County, went to Alexandria when all
this was happening in mid-March and was flabbergasted. There she found
what she thought was "the *whole world* moving toward Richmond."[3]

It was no secret in Richmond, the target of this operation, that something big was mounting in the North—a military tsunami—bound to
be moving in their direction. A Confederate officer in Yorktown awaiting this juggernaut wrote of "the thick clouds" of trouble gathering.[4]

Richmond city councilman Thomas H. Wynne saw the gathering
clouds too and concluded that Virginia was to be "the outpost, the bul-
wark against which our invaders were directing their force, and her soil
was the theatre which had been chosen for the issue."[5]

Joseph Mayo, the mayor of Richmond since 1853, a descendant of
the city's founder, and now a man in his late sixties, was steeling himself

for the worst and vowing the ultimate. For him it was do or die. "If the city of Richmond was ever surrendered to its enemies," he vowed, "it should not be by a descendent of its founder. He would sooner die than surrender our city; and if they wished a mayor who would surrender they must elect another in his place."[6]

How McClellan intended to employ this fearsome behemoth was on everyone's mind. On March 19, at the request of the War Department, he outlined his designs to Edwin Stanton. He would steer his huge armada toward Fort Monroe and Newport News and land his army there—its first base of operations. The line of operation, after landing, would run through Yorktown, to West Point (Virginia), to Richmond. From Fort Monroe, he would land a corps as near to Yorktown as possible to turn the rebel lines south of the town. He would then reduce Yorktown and Gloucester Point by siege—perhaps requiring some delay, possibly weeks.

With full and powerful support from the navy, however, he estimated the reduction of Yorktown should take not weeks but only hours. From there, he would marshal his army and march it, under cover of navy guns, up the peninsula between the York and James rivers, in adjacent lines, all in close communication. No time, he vowed, would be lost marching this force northwest to West Point, to the very gates of Richmond. Before those gates, McClellan vowed, the decisive battle would be fought. He expected the Confederates to concentrate all their available forces there, "understanding, as they will, that it involves the fate of their cause." But when Richmond would fall so would Norfolk—ideally even before the decisive battle. With Richmond and Norfolk taken, so falls all of Virginia.[7]

McClellan was banking on two, in his mind, indispensable conditions. First, the army of 100,000 to 120,000 embarked in the ships of his armada would not be enough against the concentrated rebel power, so enormous in his mind. It would need 60,000 more—the 40,000-man corps of Irvin McDowell, the 10,000-man division of Louis Blenker, and 10,000 more from Fort Monroe as a flying column in the early going from Yorktown to West Point. They had been promised and he must have them.[8]

Second, naval support was critical. "It is impossible," he wrote the War Department, "to urge too strongly the absolute necessity of the full co-operation of the Navy as a part of this programme. Without it the operations may be prolonged for many weeks, and we may be forced to carry in front several strong positions, which by [its] aid could be turned without serious loss of either time or men." Particularly critical would be absolute naval participation—"its whole available force, its most powerful vessels"—against Yorktown at the start. "There," McClellan stressed, "is the most important point—there the knot to be cut."[9]

Given all that McClellan expected, the work would still not be easy. An operation of this size foretold a task of unprecedented magnitude. Logistics alone would be a major headache. The problems, expected and unexpected, were likely to be daunting. Many factors, perhaps, would be beyond his control. Uncertain weather conditions were likely. His army would be moving through terrain unfamiliar to him, over roads not always passable—based on maps by no means wholly accurate. He could expect breakdowns in communications. War was like that.

As McClellan boarded his command vessel, *Commodore,* on April 1, he was happy to be leaving Washington, that "sink of iniquity."[10] But there was more on his mind than strategy, a huge enemy in his front, and an inconstant administration, which his arrogance had in part alienated, at his rear.

Of equal standing with his military objective as he headed for the Peninsula was his ever-governing political objective for the war. A long struggle would only aggravate the hatred of the South. Not only must the war be quickly concluded, but it must be waged, in his own way, in a relatively benign manner. Many deaths were impossible to avoid. But Southern institutions, including slavery, must not be disturbed in the waging of it. The hard hand of war must somehow be kept gloved. That, he believed, was the correct context of this war, his understanding of the proper policy. He must wage it, obey and execute orders certainly, but wage it conservatively, keep it on that limited track, running in the proper direction toward the proper outcome.[11]

Abraham Lincoln, watching this massive movement along a line he had not favored, was a man with a troubled mind. He wanted to support McClellan fully on the Peninsula but he could not stop worrying about the security of Washington. He feared for the capital's safety with its main shield now gone. He was not convinced that enough defensive muscle was being left behind, that the capital was safe from a disastrous rebel counterpunch. In every way—militarily, politically, diplomatically—letting the capital fall into Confederate hands would be catastrophic. It must not happen. Its safety was of the highest priority.[12]

The president was under the constant pressure of public opinion in the North, desperately wanting a quick end to the war. Radicals in his own party were restive, demanding results. But Lincoln could succeed only to the extent that McClellan would succeed. And nothing would succeed if his capital city fell.

McClellan and his four corps commanders believed 40,000 troops were enough to assure Washington's safety. But he had trumped that, leaving some 73,000 men in and around Washington—18,000 in the encircling forts, nearly 8,000 at Warrenton, nearly 11,000 at Manassas Junction, more than 1,000 on the lower Potomac, and more than 35,000 guarding Washington's back door in the Shenandoah Valley. All of this was within call and could be quickly concentrated to repel a Confederate attack. Lincoln and Stanton, however, saw it differently and counted differently. They saw only the troops in the immediate works in Washington as padding against a rebel blow. So as McClellan sailed for the Peninsula, another war of numbers was raging.[13]

McClellan believed his count the proper one, far more than enough to keep the capital as safe as if encased in steel, perfectly secure—and that to think and argue otherwise "is an untruth which proves either complete ignorance or willful malevolence. The quality of the troops I left was amply good for the purposes in view."[14]

When Confederate General Johnston pulled his army back from before Washington, he had destroyed the railroad bridges across the Rappahannock and would have to rebuild them to turn back and attack the capital. In McClellan's mind, that was not remotely in the books. It seemed clear to him "that we have no reason to fear any return of the rebels in that quarter."[15]

McClellan believed all these things unflinchingly. He believed what he was now doing—threatening Richmond on its flank, drawing all the Confederate forces there for its defense—was ironclad insurance against an assault on Washington. But as he believed all those things so strongly and did not recognize anyone could believe otherwise, he made no effort to explain it adequately to Lincoln and Stanton, no effort to calm their fears and ease the president's mind. In part, he had excited the fear himself with his inflated estimates of Confederate strength. He had told Lincoln that the Confederate army numbered 150,000 well-trained, well-led fighting men. Why could not even a part of that force turn on Washington while a strong force still guarded Richmond?[16]

Out of his abiding concern for the capital's safety, Lincoln had a nervous finger on the recall trigger—to withhold, if necessary, the added troops McClellan figured he needed to confront the Confederate monster on the Peninsula.

Stanton was no less reassured than Lincoln. This erstwhile McClellan ally seemed of two minds now about the general: to support him or to undercut him, both of which he professed to practice at one time or another. On March 19, he had told General Barnard, McClellan's chief engineer, "General McClellan has no firmer friend than myself...I think [he] ought not to move till he is fully ready."[17]

But a few days later, before a group of legislators, Stanton was saying the opposite, severely slamming McClellan and his reluctance to fight, "particularizing his blunders and branding them" and wishing him sacked and replaced.[18] "He told Lincoln's Illinois friend, Senator Browning, during a carriage ride that McClellan "ought to have been removed long ago," that he (Stanton) suspected that "he was not in earnest," that he did not think that "he could emancipate himself from the influence of Jeff Davis"—and feared "he was not willing to do anything calculated greatly to damage the cause of secession." However, four days later, Stanton was writing McClellan lodging full confidence in him and pledging all the support he and the War Department could give.[19] The secretary of war was working both sides of the street.

Even as McClellan was loading his army onto his armada, Lincoln, notwithstanding his fears, assured him that the augmenting troops, McDowell's corps most particularly, would positively be heading south from Fredericksburg to join him on the Peninsula within a few days. At the same time, however, McClellan's West Point classmate, the Confederate Stonewall Jackson, was making threatening moves in the Shenandoah Valley. McClellan recognized this for what it was, a diversion to keep federal troops in the Valley from augmenting his assault on Richmond.

Jackson's as-yet indecipherable intentions were, however, making Lincoln nervous. The president saw him as a palpable threat to Washington's security. On the last day of March, Lincoln advised McClellan that he was—however regretfully and painfully—withholding Blenker's 10,000 troops.[20] Lincoln's itchy finger had begun pulling the trigger. The hammer had started to fall.

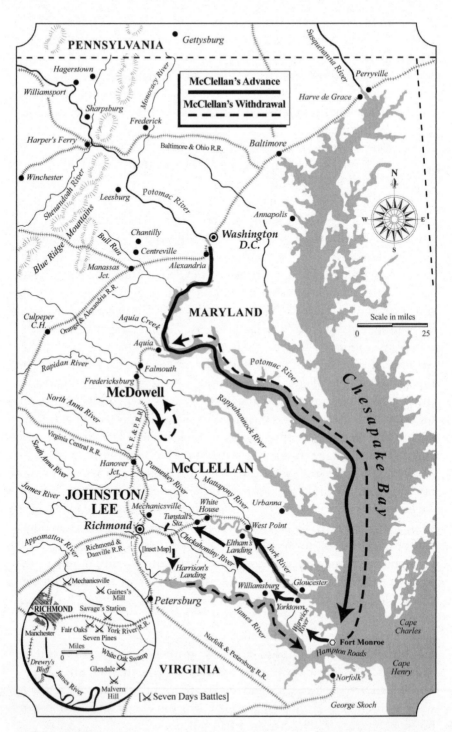

CHAPTER 11

YORKTOWN BLUES

McClellan arrived in Hampton Roads aboard *Commodore* about 4 P.M. on April 2, 1862, still believing he would have at his beckoning "an active army of 146,000 and the full control of my base of operations, and that I should receive efficient support from the navy."[1]

The steamer tied up at the wharf, unloaded the horses, and anchored in the Roads. He stayed aboard, up late into the night and deep into the next morning, making arrangements, not stepping ashore on the Peninsula until the afternoon of the third. While still aboard, he outlined his strategy in a long letter to Nelly.

His army, he told her, would begin to move on the fourth—three divisions taking the direct road to Yorktown, two divisions marching along the James River road to Young's Mills. The reserve would go to Big Bethel, where he would follow and make his headquarters that night. He intended before nightfall to take possession of a new landing some seven or eight miles from Yorktown and to have possession of Yorktown the next day—the fifth.

From there he would march his army up the Peninsula to West Point, where the Pamunkey and Mattapony rivers met to form the York and where the Richmond and York River Railroad terminated. From there, supplied by the railroad, he would move toward "the great battle...near Richmond as I have always hoped & thought. I see my way very clearly—with my trains once ready will move rapidly."[2]

What he saw clearly on April 2 began to dim almost immediately. Dark news came from both land and sea. He first learned that the order folding the 10,000 troops at Fort Monroe in under his command had been rescinded. He could no longer count them into his plans. This deprivation, combined with the loss of Blenker's division the day before he embarked for the Peninsula, cut McClellan's expected strength by 20,000 troops.

Immediately in the wake of that news came a wire telling of the most staggering further deprivation of all. The wire read: "The President, deeming the force to be left in front of Washington insufficient to insure its safety, has directed that McDowell's army corps should be detached from the forces operating under your immediate direction."[3]

A particularly edgy Brigadier General James Wadsworth, commanding the troops defending Washington, had just told Lincoln, who was edgiest of all, that his immediate force for the capital's defense numbered but 19,000 men, nearly all of them "new and imperfectly disciplined....In my judgment entirely inadequate and unfit for the important duty to which it is assigned."[4] Fearing for his capital city, Lincoln was further parsing McClellan's army.

In the space of five days, 50,000 to 60,000 men McClellan had been counting on were no longer his to have, leaving him ultimately with something less than 100,000 men. It was still the biggest army on the planet, but it was insufficient in McClellan's mind to do what he had intended and wanted to do on the Peninsula.

The loss of McDowell's First Corps in particular unstrung him. McClellan had been counting on throwing it on the rear of Yorktown, turning that fortified rampart and clearing the way for a rapid march to Richmond.[5] Virtually in a panic, he wired Lincoln the night of April 5, begging him to "reconsider the order detaching the First Corps from my command. In my deliberate judgment the success of our cause will be imperiled by so greatly reducing my force when it is actually under the fire of the enemy and active operations have commenced....I am now of the opinion that I shall have to fight all the available force of the rebels not far from here. Do not force me to do so with diminished numbers." He urged that at least he not lose William Franklin's 11,000-man division.[6]

"Nothing," he complained that same night in a message to flag officer Lewis M. Goldsborough, commanding the naval forces on

Hampton Roads and the lower Chesapeake, "could have astonished me more—I received the dispatch while listening to the rebels' guns when well assured that I required all the force I had counted upon." He vented his true horror in a letter to Nelly the next day, April 6. "It is the most infamous thing that history has recorded," he raged. "The idea of depriving a General of 35,000 troops when actually under fire!"[7]

On the same day he was writing her came yet another body blow to his strategy—this one from Goldsborough himself, advising that he was withdrawing promised naval support for the general's planned attack on Yorktown and Gloucester Point. "As things now stand," Goldsborough, charged with keeping the CSS *Virginia* from going on another rampage against the Union fleet in Hampton Roads, wrote him, "you must not count upon my sending any more vessels to aid your operations than those I mentioned to you." Gone also, then, with McDowell's legions was the full cooperation of the navy, which he had told the War Department was essential.[8]

As if being stripped from the rear by the administration and now the navy were not setbacks enough, things were not going well on the ground in McClellan's front either. They had not been going well since his army landed. Beginning April 5, heavy rain pounded his army, turning the roads into virtually impassable sinkholes. A Union officer reported seeing a mule sink out of sight in the middle of a main road—only the tips of his ears showing.[9] "If Virginia was once in the Union," a soldier marveled, "she was now in the mud." Another said the army resembled "more than anything else a congregation of flies, making a pilgrimage through molasses."[10]

The rain-drenched, ill-mapped topography continued to be little known, further frustrating all movement. McClellan wrote Stanton that he had "absolutely no information in detail of the country in our front and are obliged to grope our way." His cavalry commander and West Point classmate Brigadier General George Stoneman complained, "The map is wrong as regards this and every other road."[11]

Moreover, McClellan found himself unexpectedly blocked in his front by yet another obstacle he had not counted on: a tightly dug-in force under Confederate Major General John B. Magruder in Yorktown. Magruder had only 11,000 men, but he had a bent for the theatrical. He put on a marching and remarching show, running the same troops into the Union army's line of vision over and over. This convinced

McClellan, who was always ready to believe in higher enemy numbers, that Magruder had a force at least twice what he actually had—up to 30,000 men—with reinforcements pouring in steadily from Richmond and Norfolk.

Yorktown was the knot—so much more gnarly than McClellan first believed—that had to be cut. Given the changed circumstances and the inconstancy of the administration—not to mention the high Confederate troop count—he ordered up his siege train. He had admired sieges in Mexico and the Crimea and had come prepared to mount one against Yorktown if necessary. It now seemed necessary, the safer, surer way.[12]

McClellan felt compelled to adopt this, a different and less effective plan of campaign. He believed the loss of McDowell's corps had made rapid and brilliant operations impossible, that it had been "a fatal error."[13] He saw it as "an abominable design" of the administration to deny him his great victory at Richmond and a reknitting of the Union in the way he envisioned. He would soon be writing his friend Barlow in New York that the enemy in Washington "have done their best to sacrifice as noble an Army as ever marched to battle."[14]

He wrote Nelly, "the wretches...have done nearly their worst & can't do much more. I am sure that I will win in the end, in spite of their rascality. History will present a sad record of these traitors who are willing to sacrifice the country & it's army for personal spite & personal aims. The people will soon understand the whole matter & then woe betide the guilty ones."[15]

McClellan saw his own fault in none of this, even though there were those who believed that doing an end run around Magruder at Yorktown instead of laying a siege would have put him at the gates of Richmond by April 11, the earliest that McDowell's corps could have reached him in any event. Rapid and brilliant operations might have been possible, and the Confederate line quickly broken. It could have been argued—and it was being so in critical quarters—that the campaign-delaying siege itself was the fatal error, not the loss of McDowell's corps.[16]

Even Lincoln believed so. He later told Welles, "there was no reason why he [McClellan] should have been detained a single day in Yorktown." His waiting, Lincoln believed, was giving the enemy "time to gather his forces and strengthen his position."[17] The president had concluded in his dealings with McClellan that the general was slow to seize initiatives. It had to do with an inbred caution that seemed to stop the general from seizing the hour.

McClellan had shown at Rich Mountain in western Virginia that he was not at his best when confronted with the unexpected. And here was the unexpected, in abundance. The situation—the reduction in force, the withdrawal of half of a hundred thousand men in particular—he confessed to Goldsborough, "necessitates more caution on my part."[18]

More caution was not what Lincoln wanted from his general. John Hay, writing his fellow presidential secretary John Nicolay on April 3, said, "Gen. McC is in danger. Not in front but in rear. The President is making up his mind to give him a peremptory order to march. It is disgraceful to think how the little squad at Yorktown keeps him at bay."[19] On April 6, Lincoln prodded McClellan. "I think you better break the enemies' line from York-town to Warwick River, at once," he said. "They will probably use *time,* as advantageously as you can."[20]

This triggered another outburst to Nelly: "The Presdt very coolly telegraphed me yesterday," McClellan wrote her, "that he thought I had better break the enemy's lines at once! I was much tempted to reply that he had better come & do it himself."[21]

On April 9, Lincoln wrote a long, frank, fatherly letter to McClellan. He began, "Your dispatches complaining that you are not properly sustained, while they do not offend me, do pain me very much." He explained to McClellan again his deep concern for Washington's safety, "After you left," he wrote, "I ascertained that less than twenty thousand unorganized men, without a single field battery, were all you designed to be left for the defence of Washington."

Lincoln suggested there was confusion and disagreement over numbers. "There is a curious mystery," he wrote McClellan, "about the *number* of the troops now with you. When I telegraphed you on the 6th saying you had over a hundred thousand with you, I had just obtained from the Secretary of War, a statement, taken as he said, from your own returns making 108,000 then with you, and *en route* to you. You now say you will have but 85,000, when all *en route* to you shall have reached you. How can the discrepancy of 23,000 be accounted for?"

Whatever the numbers, Lincoln said, "I suppose the whole force, which has gone forward for you, is with you by this time; and if so, I think it is the precise time for you to strike a blow. By delay the enemy will relatively gain upon you—that is by *fortifications,* and *re-inforcements,* than you can by re-inforcements alone."

The president continued: "And, once more let me tell you it is indispensable to *you* that you strike a blow. *I* am powerless to help this. You will do me the justice to remember I always insisted, that going down the Bay in search of a field, instead of fighting at or near Mannassas, was only shifting, and not surmounting, a difficulty—that we would find the same enemy, and the same, or equal, intrenchments, at either place. The country will not fail to note—is now noting—that the present hesitation to move upon an intrenched enemy, is but the story of Manassas repeated."

Lincoln ended his letter, "I beg to assure you that I have never written you, or spoken to you, in greater kindness of feeling than now, nor with a fuller purpose to sustain you, so far as in my most anxious judgment, I consistently can. *But you must act.*"[22]

McClellan believed he was already acting as he should and could, that "all is being done that human labor can accomplish." He would soon be telling Nelly, "If they will simply let me alone I feel sure of success—but, will they do it?"[23]

On April 10, the president agreed to send Franklin's division to McClellan as requested. But the patient president's growing impatience with McClellan's "sluggishness of action" was showing. Lincoln's discontent was apparent to his friend Senator Browning, who visited the president that day.[24] This strain in the Lincoln-McClellan relationship, however, paled alongside the knives being flashed by the angry Radicals in Congress. Ben Wade, of the Joint Committee on the Conduct of the War, was viewing McClellan as an out-and-out traitor, a pro-Southern Democrat, purposely stalling, not bringing the Confederates to battle on the Peninsula and working against the best interests of the Union.[25]

John Hay was writing Nicolay on April 9: "Glorious news come borne on every wind but the South Wind. While Pope [Union Major General John Pope] is crossing the turbid and broad torrent of the Mississippi in a blaze of enemy's fire [to compel the surrender of Island No. Ten] and Grant [Major General Ulysses S. Grant] is fighting the overwhelming legions of Beauregard at Pittsburgh [Landing], the Little Napoleon sits trembling before the handful of men at Yorktown afraid either to fight or run. Stanton feels devilish about it. He would like to remove him if he thought it would do."[26]

Even the Confederates were critical. General Joe Johnston, McClellan's old friend from the Mexican War days, now commanding the Confederate legions on the Peninsula, arrived near Yorktown April 22 and said, "No one but McClellan could have hesitated to attack. The defensive line is far better for him than for us."[27]

If there was mystery in what numbers McClellan had to attack with, there was even deeper mystery—still—over what numbers the Confederates had to defend with. McClellan believed those numbers were astronomical, and concentrated immediately in his front. Pinkerton's interrogators were quoting prisoners, saying Johnston had arrived in Yorktown with massive reinforcements. "It seems clear," McClellan wired Stanton, "that I shall have the whole force of the enemy on my hands, probably not less than one hundred thousand (100,000) men & possibly more. In consequent of the loss of Blenkers Division & the First Corps my force is possibly less than that of the enemy, while they have all the advantage of position."[28] In what must have been a major news leak, the Associated Press was repeating and agreeing with McClellan's estimate, calling the Confederate's 100,000 "the flower of their army," adding that it was entrenched and backed by 500 guns.[29]

James Russell Lowell, the American man of letters, later wrote that one had to go back to Cervantes's *Don Quixote* to find a self-deception comparable to General McClellan's.[30]

Whether the Yorktown siege was wearing down the Confederates or not, after twenty-nine days it was wearing down McClellan. By May 3, he was feeling blue, exhausted, and abandoned, as much under siege as Yorktown was, under fire again from Lincoln. McClellan had ordered more giant rifled Parrott guns from Washington, and Lincoln was alarmed because it augured "indefinite procrastination." "Is anything to be done?" the president demanded.[31]

McClellan wrote Nelly on May 3: "I need rest—my brain is taxed to the extreme—I feel that the fate of a nation depends upon me, & I feel that I have not one single friend at the seat of Govt—any day may bring an order relieving me from command—if such a thing should be done our cause is lost."[32]

He was, however, not reading Lincoln correctly—a mistake he commonly made about the president. Lincoln seemed to be trying to do his best by McClellan, given the circumstances. McClellan's friend

J. C. G. Kennedy wrote him, after speaking with Lincoln, that the president "in very kind terms, spoke feelingly of the efforts made by political men of influence to underrate your qualities....He said he never wavered in his good opinion of your merits although he had not at all times the courage to withstand the demands of those who differed with him in sentiment. He expressed an earnest hope and confident belief that you would fulfill the expectations of your friends."[33]

But something was now amiss in McClellan's front. Looking over the barrels of his siege guns toward Yorktown, something did not feel right. "I don't half like the perfect quietness which reigns now..." he told Nelly, "—it don't seem natural." The eerie silence was causing him to suspect either an enemy sortie of some sort or an evacuation. If either, he told Nelly, "I hope it may be the former. I do not want these rascals to get away from me without a sound drubbing, which they richly deserve & which they will be sure to get if they remain."[34]

However, the drubbing would have to wait. It appeared the other alternative—an evacuation—was afoot. The next morning, May 4, sentries had disappeared from the enemy lines. It was then that McClellan found an empty Yorktown and midday before he organized a pursuit. He wired Stanton, "Yorktown is in our possession." He assured the secretary, "No time shall be lost...I shall push the enemy to the wall."[35]

The truth, however, was that McClellan had been caught flatfooted. There was no plan in place for an organized pursuit to cut off the rebel retreat. Johnston's army was withdrawing unhampered, with the idea of concentrating a powerful augmented counterforce around Richmond. It had come down to a chase, a race up the Peninsula.[36]

Nevertheless, McClellan was viewing it as a stunning victory. He predicted that "it and Manassas [that other voluntary Confederate evacuation before Washington two months earlier] will be my brightest chaplets in history; for I know that I accomplished everything in both places by pure military skill."[37]

CHAPTER 12

AT THE GATES OF RICHMOND

N ature and technology, however, were not smiling on the pursuit, which began on May 4. It rained hard most of the night of the evacuation and was still pouring the next morning. The roads, McClellan reported to Stanton, are "consequently infamous.... Several of our batteries are actually stuck fast in the mud." The Confederates were also planting torpedoes—land mines—in the wake of their retreat, another nuisance, "the most murderous & barbarous thing I ever heard of," McClellan complained to Nelly.[1]

Slogging likewise through driving rain on mud-bogged roads, Johnston's army reached Williamsburg, a dozen miles from Yorktown, on May 5 and turned to confront its pursuers, who were breathing hard on its wagon trains. A wicked fight opened. By late afternoon, McClellan had caught up to the van of the pursuit himself and found his army on the edge of a major repulse.

"We came very near being badly beaten at Williamsburg," McClellan wrote his old friend Major General Ambrose Burnside. "I arrived on the field at 5 P.M. and found that all thought we were whipped and in for a disaster." He recounted to Burnside how "the men cheered and brightened up when they saw me. In five minutes after I reached the ground a possible defeat was changed into certain victory."[2] He hailed it, as he had the evacuation of Yorktown, a brilliant victory. "Had I been one half hour later on the field on the fifth," he wired Stanton, "we would have been routed & would have lost everything."[3]

Brilliant Union victory or not, Johnston's army extracted itself and was soon out of danger beyond the Chickahominy River, with the gates of Richmond at its back.

McClellan followed cautiously over the boggy roads and, by May 16, he was at West Point, at White House, the old Virginia mansion home of George Washington's wife, Martha. The mansion rested on a grass-covered plateau on the banks of the Pamunkey. This was where Washington had courted Martha when she was a Custis and where they had spent their honeymoon.

The mansion had come down to Robert E. Lee's wife, Mary Anne Custis Lee, Martha's descendent. When Lee went with the Confederacy in the war and abandoned his home at Arlington, White House became the Lee family seat in Virginia. Mrs. Lee had fled from it as the Union army approached, and now McClellan was treating it somewhat as holy ground. Trying to protect it from being despoiled, he permitted none of his troops to enter the house and did not stay in it himself, but tented among the "bivouac-fires" at Tunstall's Station six miles away.[4]

After Williamsburg, McClellan's pursuit had slackened. He had lingered there longer than many thought he should, and the lack of forward motion stirred yet more disgust in Washington. Secretary of the Treasury Salmon Portland Chase, heretofore one of McClellan's staunchest champions, although a Radical, was now thoroughly alienated along with the rest of the Radicals. Since Chase's main business was counting dollars and financing the war, he now considered McClellan "a clear luxury—fifty days—fifty miles—fifty million dollars—easy arithmetic, but not satisfactory. If one could have some faith in his competency in battle—should his army ever fight one—if not in his competency for movement, it would be a comfort."[5]

For his part, McClellan was beginning to feel as he had felt those first days at another West Point, in New York—as alone as if in a boat in the Atlantic—and facing in his mind a desperate battle in front of Richmond against vastly superior numbers, well entrenched, without help from Washington. "The Government have deliberately placed me in this position," he complained to Burnside. "If I win, the greater the glory. If I lose, they will be damned forever, both by God and men."[6]

He was, however, painting his accomplishments so far in a vivid light. Without much help from Washington, he had forced the evacuation of Yorktown, snatched victory from defeat at Williamsburg, and pushed the Confederates to the gates of Richmond—all with a perceived inferior force. But nothing in what he was saying indicated that he now intended to undertake an immediate offensive. There was no idea in his mind of attacking the enemy now and driving him back on Richmond. McClellan wasn't ready. His mind-set, until the great battle was to be fought, very likely at the Chickahominy, was to resist attack until reinforced.[7]

Reinforcement was now his most pressing priority. He was urgently sending requests for massive injections of more men to bring his army to a level matching the rebels and predicting disaster if they were not forthcoming. Every other consideration in every other theater of the war must give way to what he thought was his urgent need. He wished all the government's energies and means concentrated before Richmond. He wrote Lincoln on May 14, "I beg that you will cause this Army to be reinforced without delay by all the disposable troops of the Government. I ask for every man that the War Department can send me."[8]

This was the sort of appeal McClellan generally deplored in others. He had no compunction to ask for more but resented it when someone else did. In western Virginia in early July 1861, when one of his subordinates, Brigadier General Thomas A. Morris, commanding the Indiana Volunteers, asked for more troops to defend Philippi, McClellan reprimanded him:

> I can give you no more re-enforcements. I cannot consent to weaken any further the really active and important column [his own] which is to decide the fate of the campaign. If you cannot undertake the defense of Philippi with the force now under your control, I must find some one who will.…Do not ask for further re-enforcements. If you do, I shall take it as a request to be relieved from your command and to return to Indiana.

> The crisis is a grave one, and I must have generals under me who are willing to risk as much as I am, and to be content to risk their lives and reputation with such means as I can give them. Let this be the last of it. Give me full details as to the information you obtained— not mere rumors, but facts—and leave it to my judgment to determine what force you need. I wish action now and determination.[9]

Now, in May 1862, on the Peninsula, it was McClellan feeling the reinforcement pinch. He would not himself welcome such a reprimand.

But his situation was different—far more serious and urgent, and on a far bigger stage. Pinkerton was assuring McClellan that the rebel army numbered at least 100,000, more likely 150,000 or more—the figure 250,000 was being bandied about. "If I am not reinforced," McClellan told Stanton on May 10, "it is probable that I will be obliged to fight nearly double my numbers, stronger entrenched," and "I do not think it will be at all possible for me to bring more than seventy thousand men upon the field of battle."[10]

Bombarded by McClellan's urgent pleas for more men, Lincoln wired him on May 15: "Have done, and shall do, all I could and can to sustain you." However, the president was still worried about the threat to Washington, "still unwilling to take all our force off the direct line between Richmond and here."[11]

Stanton, through whom many of McClellan's pleas for reinforcements were being funneled, was not sympathetic. Indeed, Stanton had made a move on April 3, when the general had first arrived on the Peninsula, that had deepened the McClellan's rage and depression. The secretary had decided, given all the force McClellan already had, to shut down recruiting in the country and close recruiting stations, drying up the source for the thousands more troops McClellan was clamoring for.[12]

"Never in the whole history of nations," McClellan would later write, "was anything more absurdly and recklessly managed than the whole system of recruiting, drafting, and organization under the regime of Secretary Stanton....Unparalleled in history for blunders and ignorant self-assertion."[13]

A disenchanted Stanton believed that if McClellan had 1,000,000 men, "he would swear that the enemy had 2,000,000 men, and then would sit down in the mud and holler for another 1,000,000."[14] Lincoln was thinking along the same lines. He told Senator Browning that if by magic he could reinforce McClellan with 100,000 men, he would "be in ecstasy over it, thank him for it, and tell him that he would go to Richmond tomorrow, but that when tomorrow came he would telegraph that he had certain information that the enemy had 400,000 men, and that he could not advance without reinforcements."[15]

McClellan's view, however, was that the villains in Washington were "determined to ruin me in any event and by any means; first by endeavoring to force me into premature movements, knowing that a failure would probably end my military career; afterwards by with-holding the means necessary to achieve success."[16]

He believed that the Radical Republicans were plotting and attack-ing from the rear, purposely interfering to prevent a quick and decisive victory, lest the war should end without the abolition of slavery. The Radicals at the same time were claiming that McClellan was purposely postponing the decisive battle, "lingering" out the war with the hope that some sort of compromise could be reached, the Union saved but the South still left with its slaves—the Union as it was.[17] That would be anathema in the Radical lexicon.

In mid-May, the Confederates had something over 62,500 men on the Peninsula—nothing approaching the McClellan-Pinkerton figures—and Johnston was as intent on preventing Union reinforcements as McClellan was getting them. Johnston ordered the audacious Stonewall Jackson to keep things stirred up in the Valley and Washington threatened, to keep McDowell from being detached and sent to McClellan's side.[18]

Nonetheless, by this time Lincoln's concern for the safety of the capital had eased, and Stanton informed McClellan on May 17 that the president would begin sending McDowell's corps to the Peninsula after all. However, it was conditional. McDowell was to cooperate with McClellan and obey his orders, but keep separate command and not allow his corps to be "disposed otherwise than so as to give the greatest protection to this capital which may be possible from that distance."[19]

But within a week, Jackson began a rampage against Union forces in the Shenandoah Valley that brought the planned movement of McDowell's corps to an abrupt halt. On May 23, Jackson went on the offensive. He invaded Front Royal and assaulted the retreating Union army under Major General Nathaniel Banks. All this was happening far too close to Washington for Lincoln's comfort. More on edge than ever, still giving first priority to the safety of the capital, he believed that Jackson's movements were a direct and immediate threat.

On May 24, the president wired McClellan, "In consequence of Gen. Banks' critical position I have been compelled to suspend Gen. McDowell's movement to join you." The next day he wired McClellan again: "I think the time is near when you must either attack Richmond or give up the job and come to the defence of Washington. Let me hear from you instantly."[20]

The next person to hear instantly from McClellan, however, was not Lincoln but Nelly. The general had been "rather under the weather" for the past three days, and this latest telegram from Lincoln looked to him like a last straw. He exploded to Nelly, "I have this moment received a dispatch from the Presdt who is terribly scared about Washington—& talks about the necessity of my returning in order to save it! Heaven save a country governed by such counsels! ... It is perfectly sickening to deal with such people & you may rest assured that I will lose as little time as possible in breaking off all connection with them—I get more sick of them every day—for every day brings with it only additional proofs of their hypocrisy, knavery & folly."[21]

May on the Peninsula was spring in full bloom, and nature was putting on a spectacular show, even if the army was not. Dogwood, magnolias, jessamines—all of the flowers of the season—"were blooming in rich profusion, and multitudes of birds answered the soldiers' songs with their springtime melody."[22] However, whether he was reinforced or not, McClellan would not be springing to the defense of Washington. Moving cautiously, now headquartered near Cold Harbor, he had a big battle on his mind despite the perceived huge disparity in numbers favoring the rebels.

He had been gingerly pushing part of his army over the Chickahominy, which rises some fifteen miles northwest of Richmond, empties into the James forty-five miles below, and was prone to "sudden inundations."[23] By May 21, he was astraddle that river, with three of his five corps north of it.

Despite the perceived odds against him, McClellan figured the time had come. Terse orders were going to the troops on May 25: "Upon advancing beyond the Chickahominy the troops will go prepared for battle at a moment's notice and will be entirely unencumbered...will carry three days rations in their haversacks...the cartridge boxes...will contain at least 40 rounds. Twenty additional rounds will be carried by the men in their pockets. Commanders of batteries will see that their limber and caisson boxes are filled to their utmost capacity....The ammunition wagons will be held in readiness to march to their respective brigades and batteries at a moment's warning."

In the approaching battle, McClellan told them, "the general commanding trusts that the troops will preserve the discipline which he has been so anxious to enforce and which they have so generally observed. He calls upon all officers and soldiers to obey promptly and intelligently all orders they may receive." He said, "Let them bear in mind that the Army of the Potomac has never yet been checked; let them preserve in battle perfect coolness and confidence, the sure forerunners of success. They must keep well together; throw away no shots, but aim carefully and low, and above all things rely upon the bayonet."[24]

McClellan wired Lincoln that day, "[T]he time is very near when I shall attack Richmond....All the information obtained from balloons, deserters prisoners & contrabands agrees...that the mass of rebel troops are still in immediate vicinity of Richmond ready to defend it." He told Lincoln, "I have two Corps across Chickahominy within six miles of Richmond—the others on this side at other crossings within same distance & ready to cross when bridges completed."[25]

On May 26, a storm raged overnight and by morning had "converted everything into mud again & raised Chickahominy." Despite the mud, McClellan wired Stanton that morning, "Every day is making our result more sure & I am wasting no time."[26]

On the twenty-seventh, fighting broke out at Hanover Court House between the rebels and Major General Fitz John Porter's Fifth Corps. That evening McClellan wired Stanton of "truly a glorious victory....The rout of the rebels was complete—not a defeat but a complete rout." But it was only a prelude. "There is no doubt," he wrote Stanton, "that the enemy are concentrating everything on Richmond....The real issue is in the battle about to be fought in front of Richmond." It could not be ignored, he said, "that a desperate battle is before us."[27]

The desperate battle materialized on May 31, following a night swamped by a violent pounding rainstorm. On that day, Johnston struck the left wing of McClellan's army south of the flooded Chickahominy at Fair Oaks, or Seven Pines. McClellan, however, was not present to see it. He had fallen sick on the thirtieth, lashed with misery to match the storm—"the old Mexican complaint" again, recurring agony from the malaria he had contracted in that war. He ordered up reinforcements from his sickbed as the battle raged, and his army beat off Johnston's uncoordinated attacks. Still not feeling well, he managed to get to the battlefield the next day, June 1.[28]

The fighting, however, had ended, and the two sides stood panting in positions they held when the battle opened, six miles from Richmond, close enough for McClellan's outposts on a still night to hear church bells striking the hours and on a clear day to sight its spires and towers.[29] Lincoln could not help but wonder if the general could get near enough to throw shells into the city.[30]

The savage two-day battle had not gone as Johnston planned. He had made an all-out push to destroy McClellan's left wing. It had not happened, and he had paid a heavy personal price. He had been wounded in the shoulder by a musket shot, then unhorsed by a shell fragment in the chest and carried from the field. This was not unusual for him. He had been desperately wounded as well in Mexico and seemed prone to stopping bullets. Still, he had kept McClellan out of Richmond. It was the greatest battle yet fought in the eastern theater but not yet the great decisive one, with the war-ending outcome McClellan envisioned.

McClellan's soldiers, however, had measured up and McClellan saw it as a "complete" victory, credit "due to the gallantry of our officers & men." He told those officers and men in a message the next day, June 2: "I have fulfilled at least a part of my promise to you: you are now face to face with the rebels, who are at bay in front of their Capital. The final and decisive battle is at hand. Unless you belie your past history, the result cannot be for a moment doubtful." "Soldiers!" he said, "I will be with you in this battle, and share its dangers with you. . . . Let us strike the blow which is to restore peace and union to this distracted land. Upon your valor, discipline and mutual confidence that result depends."[31]

It was strong talk, Napoleonic. But, as if in angry epilogue to bloody battle, howling rain started coming down again. On June 7, McClellan wired Stanton, "The whole face of the country is a perfect bog."[32] The war, for both armies, had sunk again in the mud.

CHAPTER 13

SHIFTING BLAME

When Joe Johnston fell at Fair Oaks on the first day of the battle, May 31, and was carried from the field, command of the Confederate army on the Peninsula fell to Gustavus W. Smith, a Kentuckian, one of McClellan's oldest and dearest friends from West Point and the Mexican War. He had graduated from the academy in 1842, and in Mexico he had won three brevet promotions for gallantry.

His friends called him "Legs," for his tall, spare, leggy, angular frame.[1] But unfortunately Smith had no legs for this command. His performance in the field throughout the campaign as Johnston's second in command had been lackluster. When faced with action, he had shown a disposition to fall ill with some undiagnosed malady. One of Confederate President Jefferson Davis's aides believed the problem was fear of responsibility for failure. Whatever it was, Davis had been losing confidence in him. Riding to the field following the battle, Davis found Smith prostrate, unable to think or act and "endure the mental excitement incident to his actual presence with the army." After only a day in command, complaining of partial paralysis, he left the army temporarily, and would not hold important command again.[2]

Davis turned to a man he vastly preferred and implicitly trusted—his military adviser, General Robert E. Lee.

Lee, a Virginian, had been a model cadet at West Point, graduating in 1829 second in his class without drawing a single demerit in four years. He had also been a spotless star in the Mexican War, as a captain, executing several spectacular reconnaissance missions for Winfield Scott. At war's end, Scott had praised Lee as "the very best soldier that I ever saw in the field," and when this new war of brothers came, he offered him command of the Union army assembling in and around Washington. Lee, however, refused to lift a sword against his own state and defected to the Confederacy, first to command Virginia troops, then as Davis's military adviser.[3]

McClellan knew Lee well; they had served side by side as engineers for Scott in Mexico. And yet he knew him not at all. A month before the battle of Fair Oaks, McClellan had downgraded him in a private letter to Lincoln. "I prefer Lee to Johnston [as an opponent]," he wrote the president on April 20, "—the former is *too* cautious & weak under grave responsibility—personally brave & energetic to a fault, he yet is wanting in moral firmness when pressed by heavy responsibility & is likely to be timid & irresolute in action."[4]

It would soon prove to be an assessment 180 degrees wrong. Lincoln might have mused—perhaps he did—that McClellan, in describing Lee, was perfectly describing himself.[5]

As soon as Lee assumed command of the Confederate army the day after the battle of Fair Oaks, he continued withdrawing it back before Richmond.

McClellan elected not to pursue. Preparations for an offensive, however, were under way—in both armies. Buoyed by his perceived victory against Johnston, McClellan wired Stanton, "The morale of my troops is now such that I can venture much & do not care for odds against me. The victory is complete." In his congratulatory trumpet blast to his soldiers after the battle, he had written, "I ask of you now one last crowning effort. The enemy has staked his all on the issue of the coming battle. Let us meet and crush him here in the very centre of the rebellion."[6]

By June 2, the weather had lifted temporarily and the Chickahominy was falling. McClellan wrote Stanton that for a final decisive assault, he needed only to repair the bridges and get the rest of his army across the river. He wrote Nelly, "One more [battle] & we will have Richmond & I shall be there with Gods blessing this week."[7]

However, the next night, June 3, the heavens protested again, lashing the Peninsula with yet another pounding rainstorm. It encouraged introspection. From the cover of his tent, McClellan wired

Lincoln, who was anxiously awaiting word of further action: "I have to be very cautious now.... The Army of the Potomac has had serious work &...no child's play is before it."[8]

The rain continued to fall for the next two days. As it raked the Peninsula, McClellan waited in his tent. He was likely remembering the old general of the Cossacks in Napoleon's campaigns, who, when asked how the roads were in those days, said, "My son, the roads are always bad in war."[9] The skies finally began to clear on June 6, but it would take time for the roads to dry out enough to finish repairing the bridges and move the artillery. As the sun struggled to shake clear of the clouds, McClellan emerged from his tent to somewhat brighter news.[10]

In view of the heavy Union losses at Fair Oaks, Stanton had rescinded his stop-recruiting order. On June 8, the War Department advised McClellan that reinforcements were coming—the long-promised First Corps. The danger to Washington seemed to have passed. In the Shenandoah Valley, Jackson had pushed Banks's army back across the Potomac, then had evaded Union forces closing in on him from two sides and had successfully outrun them to Port Republic, beyond Staunton and Winchester. He appeared finished threatening Washington. Lincoln had halted the chase to bag him, which, despite his own diligent efforts to make it happen—masterminding strategy from Washington, constantly advising and urging on his generals in the Valley with a flurry of wires—had not succeeded.

For the third time, McDowell was ordered, "as speedily as possible" to march toward Richmond to shore up McClellan's right wing. Again, he was to operate independently of McClellan's control, with an eye to defending Washington if that again became necessary.[11]

By June 10, it was raining again harder than ever, driving McClellan back into his tent. He was feeling "almost discouraged," writing Nelly "I don't know what *will* become of us!" He wrote Stanton the same day that he was "completely checked by the weather." However, he assured the secretary, "I shall attack as soon as the weather & ground permit, but there will be a delay—the extent of which no one can foresee, for the season is altogether abnormal."[12]

McClellan's mood rather resembled the weather. To his thinking, had not McDowell's corps been withheld in the first place, he would "long before now have been in Richmond."[13] And now, within bell-hearing and steeple-sighting distance of his goal, and despite the promised reinstatement of McDowell's troops, he was unhappy not only with the weather but with his situation. He would still be underpowered for the coming battle. He wrote Stanton, "I wish it to be distinctly understood that whenever the weather permits I will attack with whatever force I may have, although a larger force would enable me to gain much more decisive results."

He was worried for the safety of McDowell's corps coming to join him by the overland route. And he was unhappy with the command arrangement. For greater speed and security, and better to mesh with his plans, he told Stanton he preferred that McDowell's men be sent to him by water and put under his undiluted control. He made a pitch for some of Henry W. Halleck's army in the West to be detached and transferred to his as well.[14]

The rain, starting and stopping over the next few days, came again on June 15, but McClellan didn't believe it would do much harm. He was telling Nelly that the chances were good now for a first advance on June 17 or 18. Lincoln was anxious for information. On the eighteenth, he wired McClellan: "I could better dispose of things if I could know about what day you can attack Richmond, and would be glad to be informed, if you think you can inform me with safety."[15] McClellan promised the president, "After tomorrow we shall fight the rebel army as soon as Providence will permit. We shall await only a favorable condition of the earth and sky & the completion of some necessary preliminaries.[16]

A week later, the preliminaries still were not yet completed. And McClellan was fretting again over enemy numbers and what he saw as enormously lopsided odds against him. Confederate forces around Richmond were growing daily. News had reached McClellan that Jackson had arrived from the Valley and that troops under Pierre G. T. Beauregard had also augmented Lee's army. Indeed, Lee's strength had been ratcheted to some 85,000 men, giving him more muscle than he would have at any time in the war.

McClellan, however, still had the numbers wrong. "It was a common conceit among the soldiers," one of them later wrote, "that the spy system of our army was run in the interests of the Confederacy."[17] That system now reported a rebel host anywhere from 130,000 to 285,000 strong. As usual, McClellan was inclined to credit these numbers—on the high side. He wired Stanton on June 25 that the rebel force "is stated at (200,000) two hundred thousand, including Jackson and Beauregard."

Assuming those figures were correct, he told Stanton, "I regret my great inferiority in numbers but feel that I am in no way responsible for it as I have not failed to represent repeatedly the necessity of reinforcements, that this was the decisive point, & that all the available means of the Govt should be concentrated here. I will do all that a General can do with the splendid Army I have the honor to command & if it is destroyed by overwhelming numbers can at least die with it & share its fate." He told Stanton that if the action, probably "tomorrow or within a short time[,] is a disaster, the responsibility cannot be thrown on my shoulders—but must rest where it belongs."[18]

This refrain appeared to be all too familiar to Lincoln. He had heard it before. He wired the general the next day that his dispatch "suggesting the probability of your being overwhelmed by 200,000, and talking of where the responsibility will belong, pains me very much. I give you all I can, and act on the presumption that you will do the best you can with what you have, while you continue, ungenerously I think, to assume that I could give you more if I would. I have omitted and shall omit no opportunity to send you reinforcements whenever I possibly can."[19]

Knowing from his own intelligence operation that McClellan was about to be reinforced by McDowell's corps, Lee on June 16 had ordered Jackson to the Peninsula to make a united front against the massed Union army. On June 25, McClellan learned that Jackson, who was enjoying a rising reputation as a lethal flanker and rearer, was on his way to attack his own right flank and rear. With Jackson in motion, the old fright took hold again in Washington. Lincoln pulled McDowell back once more. He would not send that corps to McClellan as long as he believed Washington threatened.[20]

There was no sign that the Confederates were going to leave and peaceably hand over Richmond, and McClellan believed it could be taken in only two ways: by siege or by assault. A siege would take time and a well-anchored base of supplies. Assault required a more than superior force and a full stock of reserves. And he believed he had neither.[21] However, considering the numbers, a siege seemed the better way. He was as close to Richmond now as he dared be, so he ordered up his heavy siege guns.[22]

At this moment, Lincoln, without consulting his general on the Peninsula, was making new plans and setting in motion a new move.

On June 26, he issued orders creating an entirely new army. It was to be organized from the defensive force protecting Washington, the armies of General Nathaniel Banks and John C. Fremont in the Shenandoah Valley and in the mountains—both of which Stonewall Jackson had outmaneuvered, outrun, and outfought in his spectacular Shenandoah campaign—and McDowell's corps, which had never made it to the Peninsula.

This new command, designated the Army of Virginia, was to do three things: protect Washington (still an overriding priority for Lincoln); safeguard western Virginia, which was working to shape a separate Union state; and augment the assault on Richmond.[23]

To lead this new-formed army, Lincoln had appointed a successful commander from the West, Major General John Pope, who had distinguished himself in early victories on the Mississippi, notably at Island No. 10, and in the advance on and siege of Corinth.

Pope looked a soldier. He was dashing, handsome, with a squared-off rectangular beard hardly wider than his mouth and four inches long, which shot straight down stiffly from his chin like a brush. Atop a horse, which he rode with total assurance, he appeared even more soldierly. He was sociable, energetic, and courageous, but also abrasive and impetuous.[24]

A distant descendant of George Washington, Pope was also directly connected to the top in this war, tied by marriage to Mary Todd Lincoln's family. He had been on the train that had brought Lincoln from Springfield, Illinois, to Washington for his inaugural in February 1861. Pope had graduated from West Point in 1842, the year McClellan and Jackson were entering it, in a class that boasted seventeen general officers on one side or the other in this war. He was, like so many West Pointers, a hero of the Mexican War. And in this new war he looked to be a comet.[25]

Pope was full of himself, with a gift for the bombastic and for putting down McClellan, questioning his military judgment—and his loyalty. When he arrived in Washington on June 24, he began romancing the Radicals on the Joint Committee on the Conduct of the War, the Radicals in the cabinet, and the press. To anyone who would listen, he heaped criticism on McClellan's campaign on the Peninsula. Favoring what Lincoln had favored—a direct assault on Richmond overland from Washington—he scored McClellan's strategy a failure in concept and execution, and announced that it must be terminated. He argued that McClellan's "incompetency and indisposition to active movements were so great" that he must be removed at once from command, and McClellan's army attached to Pope's own.[26]

These were words the joint committee and McClellan's detractors wanted to hear. For the Radicals in Congress, for disenchanted members of the cabinet—Stanton in particular—Pope was much more to their liking. Here was a man who shared their hard line on slavery. He was everything McClellan was not: a hard-nosed fighter who favored the hard hand of war.

CHAPTER 14

DOGFIGHT DOWN THE JAMES

As McClellan was readying a siege of Richmond and Lincoln was creating a new army, Robert E. Lee was chasing his own plans.

Shortly after taking command of the Confederate army, which he redesignated the Army of Northern Virginia, he first considered a major diversion he believed "would change the character of the war." The plan was to strongly reinforce Stonewall Jackson in the Valley with troops from North Carolina, South Carolina, and Georgia and with them threaten Maryland and Pennsylvania. It would compel McClellan to abandon his offensive against Richmond and rush to the defense of a then truly endangered Washington. However, it was a plan that died a stillbirth.[1] Instead, he had called Jackson from the Valley to join him in Richmond.

Lee dreaded a siege of any kind. He believed that it would be "a mere question of time" for the Confederacy if he was "obliged to take refuge behind the works of Richmond and stand a siege," which ultimately must end in surrender. Lee wanted to fight in the open field where he would have room to maneuver and force the Federals to attack him.[2]

He had to strike first, to take the initiative, to destroy McClellan's army or at least drive him back. Lee's idea was to set in motion a turning movement on the Union right—against Fitz John Porter's command still north of the Chickahominy. He planned to attack McClellan's vulnerable right on the day McClellan had hoped to open on the enemy's batteries in Richmond. It had come down to a race of who would deliver the first blow.

Displaying a quality of audacity that McClellan believed he lacked, Lee attacked on June 26, on a very clear, still, midafternoon—the day Lincoln launched the Army of Virginia. Lee's army slammed into McClellan's right flank north of the Chickahominy at Mechanicsville, opening a bloody week of fighting that would become known as the Seven Days battles. Porter fought the Confederates at Mechanicsville on this first day, and the battle was at best a draw—in effect, therefore, a Confederate failure. McClellan pulled back to Gaines's Mill, where an implacable Lee assailed him again the next day, June 27, in a fierce battle beginning at noon and lasting nine hours. McClellan got the worst of the encounter and the next day withdrew his army farther down the James to Savage's Station. Lee followed.

The Gaines's Mill defeat and the frustration to all his plans—the general frustration to this entire campaign—brought all of McClellan's rage against Washington rushing to the surface. From his headquarters at Savage's Station he sent a bitter wire to Stanton. He told him that at Gaines's Mill he had been "overwhelmed by vastly superior numbers," that "I have lost this battle because my force was too small," that it was not his fault, that "I should have gained this battle with (10,000) ten thousand fresh men."

Then, in a scorching coda to the wire, he said something a subordinate should never say to a superior. "I feel too earnestly tonight," he told Stanton, "—I have seen too many dead & wounded comrades to feel otherwise than that the Govt has not sustained this Army. If you do not do so now the game is lost. If I save this Army now I tell you plainly that I owe no thanks to you or any other person in Washington—you have done your best to sacrifice this Army."[3]

This blazing wire was entirely too hot for Edward S. Sanford, head of the War Department telegraph office in Washington. Before passing the dispatch on to Stanton, he took it upon himself to scissor out the incendiary indictment. It would not come to Stanton and Lincoln's attention until much later.[4]

Lincoln was by now painfully accustomed to McClellan's setbacks, and his excuses, but he still wished his general success and wanted to support the army in its desperate situation on the James. The day McClellan sent his outraged and outrageous wire to Stanton, Lincoln wired him:

> Save your Army at all events. Will send re-inforcements as fast as we can. Of course they cannot reach you to-day or to-morrow, or the next day. I have not said you were ungenerous for saying you needed re-inforcement. I thought you were ungenerous in assuming that I did not send them as fast as I could. I feel any misfortune to you and your Army quite as keenly as you feel it yourself. If you have a drawn battle, or a repulse, it is the price we pay for the enemy not being in Washington. We protected Washington, and the enemy concentrated on you; had we stripped Washington, he would have been upon us before the troops sent could have got to you.[5]

McClellan must have received this message with a snort. He had never believed Washington was in danger during this campaign. On June 29, as if to plant elsewhere the frustration he felt and cement what he had written Stanton, he wrote Major General John A. Dix, who was just then replacing Major General John E. Wool in command at Fort Monroe. "May God forgive the men who have caused the loss this army has experienced," he told Dix. "It is now clear beyond a doubt that 20,000 more men would have given us a glorious victory. I for one can never forget nor forgive the selfish men who have caused the lives of so many gallant men to be sacrificed. . . . I have at least the satisfaction of a clear conscience."[6]

Gone from McClellan's thinking now, following Lee's assault on June 26, was anything that had to do with taking Richmond. The only thing on his mind, as Lincoln suggested, was saving his army.

McClellan had been seriously contemplating a retrograde from Richmond for some days, even before Lee attacked—a run down the James to the protective cover of the navy's gunboats at Harrison's Landing, some twenty-five miles. A retreat would take McClellan from the gates of Richmond, so tantalizingly close, but that could not be helped. The situation in his mind called for a "change of base," and he set it in motion after the disaster at Gaines's Mill. It had become his strategy even as he was writing his testy wire to Stanton.

June 29, two days after Gaines's Mill, opened to dense morning fog and rain. Ignoring the weather, the Confederates both north and south of the Chickahominy crossed the river, attacked McClellan at Savage's Station, and were repulsed. They attacked, bulldog-like, again on the thirtieth—a hot, sunny day—at Glendale. The result was yet another confused, bloody encounter, called the battle of Frayser's Farm. Lee was repulsed again. So far, every Confederate attack, except at Gaines's Mill, had been thwarted. McClellan had been, in effect, snarling and clawing back like a cornered cat, and Lee's attacks had been error prone, ill timed, and disjointed—"a succession of mishaps," one Confederate general called them.[7] McClellan now had his retreating army successfully across the one great natural barrier that stood in his way, a bog called White Oak Swamp. Crossing it had not been easy. Indeed, it had been a logistical nightmare. The retreat was a slow, maddening, stressful process conducted while warding off Lee's attacks. The troops were weighed down by an artillery reserve of a hundred guns, a quarter of them heavy siege pieces, each weighing up to two tons or more. McClellan's supply train, strung out and lumbering ponderously across the swamp, numbered more than 3,000 wagons and ambulances, drawn by nearly 15,000 horses and mules, encumbered as far as Savage's Station by 2,500 head of beef cattle.[8]

On July 1, McClellan placed his army on Malvern Hill, a strong defensive position on an elevated, ravine-fronted, treeless plateau six miles from his final destination at Harrison's Landing. That morning, he had boarded the new ironclad, USS *Galena,* and sailed downriver, away from Malvern Hill, anchoring off Harrison's Landing. He went ashore in a tug to do "what I did not wish to trust to anyone else—i.e. examine the final position to which the Army was to fall back." Later in the afternoon, when word reached him that the Confederates appeared to be preparing another massive attack, he returned to Malvern Hill and rode the lines, approving troop placements for its defense.[9]

Still unrelenting, Lee launched yet another mishap, another ill-timed and disjointed attack, on the afternoon of July 1. It was another hot, still day, and again the Confederates were hurled back, even more violently. McClellan was not present where the main fighting raged—he had not been in direct command on the field in any of the encounters in this running fight—but was back on the gunboat.

The bloody battle at Malvern Hill ended the Seven Days campaign. It had been the nature of those seven days that all of the fighting had been in the afternoon, what Shakespeare called "the posteriors of [the] day."[10] There had not been a night, one of McClellan's generals later wrote, "in which the men did not march almost continually, nor a day on which there was not a fight.... Sleep was out of the question," and their only rest "was while lying down awaiting an attack, or sheltering themselves from shot and shell."[11] And now, with this last battle of the seven days done, Lee recoiled, and McClellan's army left Malvern Hill in a driving rain, marched the six miles to Harrison's Landing, and slipped under the protective barrels of the navy gunboats.

No one had ever seen such losses as in those seven days—on both sides. McClellan had suffered almost 16,000 casualties, nearly 2,000 killed, the rest wounded or missing. Lee's losses topped 20,000, nearly 3,200 killed. It is axiomatic that an attacking army generally loses more men than a defending one.[12]

Both sides had won half a loaf. For Lee it had been a Pyrrhic victory. He had saved Richmond, but he had not destroyed McClellan's army. McClellan had saved his army, but he had not taken Richmond. The Seven Days battles marked an important passage, a monumental shift in roles. From being the invading power, McClellan's army was reduced to being a retreating force pursued and seeking safety. What had begun as an offensive advance had ended as a defensive withdrawal.[13]

Lee was still in something of a quandary. McClellan's army and his communications were secure, shielded by the gunboats. The huge Federal army was still lethal, and too close to Richmond for comfort. The Confederate commander did not dare stray far from its defenses until he knew what McClellan intended to do next.[14]

The public in the North was uncertain what to call the outcome. Was it a change of base or a skedaddle? Was it a victory or a defeat? The war correspondent from *Vanity Fair* said, "Yes, my boy, we have had a great victory. And now we want to know who is to blame for it!"[15]

McClellan's critics were calling it a retreat. He was calling it a change of base and was proud of it, hailing it as "one of those magnificent episodes which dignify a nation's history and are fit subjects for the grandest efforts of the poet and the painter."[16]

Lincoln, who did not put much faith in McClellan for offensive fighting, said he did respect the general's gift for waging defensive warfare. He said he would "rather trust McClellan to get his army out of a tight place than any other general that he had."[17]

Indeed, it was a skillfully handled defense, and McClellan was now where he had always wanted to be, on the James. He credited his soldiers. "Your achievements of the past ten days," he wrote them on

Independence Day, July 4, "have illustrated the valor and endurance of the American soldier. Attacked by vastly superior forces, and without hope of re-enforcements, you have succeeded in changing your base of operations by a flank movement, always regarded as the most hazardous of military expedients." He told them, "Upon your march you have been assailed day after day with desperate fury by men of the same race and nation skillfully massed and led; and under every disadvantage of numbers, and necessarily of position also, you have in every conflict beaten back your foes with enormous slaughter. Your conduct ranks you among the celebrated armies of history. No one will now question that each of you may always say with pride, 'I belonged to the Army of the Potomac!' "[18]

Jefferson Davis was hailing his own army with similar hyperbole. "You marched to attack the enemy in his intrenchments," he told them; "with well-directed movements and death-defying valor, you charged upon him in his strong positions, drove him from field to field, over a distance of more than thirty-five miles, and despite his re-enforcements, compelled him to seek safety under cover of his gun-boats, where he now lies cowering before the army so lately divided and threatened with entire subjugation."[19]

As McClellan was writing this praise for his soldiers, his whereabouts during the seven days were coming under sharp scrutiny by his detractors in Washington. His earlier vow to his soldiers—"I will be with you [in the coming decisive battle] and share its dangers with you"— had not worked out to be literally true.[20] The Seven Days battles had certainly not been the rebellion-ending encounter he had envisioned, and he had not been present with his army on the field or witnessed any of the fighting during the change of base. It was not unusual for a commander, after positioning his army where he wanted it, to leave lieutenants to handle the actual fighting—indeed, it was the accepted practice. Lee himself was an adherent of this procedure.

Coming under particular criticism and drawing the heaviest fire were his whereabouts on the afternoon of June 30, when his army was fighting for its life at Glendale, and when the critical defense on Malvern Hill was raging in the afternoon on July 1. On both days he was aboard the *Galena*.

Whatever he had done or not done, wherever he was or was not during the fighting, McClellan had lost further cachet with his critics, who believed it just one more proof of his incompetence. More important, he had lost a little more of his standing with Lincoln. The president had hoped for a far more positive outcome on the Peninsula than this. He had hoped and expected that McClellan would crush the Confederate army and take Richmond.

McClellan's own feeling for the president was at a bitter, all-time low. To Nelly, whom he had been sending long emotional letters throughout Seven Days and the days following, he wrote: "I am confident that he [Lincoln] would relieve me tomorrow if he dared do so. His cowardice alone prevents it. I can never regard him with other feelings than those of thorough contempt—for his mind, heart & mortality."

A letter to Samuel Barlow in New York was even more incendiary. McClellan considered the politicians in his rear villains, "rascals" who, he told Barlow, "will get rid of me as soon as they dare—they all know my opinion of them. They are aware that I have seen through their villainous schemes, & that if I succeed my foot will be on their necks. I do not believe there is one honest man among them—& I know what I say—I fear that none of them wish to save the Union—they prefer ruling a separate Northern confederacy—God will yet foil their abominable designs & mete out to them the terrible punishment they deserve."[21]

On the day the fighting ended, McClellan wired Washington: "I now pray for time. My men have proved themselves the equals of any troops in the world—but they are worn out. Our losses have been very great. I doubt whether more severe battles have ever been fought—we have failed to win only because overpowered by superior numbers." He then asked for a mind-jolting injection of reinforcements, "promptly, and in mass"—50,000 more men, "and with them I will retrieve our fortunes. More would be well, but that number sent at once, will, I think enable me to assume the offensive."[22]

Lincoln wrote him immediately, on July 2: "Allow me to reason with you a moment. When you ask for fifty thousand men to be promptly sent you, you surely labor under some gross mistake of fact.... the idea of sending you fifty thousand, or any other considerable force promptly, is simply absurd." Lincoln tried, however, to reassure McClellan. "If in your frequent mention of responsibility, you have the impression that I blame you for not doing more than you can, please be relieved of such impression. I only beg that in like manner, you will not ask impossibilities of me. If you think you are not strong enough to take Richmond just now, I do not ask you to try just now. Save the Army, material and personal; and I will strengthen it for the offensive again, as fast as I can."[23]

To assess the situation himself, Lincoln traveled to Harrison's Landing on the steamer *Ariel*, arriving on the afternoon of July 8. He stayed two days. Whatever impression he took from that visit and what he intended now to do, he was not saying. What he left with in his pocket, however, was a letter of advice from McClellan.

In the letter, handed to Lincoln the day he arrived, McClellan spelled out his views not just on military affairs but on political policy—generally a subject wholly outside the purview of a military commander.

He began the letter by explaining himself. "I can not but regard our condition as critical and I earnestly desire, in view of possible contingencies, to lay before your Excellency, for your private consideration, my general views concerning the existing state of the rebellion; although they do not strictly relate to the situation of this Army or strictly come within the scope of my official duties. These views amount to convictions and are deeply impressed upon my mind and heart."

"The time has come," he advised Lincoln, "when the Government must determine upon a civil and military policy, covering the whole ground of our national trouble." He observed that the rebellion "has assumed the character of a War; as such it should be regarded; and it should be conducted upon the highest principles known to Christian Civilization." By that he meant it should be waged strictly by armies against armies, and not in any way be a war upon the people of the South and its institutions, including slavery. He bluntly said as much. "In prosecuting the War," he advised the president, "all private property and unarmed persons should be strictly protected.... Military power should not be allowed to interfere with the relations of servitude, either by supporting or impairing the authority of the master."

He argued, "A system of policy thus constitutional and conservative, and pervaded by the influences of Christianity and freedom, would receive the support of almost all truly loyal men," and "it might be humbly hoped that it would commend itself to the favor of the Almighty."[24]

The letter was a restatement of McClellan's long-held view of what the war was all about: a war solely to restore the Union as it was, not to punish innocent Southerners and abolish slavery. But it also was a resurfacing of his hubris, consistent with his view of his intellectual superiority to Lincoln. It may also have been compensation for his military failure on the Peninsula, a fallback for his failure to fight and win the one big war-ending battle—an effort to salvage something. Lincoln's two personal secretaries, Nicolay and Hay, believed it marked "the beginning of General McClellan's distinctively political career."[25]

Lincoln read McClellan's letter and thrust it in his pocket without comment. A letter on policy from McClellan was not what Lincoln needed. He needed an aggressive commander, which this one had not proved to be.

CHAPTER 15

NEW POLICY AND OLD BRAINS

As Lincoln was pocketing McClellan's letter on July 8 at Harrison's Landing, he was also incubating a 180-degree change of course against slavery in the South.

Up to this point, he too had vigorously insisted on not disturbing slavery as it existed in the Southern states. But now he was contemplating limited emancipation—as a military measure. In a carriage ride in mid-July, he told Secretary of the Navy Welles that he "had about come to the conclusion that it was a military necessity for the salvation of the Union, that we must free the slaves or be ourselves subdued."[1]

Lincoln's plan was to issue an emancipation proclamation that would declare all slaves in the states in rebellion against the Union free. Although free only by edict, they would become so in reality as Union arms advanced into new Southern territory. Slavery would not be disturbed in loyal border states, whose allegiance Lincoln needed in the war. The end of slavery everywhere could come only in a general emancipation nationwide, which was also in the back of Lincoln's mind, but whose time had not yet come.

On July 22, Lincoln acquainted his cabinet with the proclamation he had been writing. He told them he was not asking for their approval, for he had made up his mind. He simply wanted "to lay the subject-matter... before them."[2] At Secretary of State Seward's suggestion, Lincoln decided the time to issue such a document had not yet come. It needed a victory of sorts, so it would not look like a desperation move. But after McClellan's failure on the Peninsula, he did not yet have a victory. The president decided to wait and hope for a better time. Perhaps General Pope would give him that better time.

Pope had meanwhile been preparing to put his army in motion. In his greeting to the soldiers on July 14, he had written: "Let us understand each other. I have come to you from the West, where we have always seen the backs of our enemies; from an army whose business it has been to seek the adversary and to beat him when he was found; whose policy has been attack and not defense." He told his soldiers, "I desire you to dismiss from your minds certain phrases, which I am sorry to find so much in vogue amongst you—'taking strong positions and holding them,' of 'lines of retreat,' and of 'bases of supplies.' Let us discard such ideas. . . . Let us look before us, and not behind. Success and glory are in the advance, disaster and shame lurk in the rear."[3]

On the Peninsula, as McClellan was coping with his failure to take Richmond and pondering what to do next and whether he had the manpower he believed he needed to do it, a new layer was added to his frustrations with Washington.

On July 11, after Lincoln returned to Washington from his visit with McClellan at Harrison's Landing, he had called Major General Henry W. Halleck from command in the West to become his new general-in-chief. The position had been vacant since Lincoln stripped it from McClellan when he left for the Peninsula campaign. Halleck, not McClellan, had been Winfield Scott's choice to succeed him in the first place when he retired. But McClellan was the instrument Lincoln then had at hand and in whom he then had confidence. And the young general was then still riding a wave of congressional hope and public acclaim.

When Lincoln appointed Halleck, he did not consult McClellan or inform him of it. McClellan first heard of the new appointment when he read it in the evening newspapers on July 20.[4] It was not a move or a man to stir his admiration, gladden his heart, inspire his hope, or relieve his mind.

It was difficult to admire Halleck by his looks. He was five foot nine inches tall, a paunchy 190 pounds, with a double chin and an ample bald spot on the upslope of his broad forehead. His eyes bulged and his cheeks sagged. His figure was what one observer described as "slack-twisted." He moved slowly and deliberately and spoke in the same sluggish manner. He was a general who lacked magnetism.[5]

But he was paper smart. A native New Yorker, Halleck had run away from home early in life because of his distaste for farming and was adopted by his maternal grandfather. At Union College, before matriculating to West Point, he had been elected to Phi Beta Kappa. At West Point, he had been an assistant professor of engineering while still an undergraduate. When he did graduate, in 1839, it was third in the class—rarefied air. Halleck had passed most of the Mexican War in California, where he had distinguished himself in noncombat, high in the territory's military government. He had been secretary of state, chief of staff in Lower California, and lieutenant governor of the Mexican city of Mazatlán. He had been prominent in shaping the California constitution prior to statehood in 1850.

In the mid-1850s, Halleck had resigned from the army to become a lawyer in the new state. He had succeeded handsomely, marrying the granddaughter of Alexander Hamilton and refusing seats on the state supreme court and in the U.S. Senate—to amass a fortune instead. He was on the board of directors of a bank and two railroads and became part owner of the second richest quicksilver mine in the world.

When the Civil War came, he went to it like everyone else. But he started closer to the top than most. He was made an instant major general in the regular army, outranked only by Scott, McClellan, and John C. Fremont. At the outset of the war, he was assigned command of the Union armies in the Department of the Mississippi.[6]

Halleck had a high reputation in the Old Army, but as a thinker about war rather than a doer of it. Early in his military career, he had authored a well-regarded book on military science—*Elements of Military Art and Strategy*—and translated from the French works on Napoleon and international law. For those accomplishments, he was known throughout the army as "Old Brains."

Although he had been Scott's favorite, he had none of the battle-field fire of Old Fuss and Feathers. In this war, in command in the West, he had been a slow mover, implementing a strategy of inching his army along, a mile or so at a time, before digging in again. Celerity of execution was not his strong suit. The successes in the West had not been Halleck's. They had been battles won by his subordinate commanders, notably U. S. Grant at Forts Henry and Donelson and Shiloh in Tennessee; John Pope at Island No. 10 on the Mississippi;

and Samuel R. Curtis at Pea Ridge. Halleck had simply basked in reflected glory.

With McClellan tied up on the Peninsula, his hands more than full with the Army of the Potomac and Robert E. Lee, Lincoln needed a military presence to oversee military affairs, and Old Brains seemed a likely choice.

McClellan was not pleased. He called Halleck's promotion "a slap in the face," and wrote Nelly, "This of course, fixes the future for us—I cannot remain permanently in the army after this slight. I must of course stick to this army so long as I am necessary to it, or until the Govt. adopts a policy in regard to the war that I cannot conscientiously affirm—the moment either of these events comes to pass I shall leave the service." He looped Halleck in with the rest of the Washington villains. "It is grating," he told Nelly, "to have to serve under the orders of a man whom I know by experience to be my inferior."[7]

When Halleck arrived in Washington in late July, Lincoln sent him to Harrison's Landing to assess the situation on the Peninsula for himself and learn McClellan's intentions. Lincoln told his friend Senator Browning that he was concerned now that McClellan would not fight and therefore that he had told Halleck that he could keep him in command or not, as he pleased.[8]

It had become apparent to Lincoln, now that he had come to know McClellan and his background, that the general's military character had undergone a complete flip from the brave, courageous, intrepid, sometimes rash and venturesome subaltern he had been in the Mexican War—and as he appeared at this war's beginning—into a timid, irresolute, halting, and overcautious commander of an army.[9]

McClellan, however, had been talking fight since arriving at Harrison's Landing on July 1—of renewing the offensive and taking Richmond if adequately reinforced. He believed his present 85,000 to 90,000 men were "in good spirits and after a little rest will fight better than ever," that they were now "in condition to make any movement justified by its numbers, and was in an admirable position for an offensive movement."[10]

However, he did not seem to have in mind any particular movement, or had not yet thought it through, or just did not want to say. And he felt he needed still more numbers. He was hearing nothing from Washington about reinforcements, and he was proposing nothing to Washington about a specific plan of attack. Both engines were idling. "Not a word from Gomorrah," McClellan complained to his chief of staff and father-in-law, Randolph Marcy, and an advance "cannot occur without stupid insanity on my part until I have tools to work with."[11]

This was the situation when Halleck arrived at Harrison's Landing on July 24 and asked about a possible advance on Richmond. McClellan told him up front that any offensive would require 50,000 more troops. Pressed for a specific plan, McClellan proposed crossing the James and marching on Petersburg, at the southern doorstep of Richmond. Halleck frowned on that, believing it dangerous and impractical. It risked having Lee, who was proving an opportunist—in no way lacking audacity and ready to attack any opening—to slam into McClellan's exposed flank.[12]

McClellan then proposed an advance up the north bank of the James, whereupon, with 30,000 reinforcements, he might attack Richmond with "a good chance for success." He would, of course, be far more comfortable with 50,000 more. To his mind, any assault on Richmond looked to be a horrific risk, for he now believed the Confederate behemoth was some 200,000 men strong and, unlike his army, being heavily reinforced daily.[13]

Halleck told McClellan that 50,000 reinforcements for any offensive were out of the question, that he was not authorized to promise more than 20,000. He gave McClellan a choice: Initiate that plan with 20,000 reinforcements, which would bring his full strength to 110,000—in truth, nearly double Confederate numbers—or give it up and withdraw from the Peninsula. McClellan considered overnight and the next day reluctantly agreed to try the plan with the authorized 20,000 men.[14]

After Halleck returned to Washington, however, McClellan wired him, again jacking up his minimum need for reinforcements to take Richmond to 35,000. That settled things with Halleck. On August 3, he wired McClellan: "It is determined to withdraw your army from the Peninsula to Aquia Creek." He ordered him to "take immediate measures to effect this, covering the movement the best you can."[15]

The order stunned McClellan—threw him "into a rage," one of his generals wrote. It was all unendurable gall and wormwood.[16]

McClellan wrote Halleck on August 4, "I must confess [your telegram] has caused me the greatest pain I ever experienced, for I am convinced that the order to withdraw this Army to Acquia Creek will prove disastrous in the extreme to our cause—I fear it will be a fatal blow." He reiterated that his army was now in excellent discipline and condition, and only twenty-five miles from Richmond. At Aquia Landing, it would be seventy-five. He predicted that the withdrawal would demoralize the army, depress the people of the North, and cause foreign powers to recognize the Confederacy. He begged instead to be "promptly reinforced" and urged "in the strongest terms afforded by our language that this order may be rescinded, & that far from recalling this Army it be promptly reinforced to enable it to resume the offensive."

McClellan argued fiercely. "All points of secondary importance elsewhere should be abandoned & every available man brought here—a decided victory here and the military strength of the rebellion is crushed.... Here is the true defense of Washington, it is here on the banks of the James that the fate of the Union should be decided."[17]

Halleck wired McClellan two days later, justifying the decision. "You, general," he wrote, "certainly could not have been more pained at receiving my order than I was at the necessity of issuing it.... I assure you ... it was not a hasty and inconsiderate act, but one that caused me more anxious thought than any other of my life. But after full and mature consideration of the *pros* and *cons,* I was reluctantly forced to the conclusion that the order must be issued. There was to my mind no alternative."

He argued that he did not see how McClellan's army would be demoralized by "a simple change of position to a new, and by no means distant, base." Halleck believed the "political effect of the withdrawal may at first be unfavorable, but I think the public are beginning to understand its necessity." He ended his long wire with another thought not designed to comfort. He reminded McClellan that "all of your plans require re-enforcements, which it is impossible to give you. It is very easy to ask for re-enforcements, but it is not so easy to give them when you have no disposable troops at your command."[18]

Even as he turned angrily to implement the withdrawal, McClellan would argue one more time, on August 12, for authority to make a dash for the Confederate capital. He had new information that the rebel forces in front of Richmond had been dramatically diluted. "From all I can learn," he wrote, "there is not thirty-six thousand men between this & Richmond nor do I believe they can get more before we can whip them."[19] Seeing that Pope's army was now moving and that McClellan seemed no longer a factor, Lee had turned the bulk of his army to confront the new threat, leaving only a part it between McClellan and Richmond.

But Halleck wrote back, "There is no change of plans. You will send up your troops as rapidly as possible."[20] McClellan's dreams of taking Richmond with one great rebellion-ending battle had been crushed.

McClellan and his wife Mary Ellen, whom he called Nelly, and with whom he shared "all my thoughts." (Library of Congress Selected Civil War photographs, 1861–1865)

Secretary of War Edwin M. Stanton, McClellan's erstwhile friend who became his Judas. (Library of Congress Prints and Photographs Division)

Ohio Senator Benjamin F. Wade, chairman of the Join Committee on the Conduct of the War, and the very face of the McClellan-hating Radicals. (Library of Congress Prints and Photographs Division)

Union Major General Henry Halleck, McClellan's successor as general-in-chief, who was called "Old Brains" and whom McClellan thought had no brains at all. (Library of Congress Digitized Historical Collections: Civil War Photographs)

Union Major General John Pope, the Union Commander of the Army of Virginia, routed by Lee and Jackson at Second Manassas. (Library of Congress Selected Civil War photographs, 1861–1865)

Union Major General Ambrose Burnside, McClellan's dear friend who reluctantly succeeded him as commander of the Army of the Potomac. (Library of Congress Digitized Historical Collections: Civil War Photographs)

Confederate General Joseph E. Johnston, McClellan's first opponent on the Penninsula, desperately wounded at the battle of Fair Oaks and replaced by Lee. (Library of Congress Selected Civil War photographs, 1861–1865)

Confederate General Robert E. Lee, McClellan's chief rebel foe on the Peninsula and at Antietam. (Library of Congress Selected Civil War photographs, 1861–1865)

A highly pro-Lincoln political cartoon in Harper's Weekly during the 1864 presidential election campaign between Lincoln and McClellan. (Library of Congress Prints and Photographs Division)

Lincoln pictured at the time of this 1864 reelection campaign against McClellan. (Library of Congress Prints and Photographs Division)

McClellan in civilian attire, the Democratic candidate to unseat the president who had sacked him. (Library of Congress Prints and Photographs Division)

Antietam, Md. President Lincoln and Gen. George B. McClellan in the general's tent, October 1862. (Library of Congress Civil War glass negative collection)

CHAPTER 16

IN COMMAND OF NOTHING

H alleck was simply carrying out orders from the top. A new and different strategy had been set in motion and was being implemented. The new strategy was, in effect, reverting to the old and discarded one: a direct overland march on Richmond from in front that Lincoln had favored, with a new and hard-nosed commander.

That and the proposed proclamation of emancipation Lincoln contemplated in July constituted a sea change on how the war was being seen and being waged, and for what reasons. So far it had been waged by McClellan's lights—to win the war in a friendly way, crush the rebellion without breaking all the eggs; win the big battle without unduly disrupting the civilian South and its primary institution, slavery—basically, McClellan's Harrison's Landing letter approach. That—the conciliatory policy—was being discarded by Lincoln as McClellan was being recalled from the Peninsula.

McClellan did not like anything that he was seeing and hearing. None of it pleased him. It was all counter to his idea of how the war should be waged and won—and by whom. None of the advice in his Harrison's Landing letter to Lincoln was being followed.

His disagreement with events had surfaced in letters he had been writing to Nelly. "I do not like the political turn that affairs are taking," he told her on July 22.

On August 2, he wrote, "When you contrast the policy I urge in my letter to the Presdt with that of Congress & Mr. Pope you can readily agree with me that there can be little mutual confidence between the Govt & myself—we are the antipodes of each other & it is more than probable that they will take the earliest opportunity to relieve me from command & get me out of sight."

McClellan was daily expecting the worst for himself. A week later, he told Nelly, "I am trying to keep my temper & force *them* to relieve me or dismiss me from the service. I have no idea that I will be with this army more than two or three weeks longer & should not be surprised any day or hour to get my 'walking papers.'" He also expected and hoped the worst for Pope, predicting he "will be thrashed during the coming week—very badly whipped he will be & ought to be—such a villain as he is ought to bring defeat upon any cause that employs him."[1]

McClellan believed that in this miserable turn of events, the sacrifices, the loss of life, the high expense of waging the war, and the heartache would be enormous before the army ever got back as close to Richmond as he now was and had been ordered to leave. There were those in the country—in the public and in the military—who agreed with him.[2] One Union officer later wrote, "[T]he worst that could be said of the Peninsula Campaign was that thus far it had not been successful," that now it was about to be turned into a downright failure, and largely through "the agency of General Halleck."[3] McClellan was arguing that Washington was truly in danger now, in early August, with his army evacuating the Peninsula, and that he was still in much better position to save it from where he was rather than at Aquia Creek.[4]

Despite his contrary convictions, McClellan had been obeying orders. After receiving them in the first week in August, even while arguing fiercely against them, he had reluctantly set in motion the evacuation with all of its men and impedimenta—arms, animals, wagons, baggage, and stores. Elements of his army had also started moving to Pope. McClellan was beginning to send them—under orders, but not with gracious best wishes.

He was convinced more strongly than ever that Pope's campaign was doomed. "I am inclined to believe," he wrote Nelly on August 10, "that Pope will catch his Tartar within a couple of days & be disposed of. The absurdity of Halleck's course in ordering the army away from here is that it cannot possibly reach Washn in time to do any good, but will necessarily be too late."[5]

The anti-McClellan faction in Washington, believing the worst of him, suspected he was dragging his feet. Lincoln was not among them, but Stanton, now the most avid of the McClellan haters, watched the general impatiently and began canvassing various sources seeking evidence of delay. Secretary of the Navy Welles, watching Stanton, wrote that he was "so absorbed in his scheme to get rid of McClellan that other and more important matters were neglected."[6]

Stanton was continuing to work both sides of the street, however. After the Seven Days battles, he wrote McClellan: "No man had ever a truer friend than I have been to you and shall continue to be. You are seldom absent from my thoughts and I am ready to make any sacrifice to aid you.... I pray Almighty God to deliver you and your army from all peril and lead you on to victory."[7] That was a sentiment Lincoln endorsed wholeheartedly.

McClellan was spending telegraph time trying to convince the doubters in Washington that he was not foot-dragging, that he was moving as fast as inadequate wharf space at Yorktown and Fort Monroe and the shallow water at the disembarkation point at Aquia Creek permitted. On August 10, he insisted in a wire to Halleck: "There has been no unnecessary delay, as you assert—not an hour—but everything has been and is being pushed as rapidly as possible to carry out your orders."[8]

By August 16, the change of base was mostly completed. McClellan later wrote that late in the afternoon that day, "when the last man had disappeared from the deserted camps, I followed with my personal staff in the track of the grand Army of the Potomac, bidding farewell to the scene still covered with the marks of its presence, and to be forever memorable in history as the vicinity of its most brilliant exploits."[9]

Following in the army's train, McClellan left Fort Monroe on August 23 and arrived at Aquia Creek the next day. He pushed on from there to Alexandria, where he set up his headquarters on August 28.

McClellan was intent on learning what his role now was going to be. He rather suspected what was likely to happen. "I take it for granted that my orders will be as disagreeable as it is possible to make them—unless Pope is beaten," he wrote Nelly, "in which case they will want me to save Washn again. Nothing but their fear will induce them to give me any command of importance or treat me otherwise than with discourtesy. Bah!"[10]

He complained bitterly to her of the continuing silence from Lincoln, Stanton, and Halleck. "I learn nothing whatever of the state of affairs," he wrote. "Please inform me at once what my position is," he had pleaded with Halleck on the twenty-seventh, "I do not wish to act in the dark." "I expect merely a contemptuous silence," he told Nelly on the twenty-ninth. There was no answering word from Lincoln or anyone else spelling out his position and authority.

As McClellan's army passed through Aquia Creek, it was being shuttled on to Pope at Manassas, where Lee had now mobilized all of his army to confront this new threat.

By August 28, fighting was under way as elements of the two armies met in bloody combat at Brawner's Farm, seven miles south of Manassas Junction. McClellan had been telling Nelly that Pope was in trouble and the campaign was headed for disaster. He wrote her, "Pope is in a bad way." He also wrote, "I have a terrible task on my hands now—perfect imbecility to correct. No means to act with, no authority—yet determined if possible to save the country & the Capital. I find the soldiers all clinging to me—yet I am not permitted to go to the post of danger! Two of my Corps will either save that fool Pope or be sacrificed for the country."[11]

On August 29, McClellan had wired Lincoln advice. "I am clear that one of two courses should be adopted," he wrote the president. "—1st To concentrate all our available forces to open communication with Pope—2nd To leave Pope to get out of his scrape & at once use all our means to make the Capital perfectly safe. No middle course will now answer."[12]

The second alternative froze Lincoln's blood, then set it boiling. John Hay wrote in his diary: "The President was very outspoken in regard to McClellan's present conduct. He said it really seemed to him that McC wanted Pope defeated.... The President seemed to think him a little crazy. Envy jealousy and spite are probably a better explanation for his present conduct. He is constantly sending dispatches to the President and Halleck asking what is his real position and command. He acts as chief alarmist and marplot of the Army."

Hay also wrote, "Stanton was loud about the McC. business. He was unqualifiedly severe upon McClellan. He said that after these battles, there should be one Court Martial, if never any more. He said that nothing but foul play could lose this battle & that it rested with McC. and his friends."[13]

While McClellan's suggestion—in effect, leave Pope to get out of his scrape as best he can—was unfortunate and hackle-raising, it conveyed the idea. It made sense, but the phrase was unfortunate, written in haste without weighing the words. But it was widely construed to mean that he wished the destruction of Pope and his army.[14]

McClellan was in his headquarters in Alexandria, where all day August 30 he listened to heavy firing from the direction of Manassas. The battle seemed to be roaring toward a climax, and he expected the worst. He wrote Nelly, "I have sent up every man I have, pushed everything, & am left here on the flat of my back without any command whatever. It is dreadful to listen to the cannonading & not be able to take any part in it."

Such, he figured, was his fate, but that was no consolation. "I feel too blue & disgusted to write any more now," he told her, "so I will smoke a cigar & try to get into a better humor. They have taken *all* my troops from me—I have even sent off all my personal escort & camp guard & am here with a few orderlies & and the aides. I have been listening to the distant sound of a great battle in the distance—my men engaged in it & I away! I never felt worse in my life."[15]

Although not under enemy fire, McClellan was under stepped-up fire from his detractors, particularly Pope. The notion that McClellan had knowingly held back and delayed sending troops before it was too late was so intense and well known that damage control had become necessary. McClellan wired the faithful Fitz John Porter on September 1, "I ask of you for my sake that of the country & of the old Army of the Potomac that you and all my friends will lend the fullest & most cordial cooperation to Genl Pope in all the operations now going on. The destinies of our country the honor of our arms are at stake, & all depends now upon the cheerful cooperation of all in the field." He admonished Porter and all friends and supporters to "extend to Genl Pope the same support they ever have to me."[16]

As he was writing this, the disaster had happened. The second battle of Manassas had ended with a Union defeat as devastating as the first one the year before. Pope was routed at Manassas on August 30 and was falling back on Washington and blaming McClellan. The satisfaction McClellan's friends took in Pope's misery was ill hidden. One of Pope's officers bitterly wrote, "It is interesting, but saddening to witness the brightening of countenances among some of the staffs of the army of the Potomac, whilst listening to or reading reports of the repulses of General Pope."[17]

An officer in McClellan's Second Corps wrote:

The campaign was destined to end in humiliation. The braggart who had begun his campaign with insolent reflections...upon the Army of the Potomac and its commander...had been kicked, cuffed, hustled about, knocked down, run over, and trodden upon as rarely happens in the history of war. His communications had been cut; his headquarters pillaged; a corps had marched into his rear, and had encamped at its ease upon the railroad by which he received his supplies; he had been beaten or foiled in every attempt he had made to "bag" those defiant intruders; and, in the end, he was glad to find refuge in the intrenchments of Washington, whence he had sallied forth, six weeks before, breathing out threatenings and slaughter.[18]

Samuel Davis Sturgis, one of McClellan's generals and another West Point classmate, rather summed up the feeling of McClellan's inner circle with this acid comment: "I don't care for John Pope one pinch of owl dung."[19] "We were badly beaten & lost a good deal," one officer wrote home. "I hope to God this will give us McClellan."[20]

On August 30, McClellan had finally seen an order defining commands, and "mine," he told Nelly the next day, "is that part of the army of the Potomac not sent to Pope—as all is sent there I am left in command of *nothing*." He told her, "I feel like a fool here—sucking my thumbs & doing nothing but what ought to be done by junior officers." Discredited and politically ignored, he had nothing to command but his staff—only "a corporal's guard," as an early biographer would describe it.[21]

However McClellan's men felt about Pope, however Pope felt about them and McClellan, however McClellan felt about Washington or Washington felt about him, the problem now was how to regroup. Despite his dismay over what he saw as McClellan's ungracious conduct during the second battle of Manassas, Lincoln knew what had to be done. And it was what McClellan expected would happen.

On the night of August 31, with Pope in retreat back into the fortifications of Washington, McClellan, who had relocated to Washington, "had just finished a very severe application for a leave of absence when I received a dispatch from Halleck begging me to help him out of the scrape & take command here." On the morning on September 2, McClellan was at breakfast when both Lincoln and Halleck paid him a surprise visit. Lincoln, as McClellan recounted it, "expressed the opinion that the troubles now impending could be overcome better by me than anyone else."[22]

The president, McClellan later wrote, told him "that there were 30,000 stragglers on the roads; that the army was entirely defeated and falling back to Washington in confusion," that he regarded the city as lost, "and asked me if I would, under the circumstances, as a favor to him, resume command and do the best that could be done." Lincoln, McClellan wrote, asked him to "take steps at once to stop and collect the stragglers, to place the works in a proper state of defence, and to go out to meet and take command of the army when it approached the vicinity of the works; then to put the troops in the best position for defence—committing everything to my hands." McClellan accepted instantly. "Without one moment's hesitation and without making any conditions whatever, I at once said that I would accept the command and would stake my life that I would save the city."[23]

Halleck then issued a general order, saying "Major-General McClellan will have command of the fortifications of Washington and of all the troops for the defense of the capital."[24]

Lincoln's unilateral reappointment of McClellan to command landed like a bomb blast in Washington, and with particularly explosive power in a cabinet meeting on September 2. As Pope's army was retreating back to Washington, on September 1, Stanton and Chase had drafted a letter to Lincoln demanding McClellan's immediate firing and were ready to present it to the president. It was two-fisted and designed as a knockout punch. Welles believed it amounted to "a fixed determination to remove, and if possible to disgrace McClellan."[25]

The letter called for the immediate removal of McClellan from command. It called him incompetent and cited his "sad and humiliating trial of twelve months" and the waste of lives and millions of dollars at his hands. It scorched his disobedience of orders, which they charged had imperiled the army under Pope. Keeping him in command, the letter insisted, will "daily hazard the fate of our armies and our national existence."[26]

The letter would never be delivered. Before Lincoln arrived for the cabinet meeting, Stanton, in a voice vibrating with emotion, said he had just learned that, instead of being sacked, McClellan had been restored to command. It was startling, cabinet-shaking news. When Lincoln arrived, he confirmed it. Chase, in a high fit of anger, predicted it would prove a national calamity, "the equivalent to giving Washington to the rebels."[27]

But Lincoln refused to back down. It was one of the rare occasions that the president and Stanton would disagree. They had been working well in tandem, generally in harmony, on all important matters concerning the war and the rebellion.[28]

McClellan was back in command, despite Stanton's wishes, and would so remain—for now at least. The president explained it to John Hay: "The Cabinet yesterday were unanimous against him. They were all ready to denounce me for it, except Blair. He [McClellan] has acted badly in this matter, but we must use what tools we have. There is no man in the army who can man these fortifications and lick these troops of ours into shape half as well as he." Lincoln told Hay, "Unquestionably he has acted badly toward Pope! He wanted him to fail. That is unpardonable. But he is too useful just now to sacrifice.... If he cant fight himself, he excells in making others ready to fight."[29]

Lincoln later expanded on his reasons to Welles, who had remained relatively detached from the destroy-McClellan campaign and had refused to sign the Stanton-Chase letter. Lincoln confessed to Welles that he might have made a mistake in the first place replacing McClellan with Pope in command of the army before Washington. He said that now he felt humiliated rewarding McClellan "and those who failed to do their whole duty in the hour of trial." But facts had to be faced. The army was undoubtedly avidly pro-McClellan, and that personal feeling must give way to the public good. "I must have McClellan to reorganize the army and bring it out of chaos," he told Welles. "There has been a design, a purpose in breaking down Pope, without regard to the consequences to the country that is atrocious. It is shocking to see and know this, but there is no remedy at present. McClellan has the army with him."[30]

Lincoln was nothing if not pragmatic, which was more than McClellan's critics were. One of the harshest, Senator Wade, the Committee on the Conduct of the War chairman, earlier in the summer had demanded Lincoln sack McClellan and get somebody else to command the army.

"Well, put yourself in my place for a moment," Lincoln told Wade. "If I relieve McClellan, whom shall I put in command?"

"Why, anybody!" Wade exclaimed.

"Wade, *anybody* will do for you, but not for me," Lincoln answered wearily. "I must have *somebody*."[31]

With his somebody reinstated, Lincoln hoped for the best. The McClellan haters expected the worst.

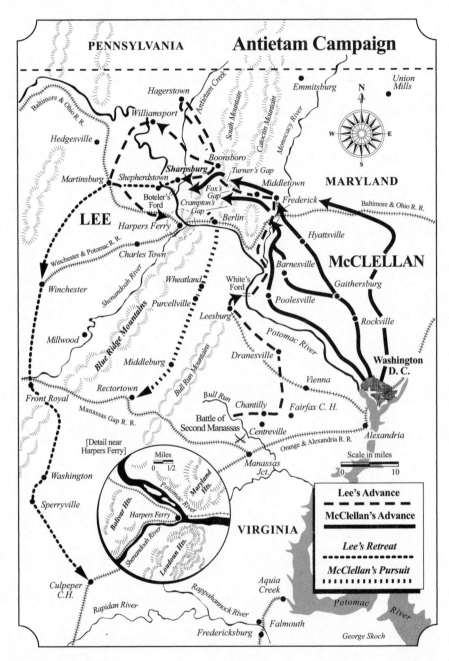

Credit: George Skoch

CHAPTER 17

THE ROAD TO SHARPSBURG

The announcement of McClellan's restoration to command reached the army in the early evening of September 2. McClellan rode out immediately toward the front to greet his retreating, disconsolate troops and give them a rebirth of hope.

One soldier wrote: "The scene that followed can be more easily imagined than described. From extreme sadness we passed in a twinkling to a delirium of delight. A Deliverer had come. A real 'rainbow of promise' had appeared suddenly in the dark political sky....Men threw their caps high into the air, and danced and frolicked like school-boys, so glad were they to get their old commander back again."[1]

"Troops cheered themselves hoarse," another soldier wrote, "our regiment, like many others, hailed him extravagantly as a savior." An officer in the Second Massachusetts wrote that McClellan was "the greatest general the country ever produced. Every body is overjoyed."[2]

"I hear them calling out to me as I ride among them," McClellan wrote Nelly. "It makes my heart bleed to see the poor shattered remnants of my noble Army of the Potomac, poor fellows! And to see how they love me even now." They crowded around shouting and cheering, embracing Dan Webster's legs. McClellan heard them calling out "George—don't leave us again! They *shan't* take you away from us again."[3]

Even as McClellan was riding out to bring home his battered army, the man who had battered it, Robert E. Lee, was seeking further gratification. His routing of Pope on the fields of Manassas demanded follow-up. He had no intention, however, of pursuing the beaten Union army into Washington and assaulting the city's fortifications. He considered that injudicious at best—a useless bit of folly. He had a mind to go on the offensive big time in another direction—to push across the Potomac into Maryland and Pennsylvania instead, to threaten Washington at its back door, and to there strike a war-deciding, independence-bestowing blow.

Lee knew that the Union army must be demoralized after its roughing up at Second Manassas. It was an excellent time to put on a different, more intense order of pressure, before that army could recuperate and heal. It would not do now to simply idle his engines in Virginia. Promise lay across the Potomac. There he could take the war out of his own backyard and fight the way he wanted to fight, in the open, isolating parts of the Union army in its own territory and crushing it in detail, weakening the North's will to continue this war.[4]

Washington, Secretary of Navy Welles observed on September 4, was a "city full of rumors and but little truth in any of them."[5] The outlook was dark for Lincoln and the Union. The Confederacy looked closer to victory than at any other time in this year-and-a-half-old war. Great Britain appeared close to recognizing the rebel government, and such a move would be disastrous. And now this—an invasion by an irrepressible rebel horde.

Lee's army, battered in its own right, began crossing the Potomac near Leesburg on September 4, with Stonewall Jackson's corps in the lead. It was one of those incomparable, warm, beautiful late summer days. The morning sun, risen in a cloudless sky, bathed the summit of the mountains to the west. The banks of the Potomac, lined by trees in full autumn dress and decked with flowers, flowed languidly around the crossing army.

The army's mood matched the weather. As they crossed at White's Ford, the soldiers laughed and shouted and sang out, "Maryland, My Maryland!" Their voices boomed across the river and into the trees.[6]

It has a happy, singing army. But it was also a spectral one, a scarecrow chorus, "coon-jawed" and "hollow-eyed," as generally was the case with Confederate soldiers in this war.[7] As the army passed through Leesburg on the way to the ford, an old lady raised her arms and with brimming tears exclaimed, "The Lord bless your dirty ragged souls!"[8]

Dirty and ragged they were, threadbare and vermin infested. When they reached Frederick, a resident named Kate looked at them in disgust and wrote her friend Minnie in Baltimore: "Oh they are so dirty! I don't think the Potomac River could wash them clean; and ragged!—there is not a scarecrow in the corn-fields that would not scorn to exchange clothes with them; and so tattered!—there isn't a decently dressed soldier in their whole army."[9] This was a common condition of Confederate soldiers in the war. Union troops were generally better supplied and better dressed, given their richer resources.

The crossing into Union territory of this ragtag but happy army gave McClellan a big problem atop an already big problem. He was nowhere near reorganizing his army to his satisfaction. He would far rather take several weeks to "hold our own army quiet until its pressing wants were fully supplied, its organization restored, and its ranks filled with recruits—in brief prepared for a campaign." But alas, "as the enemy maintained the offensive and crossed the upper Potomac to threaten or invade Pennsylvania, it became necessary to meet him at any cost, notwithstanding the condition of the troops; to put a stop to the invasion, save Baltimore and Washington, and throw him back across the Potomac."[10]

Lee, though rather unprepared himself, was not proving to be the sort to give an enemy—or himself—time under any circumstances. McClellan had no choice but to get his army moving to counter this new threat. The Confederates could not be permitted to win another decisive victory—and certainly not on Union soil.

But this was not McClellan's kind of campaign. It compelled him to react to an enemy's moves and to improvise. That kind of war was not in his comfort zone. Yet it was the only way to drive Lee back across the Potomac and give McClellan time to thoroughly restore and revitalize his own army; get its logistics, organization, morale, military efficiency, and physical well being back on track; then undertake a new, truly decisive campaign on his own terms, within his comfort zone.[11]

McClellan worried again that numbers were not in his favor. Having defended Richmond on the Peninsula with what McClellan still believed were 200,000 men and routed Pope at Manassas with at least 120,000, Lee must now be invading the North with certainly not less than that number. It must be, for McClellan himself would never attempt such a move with less than that. In truth, Lee was marching with but a third of the numbers McClellan credited him—hardly 45,000 men: forty brigades of infantry, three of cavalry, and seventy-seven batteries of artillery.[12]

Notwithstanding his disquiet, McClellan set his army on the road for Rockville and followed it himself on Sunday, September 7, with something smacking of optimism. He wrote Nelly, "I leave in a couple of hours to take command of the army in the field. I shall go to Rockville tonight & start out after the rebels tomorrow. I shall have nearly 100,000 men, old & new, & hope with God's blessing to gain a decisive victory. I think we shall win for the men are now in good spirits—confident in their General & all united in sentiment....if I defeat the rebels I shall be master of the situation."[13]

McClellan was getting little help or advice from the top. "The War Department," Welles thought, "is bewildered, knows but little, does nothing, proposes nothing."[14] Halleck had a recurrent worry about the situation. As McClellan moved out to check Lee, the general-in-chief was as obsessed with Washington's safety as Lincoln and Stanton had been in the spring and summer. Halleck fancied Lee's move was very likely only a ruse, a feint preliminary to turning suddenly in full cry on Washington. "It may be," he wrote McClellan, "the enemy's object is to draw off the mass of our forces and then attempt to attack from the Virginia side of the Potomac." He urged McClellan to "Think of this."[15]

McClellan would just as soon not think of it. It was not a theory he was buying. All the evidence told him "most conclusively that almost the entire Rebel army in Virginia, amounting to not less than 120,000 men, in the vicinity of Frederick City."[16]

Lincoln, of course, was also anxious. As McClellan was arriving in Rockville on September 8 to take command in the field, Lincoln wired him, "How does it look now?" Again two days later, he asked the same question—"How does it look now?" McClellan was not sure how it looked. He was pushing his army, divided into three wings, cautiously out along an equal number of converging roads toward the enemy, wherever that might be. He was still uncertain what Lee's intentions were. He wired the president on September 10 that he had "scouts and spies pushed forward in every direction and will soon be in possession of reliable and definite information." General Ambrose Burnside's scouts were reporting "that the mass of the Enemy was still at Frederick." Yet McClellan also had intelligence that the Confederate army might be backing off, recrossing the Potomac. He assured Lincoln, "We shall know the truth of this rumor soon."[17]

No less worried was a man with more to lose than most—Andrew Curtin, governor of McClellan's native state of Pennsylvania. The Confederate army was moving entirely too close to his state for comfort. McClellan assured him, "I will follow them as closely as I can, and fight them whenever I can find them. It is as much my interest as yours to preserve the soil of Pennsylvania from invasion, or, failing in that, to destroy any army that may have the temerity to attempt it."[18]

McClellan was telling Nelly at least as much he was telling Lincoln, Halleck, and Curtin. "It is hard to get accurate news from the front," he wrote her on September 9. His last reports, he told her, "are that the enemy have 110,000 on this side of the river. I have not so many, so I must watch them closely & try to catch them in some mistake, which I hope to do....McC has a difficult game to play, but will do his best & try to do his duty."[19]

By September 12, McClellan had more information. Unfortunately, it was wrong. The intelligence coming from his scouts and spies that the enemy might be recrossing the Potomac had led him to believe Lee might be retreating. "From all I gather," he wrote Nelly, "secesh is skedaddling & I don't think I can catch him unless he is really moving into Penna....I begin to think he is making off to get out of the scrape by recrossing the river a Williamsport....He evidently don't want to fight me—for some reason or other."[20]

The anxious Curtin, who was deeply involved in intelligence gathering himself, had advised Lincoln that Jackson was indeed crossing the Potomac at Williamsport, "and probably the whole rebel army will be drawn from Maryland." If that is so, Lincoln advised McClellan on September 12, "Please do not let him get off without being hurt."[21]

If McClellan did not have what Lee was doing accurately pegged, neither did Lee have a clear idea what McClellan was doing. At first Lee believed that "the enemy are not moving in this direction, but continue to concentrate about Washington."[22]

While both sides were speculating, Lee's army had passed through Frederick headed west over South Mountain on September 10, with all except his cavalry. The last of it did not clear Frederick until the twelfth. McClellan's troops began entering on its heels the same day, and it was into a cheering city.

When McClellan arrived the next morning and rode through the flag-bedecked town with his staff, it was to "a spontaneous ovation that stirred every soul to its depths."[23] One observer wrote that the general was "received on all sides with the most unlimited expressions of delight. Old and young shouted with joy; matrons held their babes toward him as their deliverer from the rule of a foreign army, and fair young ladies rushed to meet him on the streets, some even throwing their arms around his horse's neck. It was a scene difficult to realize in this matter-of-fact age, but deep seated feeling of gratitude found expression in every possible form."[24]

"I was nearly overwhelmed & pulled to pieces," McClellan told Nelly. "I enclose with this a little flag that some enthusiastic lady thrust into or upon Dan's bridle. As to flowers!!—they came in crowds! In truth I was seldom more affected than by the scenes I saw...& the reception I met with."[25]

The very same day McClellan arrived in Frederick to such loving acclaim, Union soldiers found, in a nearby field, wrapped around three cigars, a copy of Lee's Special Orders No. 191, issued four days earlier and spelling out in stunning detail his invasion strategy.

When he advanced on Frederick, Lee had supposed that threat alone would dislodge Federal troops from isolated Martinsburg and Harpers Ferry. But it had not happened, so he must forcibly see to it. He could not afford to have them menacing his rear and flank. The special orders had Stonewall Jackson going to Harpers Ferry to handle the matter. When Union intelligence had Lee recrossing the Potomac at Williamsport, it was only Jackson crossing on his errand for Lee. The Confederate plan for Harpers Ferry was a three-pronged assault. Lafayette McLaws was to seize Maryland Heights above Harpers Ferry, and John G. Walker was to occupy Loudoun Heights. With Jackson approaching through Bolivar Heights in its rear, Harpers Ferry and its 12,000-man Union garrison would be clamped in a three-sided vise. When Harpers Ferry was taken and secured, all three would rejoin the main army at Boonsboro or Hagerstown.

The special orders found on the field at Frederick also told McClellan that Lee had further divided his army, positioning D. H. Hill's division at Boonsboro west of South Mountain, as the army's rear guard, and sending James Longstreet temporarily to Hagerstown to investigate the rumor of a Federal force approaching from that direction. Lee's idea was to draw the Union army across South Mountain and fight it as far from its base in Washington as possible. That was his intention, and that was the essence of the plan laid out in the special orders, now in McClellan's hands.[26]

It is axiomatic in military strategy that you do not divide an army in front of a larger foe. Doing so is much too dangerous. But Lee knew McClellan. "Are you acquainted with General McClellan?" Lee had asked General Walker as his army was passing through Frederick around September 12. "He is an able general but a very cautious one. His enemies among his own people think him too much so. His army is in a very demoralized and chaotic condition, and will not be prepared for offensive operations—or he will not think it so—for three or four weeks. Before that time I hope to be on the Susquehanna."[27]

With Lee's plans in his hands—a fact that Lee at this point did not know—McClellan was exultant. He wired Lincoln on the thirteenth: "I have all the plans of the Rebels and will catch them in their own trap if my men are equal to the emergency." He wrote, "I think Lee has made a gross mistake and that he will be severely punished for it. The Army is in motion as rapidly as possible. I hope for a great success if the plans of the Rebels remain unchanged."[28]

That same evening McClellan told John Gibbon, a onetime West Point classmate, "Here is a paper with which if I cannot whip 'Bobbie Lee,' I will be willing to go home." He turned down one corner of the precious document for Gibbon, now a brigade commander in his army, to see. "I will not show you the document now," he told Gibbon. "But there is the signature." Gibbon read the signature. The orders were signed by R. H. Chilton, Lee's adjutant general. They were genuine, no doubt about that.

"It gives the movement of every division of Lee's army," McClellan explained. "Tomorrow we will pitch into his centre and if you people will only do two good, hard days' marching I will put Lee in a position he will find hard to get out of."[29]

Despite this rare stroke of fortune, McClellan's army was not in motion "as rapidly as possible," whatever the general had promised Lincoln. The document answered some questions, but not all. Although it spelled out Confederate movements and intentions, it lacked some other important information: specifically, numbers, either about over-all Confederate strength or its parts. McClellan still believed Lee's army was at least 120,000 strong. All he really knew now was that it was clearly in his front and not skedaddling. But it was divided.

Lacking numbers, McClellan was proceeding cautiously, deciding not to make any rash changes in his already well-laid out operational plan for September 13. Following his message to Lincoln, he waited several hours for more information from his advance that might make a few things clearer. As yet he had nothing definitive about whether Lee was still following this lost order. McClellan decided from what information he did have, however, that it was enough to set plans for an advance the next day.[30]

He wired Halleck: "Unless Genl Lee has changed his plans I expect a severe general engagement tomorrow. I feel confident that there is now no rebel force immediately threatening Washington or Baltimore, but that I have the mass of their troops to contend with & they out-number me when united."[31]

The morning of September 14 opened to a bright rising sun. McClellan was up with it, pushing his army toward the South Mountain gaps. Moving up into the mountain, the Union army struck one sol-dier as "a monstrous, crawling, blue-black snake, miles long, quilled with the silver slant of muskets, at a 'shoulder,' its sluggish tail writhing slowly up over the distant eastern ridge."[32]

Snaking thus toward South Mountain, the soldiers saw their general sitting astride Dan Webster beside the road of march. One wrote:

> As each organization passed the general, the men became appar-ently forgetful of everything but their love for him. They cheered and cheered again, until they became so hoarse they could cheer no longer. It seems as if an intermission had been declared in order that a reception might be tendered to the general-in-chief. A great crowd continually surrounded him, and the most extravagant demonstra-tions were indulged in. Hundreds even hugged the horse's legs and caressed his head and mane. While the troops were surging by, the general continually pointed with his finger to the gap in the moun-tain through which our path lay. It was like a great scene in a play, with the roar of the guns for an accompaniment.[33]

What was happening struck Lee as very un-McClellan-like. He was coming on at a faster clip than normal for him—faster than Lee expected, and Lee with his army scattered in every direction. He was not the only surprised Confederate. Stonewall Jackson, taking care of business at Harpers Ferry, confessed to General Walker, "I thought I knew McClellan," he said of his old West Point classmate, "but this movement of his puzzles me."[34]

Even so, McClellan was coming slow enough that Jackson's brother-in-law, Confederate Major General D. H. Hill, was able to position troops on South Mountain to meet the onslaught and try to buy Lee time to reassemble his scattered army. Hill dug in. He looked out on McClellan's huge army snaking up the mountain toward him, extending "back as far as eye could see in the distance," and thought it "a grand and glorious spectacle, and it was impossible to look at it without admiration. I had never seen so tremendous an army before, and I did not see one like it afterward." With only 5,000 men, Hill knew he would be vastly outmanned and outgunned, even though eight brigades were being hurried to him by James Longstreet from Hagerstown.[35]

The battle was joined in two passes, Fox's Gap, the point of McClellan's main attack, and Turner's Gap, a mile north. All morning and into the afternoon Hill was not able to drive the Federals back. But neither had McClellan, attacking in the two gaps, been able to force his way over the mountain—not until late afternoon, when he made a breakthrough at Fox's Gap and Hill withdrew down the other side of the mountain.

There was yet another important fight that day, September 14, at a third gap—Crampton's, South Mountain's southernmost defile five miles south of Fox's and a few miles northeast of Harpers Ferry. The Union garrison at Harpers Ferry was besieged by Jackson's command and the two others Lee had sent to neutralize it. McClellan that morning sent Major General William B. Franklin's 12,000-man Sixth Corps to attempt to storm through the gap, destroy Confederate Major General McLaws's command on Maryland Heights, and relieve the surrounded garrison. Barring the way at Crampton's Gap were two Confederate cavalry and three infantry regiments, only one tenth the size of Franklin's force. The small Confederate line held off the Union attack for several hours before breaking and running. Confederate reinforcements set up another line in Pleasant Valley a mile and a half below the gap. Franklin, overestimating Confederate strength, stopped short, and night ended the effort, dooming the Union garrison at Harpers Ferry.[36]

Although the assault at Crampton's Gap failed, the breakthroughs at the other two gaps buoyed McClellan. He exultantly wired Washington the next morning: "[T]he Enemy...in a perfect panic & Genl Lee last night stated publicly that he must admit they had been shockingly whipped." Lincoln responded, "Your dispatches of to-day received. God bless you, and all with you. Destroy the rebel army, if possible."[37]

When McClellan occupied the South Mountain passes, Lee began backing away. In Boonsboro on September 15, McClellan learned that the Confederates appeared to be making for Sharpsburg, a small town half a dozen miles away hard on the Potomac on the Maryland side, possibly to concentrate the army there and make a stand across a creek called the Antietam.[38]

It was so. Lee had called Longstreet back and called home Jackson, who was not quite finished at Harpers Ferry. But he would be that day, September 15. Harpers Ferry would fall to him then, with its more than 12,500 Union soldiers, more than 70 artillery pieces, 13,000 muskets, and a large cache of valuable military stores, including uniforms.[39]

As was his way, McClellan followed cautiously that day. He still believed that Lee, though cornered, had monstrous muscle—80,000 to 120,000 men—and nothing in the way of intelligence convinced him otherwise. He must not attack rashly. When McClellan reached the Antietam in Maryland and stared across the open rolling ground, so different from heavily forested Virginia, he found Lee not yet fully reinforced, perhaps, but strongly dug in and waiting. The Confederate appeared to be readying himself for a strong defensive stand. Surveying the setting, McClellan saw that to win this fight, he would have to cross three bridges and attack chiefly over that open rolling farmland. Lee clearly held a strong position and would have the advantage. But his back would be to the Potomac, with nowhere to escape if beaten.[40]

It was now late in the day—no time, in McClellan's mind, for anything but a frontal assault, and that appeared to be foolish. Only two of his divisions were at hand, and an assault now would be a waste of lives. He decided to wait, call it a day, and plan for tomorrow.[41]

CHAPTER 18

HELLFIRE ON
THE ANTIETAM

S eptember 16 dawned on the Antietam uninviting: misty, cloudy, and damp. An early morning fog lay across the rolling terrain. McClellan had set up headquarters at the Philip Pry farmhouse on a rise across the creek, and when the fog lifted, he launched a reconnaissance.

It was placid, inviting ground, in no way suggesting violence, with its green fields where herds of cattle were grazing and with richly laden orchards and yellow harvests ripening in the September sun. It was ground of undulating hills, fertile meadows, and comfortable farmhouses, some standing out boldly on rises, others half hidden by fruit trees. Antietam Creek itself was mostly obscured from view by trees that fringed its winding course.[1]

The supposed disparity in numbers—McClellan was clearly outmanned again in his mind—advised caution. He still had uncertain intelligence about the whereabouts of all of Lee's force, and its size. But he did know, despite the fog, that "some of the enemy was still there." He advised Halleck that he planned to attack "as soon as situation of the enemy is developed." There would be no assault, however, until he was fully ready. By evening he had not attacked, but he had devised a plan for the next day that he called his "design."[2]

The next morning, September 17, McClellan would unleash his main assault across the upper bridge against Lee's left. When that showed progress, he would unleash an attack on the Confederate right across the Antietam at the lower bridge, to interpose his force between Lee and the single Potomac crossing. As soon as one or both of these attacks had broken through, he would smash into the rebel center with a crushing blow.

That was the plan, and it was an excellent one. McClellan began late in the afternoon of September 16 putting his corps into position on both ends of the line.

The Union First Corps under Major General Joe Hooker, nicknamed "Fighting Joe" for aggressive and courageous fighting in the Peninsula campaign, crossed the creek at the unguarded upper bridge and approached the Confederate left. Major General Joseph K. F. Mansfield, nearly sixty years old, in the army since he was thirteen and now white-haired and white-bearded, followed him across with his Twelfth Corps. By nightfall, everything was in place on that end of the line. The Ninth Corps under Ambrose Burnside was filing into the hills overlooking the quiet bridge that spanned the creek on the Confederate right.[3] Edwin Vose Sumner's Second Corps and Fitz John Porter's Fifth Corps would be held in reserve. William Franklin's Sixth Corps, camped in Pleasant Valley, some six miles to the east, would arrive by noon on the seventeenth.

McClellan's decision not to attack in the remaining daylight hours of September 15 and his studying of the ground, preparation, positioning, and planning throughout the day on the sixteenth had given Lee time to reassemble his outmanned army. The Confederate commander had positioned what he had with him now—about 18,000 men—at Sharpsburg along a north-south line paralleling the creek and had called Stonewall Jackson, John Walker, and Lafayette McLaws in from Harpers Ferry, seventeen miles away. They were marching hell-bent for Sharpsburg.

Even when they arrived, Lee would have no more than 40,000 men to throw against the McClellan juggernaut of some 85,000 troops. Nevertheless, as McClellan was looking and planning and adjusting his lines, Lee was thinking attack, despite the disparity in numbers. He was not happy with the thought of retreating back into Virginia. Nor was he content merely to await McClellan's next move. On the night of September 15, he was considering how he might go on the offensive the next day—a turning movement, marching north to Hagerstown. He sent his cavalry under J. E. B. Stuart to scout routes.

But events conspired against any Confederate offensive. After a grueling march from Harpers Ferry, Jackson's force would likely be in no
condition for another punishing push the next day. Hooker's crossing of the upper bridge late on September 16 finally killed the idea
altogether.

As the Union troops moved into position, Lee's men waited around
their campfires and listened. They heard what they were listening for
first as a faint cheering in their rear. Gradually it grew into the unmis-
takable sound of mounted men, the distant strains of artillery bugles,
and the tramp of marching feet. It was a good sound, a reassuring
sound: the sound of reinforcement. Couriers arrived and soon the jin-
gle of artillery caissons left no doubt. Jackson's corps was arriving and
taking its place in the line. They came in such order and made such a
rustle among the deep layer of fall leaves as to magnify their numbers
and strength. Swiftly, as was Jackson's way, they passed through the
wood and took their position on the left, directly facing Joe Hooker.[4]

All this movement, presaging something brilliant and terrible, continued though the twilight hours of September 16. On both sides of
Antietam Creek shadows moved, dimly seen in the night. A soldier in
Union Major General Burnside's corps, positioned at the lower bridge,
on the Confederate right, wrote: "There was something weirdly
impressive yet unreal in the gradual drawing together of those whis-
pering armies under cover of the night—something of awe and dread,
as always in the secret preparation for momentous deeds."[5]

The next morning, September 17, a low-hanging mist was lifting from
Antietam Creek as the two sides stirred. The corn in the thirty-acre
field between Hooker and Jackson stood as high as a man, and the
orchards around were tinted with the flush of red ripening apples.[6]
The Confederates were up long before daylight. The most provident
fixed themselves breakfast, then sat in groups, smoking their pipes,
chatting sociably, not knowing at what moment all would be sum-
moned to "fall in."[7]

At first light, Hooker set his corps in motion, its vision fixed on a
small, white Dunkard church house in the distance, the only landmark
clearly seen in the early-morning light. Suddenly the roar of battle
erupted across the cornfield.

In Hagerstown, a dozen miles north of Sharpsburg, the town awoke
to the cannonade. "The people of the town," wrote Charles Carleton

Coffin, a newspaper correspondent, "were at the windows of the houses or in the streets, standing in groups, listening to the reverberations rolling along the valley." The thunder of the cannon rolled and echoed "from cloud to mountain and from mountain to cloud." Coffin listened as it grew into "a continuous roar, like the unbroken roll of a thunder-storm." Soon a counterpoint of musketry fire began to penetrate the thunder-roar of the cannon. Coffin thought it at first like the patter of rain on a roof. But it soon mounted to "a roll, crash, roar, and rush, like a mighty ocean billow upon the shore...wave on wave."[8]

Hooker's men charged through the cornfield, the corn and his men cut down in a terrible fusillade. McClellan, watching through his field glass, believed his plan was unfolding as it should and on schedule. Despite his appalling losses, Hooker was slowly pushing Jackson's men back. McClellan sent word to Burnside on the left to get his men into position to attack and await instructions.

But after that first hour, bad news started coming in. Hooker was not holding what he had won. Jackson had sent Brigadier General John Bell Hood's Texas Brigade into the breech, slamming into Hooker's flank, driving him back. McClellan ordered Mansfield's Twelfth Corps, backing up Hooker, into the fight. It charged and hammered Hood, in turn driving him back. But the Confederates, reinforced by three of D. H. Hill's five brigades posted in Lee's center, first slowed, then checked Mansfield's surge.

McClellan, watching from Pry house, now committed Sumner's Second Corps. Hurrying over the creek into the chaos, Sumner's lead division, under Major General John Sedgwick, penetrated deeper into the Confederate line than any drive so far. But John Walker's division, back from Loudoun Heights at Harpers Ferry, hurried up the interior Confederate line and struck Sedgwick. Lafayette McLaws, back from Maryland Heights, also slammed into him. Sedgwick was wounded, and 2,200 of his 5,200 soldiers became casualties in twenty minutes in what became known as the West Woods Slaughter.

By midmorning, the fighting on the Confederate left was over with no breakthrough. Jackson's 8,000 hungry, march-weary, ragged Confederates, with timely help sent up through his interior line by Lee, had held off nearly 30,000 fiercely attacking Union troops.

It had been a slaughter pen, the casualties on both sides appalling. Hooker had been shot through the foot, and Mansfield lay dying. When it became apparent that the attack on the north end of the Confederate line had stalled, McClellan knew he must deviate from his plan and make Burnside's operation on the south end the main point of assault. He sent a courier down to the lower bridge with the order to attack.[9]

Meanwhile, something McClellan had planned as the coup de grace for when the battle had been fought and won on both ends of the line was developing—prematurely and without his orders—in the center. McClellan's attention suddenly, mid-morning, became riveted there. A second division of Sumner's Corps under Major General William French, following Sedgwick, had lost contact and veered off toward the center and into a nest of Confederates commanded by D. H. Hill posted in a sunken road, which would shortly become known as Bloody Lane.

Without any instructions, without any reconnoitering or even knowing who or how many rebels were in his front, French hurled his division at the sunken road and was repulsed. Sumner's third division in line under Major General Israel Richardson—following French, also without orders from McClellan—charged the sunken road.

It was becoming a battle of disconnected assaults fought "in driblets,"[10] pitched battles under a pounding sun over open ground. On the Union side, there had been no concert of action, no hammering all along the line at the same time, no follow-up of heavy coordinated blows. The sound effects were deafening, cannon bellowing and thundering over all. A Confederate colonel called it an "Artillery-Hell."[11] And the suspense had been nerve crushing. "Mars was striking with iron and fire," one of Jackson's lieutenants later wrote, "time moving with leaden heel."[12]

Richardson's attack was also hammered back, but then, in a mix-up in orders, the Confederate center anchored on the sunken road gave way and rebel soldiers began leaping out and running to the rear. Just as the attack in the center had been unexpected and mindless, the battered Union troops were handed an unexpected and mindless victory. The sunken road was in Union hands. But there was no pursuit, no troops to follow up, and Richardson was mortally wounded. The Confederate line had sagged and nearly snapped, "already badly whipped," James Longstreet, commanding Lee's First Corps, later wrote, "only holding our ground by sheer force of desperation." One more push and Lee's army would have been cut in half. It had been a battle won, but nobody knew it.[13]

Nothing was going quite as McClellan planned. Several couriers had been sent down to Burnside, and maddeningly, he still had not crossed the lower bridge. "What is Burnside about?" McClellan snapped. "Why do we not hear from him?"[14]

Burnside was wrestling with his own frustrations. Only 2,000 Confederates stood between his Ninth Corps and Sharpsburg, if only he could get across that damnable bridge. God knows he had tried. But about 500 Georgians with muskets had been planted on the bluffs on the other side of the creek. They had raked the bridge with withering fire, frustrating every run Burnside had made to cross it.

It was not until one o'clock that, in one final push, Burnside finally managed to cross and drive the Confederates back from the creek. And that, in Burnside's mind, was enough for the moment. His men were spent and out of ammunition. So for the next two hours, all activity along the line seemed to stop as Burnside regrouped.

McClellan took that moment to wire Halleck, "We are in the midst of the most terrible battle of the war, perhaps of history—thus far it looks well but I have great odds against me. Hurry up all the troops possible. Our loss has been terrific, but we have gained ground....I hope that God will give us a glorious victory."[15]

As the minutes ticked by, both sides waited. No one waited more impatiently than McClellan. The word from Burnside was only that he thought he could hold the bridge. McClellan exploded: "He should be able to do that," he raged, "with five thousand men; if he can do no more I must take the remainder of his troops and use them elsewhere in the field." Burnside was one of McClellan's closest friends. They had been at West Point together, served together in the Old Army, worked together on the railroad in civilian life, lived together in Chicago. McClellan had never spoken so harshly of him.[16]

Despite urgent repeated orders from McClellan to "drive on hard towards Sharpsburg," that it was "*imperative* not to stop at any sacrifice of life, for the day depended on it," it wasn't until three o'clock that Burnside was ready to push forward.[17]

Burnside set his corps in motion then, charging across the rolling terrain toward Sharpsburg. He outnumbered the defending Confederates in his front nearly five to one. Confederate soldiers watched this Union wave roll toward and over them. "The earth seemed to tremble beneath their tread," one of them later wrote, "It was a splendid and fearful sight, but for them to beat back [the] feeble [Confederate] line was scarcely war. The artillery tore, but did not stay them."[18]

The thin Confederate line, barely holding, was being pushed now to the extreme. It looked to be only a matter of time and the line would cave. If that happened, Burnside would be between Lee and his only avenue of escape over the Potomac. The Confederates would be boxed in, front, flank, and rear. Lee's army was facing destruction.

But there was something happening—and someone doing it—that neither McClellan nor Burnside had counted on.

CHAPTER 19

THE QUIET AFTER THE STORM

At this moment in the late afternoon, September 17, on the battle-field at the Antietam, Union Major General Ambrose Burnside did not have Confederate Major General Ambrose Powell Hill on his mind.

He knew Hill very well, however. They had graduated from West Point together in the same class in 1847, the best of friends. Hill was also one of McClellan's dearest friends, and a onetime rival for the hand of the beautiful Nelly. Burnside perhaps knew Hill's Light Division was at Harpers Ferry with Jackson. Hill's division had been left there to mop up when Jackson had answered Lee's summons to Sharpsburg the day before. But at six thirty on the morning of September 17, as Hooker was attacking through the cornfield, Hill received an urgent message from Lee. It was an order to march his division with all possible speed to Sharpsburg. Lee needed every man he could get.

An hour later, Hill had his soldiers rapidly forced-marching north-ward. The day soon turned hot, a scorcher. The sun, the dust, the heat were merciless. Hill rode up and down the line, a long-bearded demon in a red shirt he always wore in battle, cursing, prodding, exhorting with the flat of his saber. Lee needed his division in Sharpsburg, and by God, Hill was going to get it there.

As the Confederate soldiers raced on, many of them dropping from heat and exhaustion, they could hear the distant thunder of battle drawing closer and closer. At about one thirty in the afternoon, what was left of his division—nearly half of Hill's 5,000 had dropped out by this time—plunged into the cool waters of the Potomac and up the opposite bank at Boteler's Ford below Sharpsburg.

Hill galloped on ahead, looking for Lee. It had been a fretful, anxious day for the Confederate commander. He now knew that everything depended on Hill getting to Sharpsburg on time, and time was running out. Suddenly a group of hard-riding men on sweat-lathered horses pulled up before him. At their head was Hill in his red battle shirt. Lee had never seen a more welcome sight. He embraced Hill with as much a show of emotion as he was ever likely to exhibit. He now knew there might be salvation.[1]

Burnside's army was now virtually at the doorstep of Sharpsburg. A few Federal flags appeared on the hill in the rear of the town nearly astraddle Lee's only avenue of escape. The town was enveloped in battle smoke, and Lee was seeing two sets of flags in the distance. "What troops are those?" he asked a lieutenant with a field glass. "They are flying the United States flag," the lieutenant said. Lee pointed to another body of troops in the distance, nearly at a right angle from the other, and asked, "What troops are those?" "They are flying the Virginia and Confederate flags," the lieutenant said.

"It is A. P. Hill, from Harper's Ferry," Lee said.[2]

What looked to be possible salvation to Lee looked a nightmare to Burnside. At first Hill's approaching men appeared to be Federals. Many of them were wearing Union uniforms expropriated from the captured garrison at Harpers Ferry. Burnside was soon disabused of this delusion as Hill's men hit his flank in full Confederate cry.

A Confederate high private later wrote, "[A] change takes place in this panorama; a marvellous change, before our very eyes. One moment the lines of blue are steadily advancing everywhere and sweeping everything before them; another moment and all is altered. . . . Still forward came the wave of gray, still backward receded the billows of blue, heralded by warning hiss of the bullets, the sparkling of the rifle flashes, the purplish vapor settling like a veil over the lines, the mingled hurrahs and wild yells, and the bass accompaniment . . . of the hoarse cannonading." All the country, the correspondent Charles Coffin wrote, "was flaming and smoking."[3]

Burnside's corps stumbled back through the flame and smoke to the banks of the Antietam; the Confederate pursuit stopped in the battle-torn ground between the creek and the town. The two armies were spent. Men on both sides had done all they could do. "Nature has its limits," said a Carolina adjutant, "and we had reached ours, with fearful sacrifice."[4]

Darkness fell all along the bloody battle line. The fighting was done. It had been one of the longest sustained days of battle so far in the war, and it had been a standoff. Nearly 125,000 men and 500 pieces of artillery had fought through fourteen hours of hellfire. More than 12,400 Union soldiers and 10,300 Confederates were killed, wounded, or missing—a mind-boggling number of men, the bloodiest single day of the war.[5] And no one had a clear idea of who had won or lost.

It was doubtful that either of these two weary armies would be ready to fight again the next day. McClellan certainly did not have that in mind. He was not feeling well; he seemed coming down again with his old Mexican War ailment. And the battle—and its appalling death toll—had sapped his army's energy and diminished its strength. Moreover, aggressive, hurried follow-up was not in his cautious nature. So all the next day, September 18, McClellan laid low with his army, not intending to attack again.

Lee waited through the night of the seventeenth, ready to do battle if necessary the next day—indeed, looking for some way to launch a counteroffensive of his own. But it was not to be. McClellan wired Halleck that little occurred throughout September 18 but skirmishing, "we being fully occupied in replenishing ammunition, taking care of wounded, etc."[6]

As night fell on the eighteenth, Lee decided there was nothing to be gained in Maryland and started his army back across the Potomac into Virginia. His invasion of the North had failed, but not his resolve. He viewed the withdrawal not as the end of his campaign to take the war to the North, only a temporary falling back on a better position before trying again.[7]

McClellan was exultant, claiming untainted victory. He wired Halleck: "Our victory was complete.... The enemy is driven back into Virginia. Maryland & Penna. are now safe."[8]

He was even more expansive in his dispatches to Nelly. That same day, he wrote her, "We fought yesterday a terrible battle against the entire rebel army. The battle continued *14* hours & was terrific—the fighting on both sides was superb. The general result was in our favor, that is to say we gained a great deal of ground & held it. It was a success, but whether a decided victory depends upon what occurs today." He told her, "The spectacle yesterday was the grandest I could conceive of—nothing could be more sublime. Those in whose judgment I rely tell me that I fought the battle splendidly & that it was a masterpiece of art."

On September 19, after Lee had re-crossed the Potomac, McClellan wired Nelly as he had wired Halleck: "Our victory complete." And the next day, he wrote her a long dispatch: "Yesterday the enemy completed his evacuation of Maryland—completely beaten...its dreams of 'invading Penna' dissipated for ever." He told her, "I feel some little pride in having with a beaten and demoralized army defeated Lee so utterly & saved the North so completely...my military reputation is cleared—I have shown that I can fight battles & *win* them!"[9]

McClellan was not deluded into thinking the Army of Northern Virginia was no longer dangerous. But the fact that it had retreated back across the river and off Northern soil was enough for him to think he had indeed worked a masterpiece of military art.

The situation was, however, not so clear-cut. The outcome at Antietam was a mixed bag. And there were naysayers, even on McClellan's staff. One of these, David Strother, believed "we had not done enough...and had lost an opportunity which may never again be presented to us. The empty name of victory is not sufficient; we needed a result crushing and conclusive, and have failed to obtain it."[10]

Although it was a drawn battle—hardly a Napoleonic victory—it was a success for the Union in important ways. Lincoln drew a small breath of relief. "Well," he said, "I suppose our victory at Antietam will condone my offense in reappointing McClellan. If the battle had gone against us, poor McClellan (and I too) would be in a bad row of stumps."[11] It was again, as on the Peninsula, not the outcome Lincoln had wished. He sought more than an enemy driven from Union soil. He wanted Lee's army destroyed. It should have happened and it hadn't. A clear-cut, Lee-destroying victory would have likely ended the war.[12]

However, short of that, it had been a strategic success. The Confederates had been driven out of Maryland, and McClellan had aborted another stunning Confederate triumph. Diplomatically it had also been a success. Now there seemed no likelihood that Great Britain would recognize the Confederacy or intervene and mediate in the war. There had been that danger after the Peninsula and the disaster at Second Manassas and when Lee had boldly crossed the Potomac into

Maryland. "Designed as an invasion," one war correspondent wrote, "it degenerated into a raid."[13]

The result also signaled another sudden reversal of roles. Confederate Major General James Longstreet was to say of it: "The razing of the walls of Jericho by encircling marches of priests and soldiers, at the signal of long-drawn blasts of sacred horns and shouts of the multitude, was scarcely a greater miracle than the transformation of the conquering army of the South into a horde of disordered fugitives before an army that two weeks earlier was flying to cover under its homeward ramparts."[14]

However, Lee had worked an undeniable defensive masterpiece at Sharpsburg. It had been brilliant—against all odds. It was difficult also not to conclude that McClellan had blown his chance. He had missed the best opportunity yet to destroy Lee's army. The unhappy Strother wrote, "[I]n concluding to sit down on this side of the Potomac, and permitting the public enemy to escape, I fear our General has thrown away the thread of his fortunes with the probability that he will never find it again."[15]

Even with Lee boxed in with his back to the Potomac and only one avenue of escape, McClellan had been slow to bring him to battle. He had failed to fix on and execute boldly a definite plan of attack in the thirty-six hours after he had found Lee's lost orders. And when he finally did bring Lee to battle at Sharpsburg on September 17, he fought piecemeal, feeding in a division at a time and holding much of his army in reserve. There had been no coordinated simultaneous all-out attack along the entire front, which would likely have overwhelmed the undermanned Confederate line. McClellan had not been a bold commander.

Edward Porter Alexander, the Confederate artilleryman, later wrote: "Common Sense was just shouting, 'Your adversary is backed against a river, with no bridge & only one ford, & that the worst on the whole river. If you whip him now, you destroy him utterly, root & branch & bag & baggage. Not twice in a life time does such a chance come to any general. Lee for once has made a mistake & given you a chance to ruin him if you can break his lines, & such a game is worth great risk. Every man must fight & keep on fighting for all he is worth.' "[16] But McClellan had not fought every man for all he was worth. He had not thrown his entire army against Lee's thin line. He had not fought a bold, risk-all fight.

Strother, something of a different thinker in McClellan's inner circle, was quoting the grand duke Constantine, a royal Russian martinet
who was reported to have said he hated war because "it was ruinous to
the army." Strother wrote in his daily journal, "I think there is some
vague idea of the sort around these head-quarters."[17]

Would McClellan now boldly pursue? Pursuit is not an easy thing,
offering danger for the pursuer as well as the pursued—perhaps even
more danger. Disorder is often as rampant in the army of the victor as
in the army of the defeated. Pursuit is often only as good as the supply lines supporting it, and a wounded enemy can be rattlesnake dangerous, capable of vicious rearguard fighting. And there was always
that problem of unreliable information bringing unreliable intelligence of inflated enemy numbers. Failure to pursue and destroy an
enemy, for all these reasons, had its precedent. Lee himself had failed
to destroy McClellan's army in his pursuit in the Seven Days battles on
the Peninsula.[18]

McClellan's soldiers knew that pursuing and destroying an enemy
was easier said than done. A lieutenant in his army, resenting the impli-
cation that McClellan had allowed Lee to escape, said that if people at
home "think the Rebble army can be Bagged let them come & bagg
them....Bagging an army is easy to talk about."[19]

It was, however, what Lincoln was talking about. When McClellan
informed him of his "complete victory" after the battle, the president
wired back: "God bless you, and all with you. Destroy the rebel army,
if possible." Lincoln believed McClellan "should have prevented Lee
from escaping into Virginia" and should have "pursued him vigorously
without giving his army time to recuperate."[20] Again, Lincoln wanted
more. As McClellan had failed to bag the enemy, the president now
wanted a speedy, vigorous pursuit.

McClellan did not believe, under the circumstances, that this was
possible. Nor was it something he had his heart in. He did not believe
his army was ready for pursuit. For McClellan, it was enough that he
had driven Lee back into Virginia, saved the North, and put himself
in a position to mount a campaign more to his liking—more in his
comfort zone.

When he had once again reorganized his army, resupplied it,
reinforced it, properly retrained and redisciplined it, then he would
undertake a new and truly decisive McClellan-style campaign against

the rebels. What he wanted in his heart of hearts was not to undertake a major campaign before winter but to wait until the next year, 1863, and return his army to its proper line of operations: back on the Peninsula stalking Richmond on the James River, and ending the war there.[21]

CHAPTER 20

McCLELLAN'S
BODYGUARD

Abraham Lincoln was thinking two things after Antietam, neither tailored to George McClellan's liking. Here, Lincoln instantly saw, was victory enough on which to hang his preliminary emancipation proclamation, which he had shelved in the summer to wait a turn of fortune on a battlefield. This was not an emphatic opportunity, but it was opportunity enough. On September 22, five days after that most bloody day of the war, he issued it.

"I, Abraham Lincoln," he proclaimed to the world, "President of the United States of America, and Commander-in-chief of the Army and Navy thereof, do hereby proclaim and declare... That on the first day of January, in the year of our Lord, one thousand eight hundred and sixty-three, all persons held as slaves within any State, or designated part of a state, the people whereof shall then be in rebellion against the United States shall be then, thenceforward, and forever free."

Lincoln made it clear up front, in the proclamation's opening lines, that he was doing this purely as a war-winning measure. As heretofore, he proclaimed, "the war will be prossecuted for the object of practically restoring the constitutional relation between the United States, and each of the states and the people thereof, in which states that relation is, or may be suspended, or disturbed."

The three-month window between the proclaiming of emancipation and its becoming law on January 1, 1863, was intended to permit those slaveholding states to end the rebellion and return to the Union. Only then would their slaves be immune to the proclamation.[1]

McClellan was outraged. He was unhappy enough seeing, a week after his "complete victory," that his two chief enemies in Washington, Stanton and Halleck, were still in harness. But now this. Freeing slaves was in no way his idea of what the war was about; it did not fit into his strategy for how it should be waged and won. "The Presdt's late proclamation," he wrote Nelly, "the continuation of Stanton & Halleck in office render it almost impossible for me to retain my commission & self respect at the same time. I cannot make up my mind to fight for such an accursed doctrine as that of a servile insurrection—it is too infamous."[2]

For a short time he considered open opposition to it. But that would also be open rebellion against authority. He didn't go that far, and neither did he resign.[3]

The other thought on Lincoln's mind, equally unwelcome to McClellan, continued to be immediate pursuit of the battered Confederate army. The word coming to McClellan from Washington was not the undiluted praise he believed he richly deserved for chasing the Confederate army out of Maryland but the urgent expectation that he would now do more—deliver that crippled army a mortal blow.

"Not yet even," McClellan complained to Nelly on September 29, two weeks after the battle, "have I a word from anyone in Washn about the battle of the Antietam & nothing in regard to South Mountain except from the Presdt in the following *beautiful* language. 'Your dispatch received. God bless you & all with you, Can't you beat them some more before they get off?'!!! I don't look for any thanks at their hands & believe that they scarcely pretend to conceal their malevolence."[4]

McClellan's animosity for Stanton and Halleck was more bitter even than his disdain of the Emancipation Proclamation. In his mind, they had thwarted him, denied him the tools he needed for victory, undercut him at every turn. He had expected that his victory at Antietam would not only restore his reputation but doom theirs, whom he now loathed equally. He had thought Antietam would rid him of them.

McClellan wrote Nelly on September 20, "I think my enemies are pretty effectively killed by this time! May they remain so!!" He told her, "Thro' certain friends of mine I have taken the stand that Stanton must leave & that Halleck must restore my old place to me. Unless these two conditions are fulfilled I will leave the service. I feel I have done all that can be done in twice saving the country. If I continue in its service I have at least the right to demand a guarantee that I shall not be interfered with—I know I cannot have that assurance so long as Stanton continues in the position of Secy of War & Halleck as Genl in Chief."[5]

By now he had concluded, if he had not long since, that Stanton was "as great a villain as ever" and that Halleck was "as great a fool—he has no brains whatever!"[6] "Of all men I have encountered in high position," he would later write, "Halleck was the most hopelessly stupid. It was more difficult to get an idea through his head than can be conceived by any one who never made the attempt. I do not think he ever had a correct military idea from beginning to end." Even Stanton, McClellan later came to believe, thought Halleck "probably the greatest scoundrel and most barefaced villain in America . . . totally without principle."[7]

All this flew in the face of Halleck's reputation in the Old Army as "Old Brains." But more, in this new Civil War army, were coming to view him as McClellan did: brainless. Even soldiers in the ranks seemed to think so. "Halleck, while holding his exalted position . . . ," one of them later wrote, "showed his greatest ability in anticipating and acting in unison with the designs of the enemy."[8]

Lincoln himself was coming to the conclusion that Halleck was "little more . . . than a first rate clerk."[9] He had repeatedly failed to take charge, assume responsibility, and perform the role of an assertive general-in-chief. Others also wondered about his intangibles. Union Major General Ben Butler said, "[N]ow there is General Halleck, what has *he* to do? At a moment when every true man is laboring to his utmost, when the days ought to be forty hours long, General Halleck is translating French books at nine cents a page and, sir, if you should put those nine cents in a box and shake them up, you would form a clear idea of General Halleck's soul."[10]

Navy Secretary Gideon Welles, who registered an opinion about nearly everyone, wrote in his diary: "[Halleck] has a scholarly intellect and, I suppose, some military acquirements, but his mind is heavy and irresolute. It appears to me that he does not possess originality and that he has little real talent. What he has is educational." Otherwise, Welles found him "dull, stolid, inefficient, and incompetent"—"he originates nothing, anticipates nothing, to assist others; takes no responsibility, plans nothing, suggests nothing, is good for nothing." Halleck's habit of rubbing his elbows on a regular basis caused Wells to wonder if they, and not his brain, might be his "seat of thought."[11]

Wherever Halleck's seat of thought was, after Antietam he was continuing to fear and anticipate a sudden Confederate attack on Washington. He had radiated this fear from the minute Lee had crossed over the Potomac into Maryland. He had radiated it even as McClellan was peering at Lee's army across the fog-shrouded battle-field at Sharpsburg and thinking it bigger than it was. Now that Lee had passed back across the Potomac into Virginia, Halleck thought it likely that he would next take aim on Washington while McClellan idled away the days on the other side of the river.[12]

As much as McClellan deplored Halleck and his lack of brains, it was his old friend Stanton whom he saw as the greatest scoundrel and most barefaced villain in America. "I think," he told Nelly, "that he is the most unmitigated scoundrel I ever knew, heard or read of; I think that (& I do not wish to be irreverent) had he lived in the time of the Saviour, Judas Iscariot would have remained a respected member of the fraternity of the Apostles, & that the magnificent treachery & rascality of E. M. Stanton would have caused Judas to have raised his arms in holy horror & unaffected wonder."[13]

What McClellan wanted after the battle of Antietam, besides more credit for a great victory, was to be left alone. In his mind, he had done what he set out to do—repelled the invader and saved Washington. From the first, he had not contemplated doing more than that. On September 27, he informed Halleck that his army "is not now in con-dition to undertake another campaign nor to bring on another battle, unless great advantages are offered by some mistake of the enemy or pressing military exigencies render it necessary."[14]

McClellan's army desperately needed refitting and restocking—in matériel and personnel. Its regiments were depleted. It lacked essen-tial supplies, clothing, shoes, tents, armament, horses—and officers and men. He wrote Halleck that he had lost ten general officers in the battles on South Mountain and Antietam, many regimental and com-pany officers, and huge numbers of enlisted men. Not a day should be lost, he said, "in filling the old regiments, our main dependence, and in supplying vacancies among the officers by promotion." Until then, he told Halleck, "My present position is to hold the Army about as it now is."[15]

Yet Lincoln wanted much more than that, and he wanted it as soon as possible. More than an opening to issue the Emancipation Proclamation, Lincoln wanted Lee's army pursued and destroyed. So again he went to the scene of action, as he had done after the Seven Days battles on the Peninsula, to see for himself and to prod his reluctant general to action—"to get him to move."[16]

Lincoln reached Harpers Ferry on October 1 and the next day traveled to the area south of Burnside's bridge to where McClellan had moved his headquarters in the days following the battle. For three days Lincoln was with the army, closeted with his general, visiting the various corps, riding the battlefields at South Mountain and Sharpsburg. McClellan later reported, "I remember well, our sitting on the hillside together, Lincoln, in his own ungainly way, propped by his long legs, with his knees almost under his chin" and saying "General, you have saved the country. You must remain in command and carry us through to the end."[17]

It was reported that Lincoln on October 3 stood on a hill with his old Illinois friend, Ozias M. Hatch, who had accompanied him to Antietam. As they gazed down on the vast encampment of the army's white tents "glistening in the rising sun," Lincoln asked Hatch, "Do you know what this is?"

The question surprised Hatch. "It is the Army of the Potomac," he replied.

"So it is called," Lincoln said sadly, "but that is a mistake; it is only McClellan's bodyguard."[18]

When Lincoln left Sharpsburg to return to Washington on October 4, he and McClellan entertained strikingly different views of what had been decided. McClellan believed he had Lincoln's approval. Lincoln left "thinking [the general] would move at once," believing "he would be a ruined man if he did not move forward, move rapidly, and effectually."[19]

But when two days passed and McClellan began to argue why he ought not to move, Lincoln issued a peremptory order through Halleck. It directly commanded McClellan to cross the Potomac immediately and give battle to the enemy or drive him south. "Your army," Halleck told him, "must move now while the roads are good."[20]

Despite the direct order, McClellan did not cross the Potomac immediately. Indeed, it would be nineteen more days before he finally began to do so, and those nineteen days would be consumed in prodding from Washington and delay from him. McClellan would not be left alone, as he wished, and Lincoln would have no advance, as he wished.

CHAPTER 21

FATIGUED HORSES

L incoln's unhappiness in early October, as frown-inducing as it was, did not match the disgruntlement in the cabinet or the animosity of the Radicals in the Congress. The meager success at Antietam had not silenced any of that.

But there was no denying that McClellan's army needed all he said it needed. Everybody in the army was feeling the pinch. Major General George Gordon Meade wrote his wife, "I have *hundreds* of men in my command without shoes, going barefooted, and I can't get a shoe for man or beast." And Brigadier General Alpheus Williams wrote, "There seems to be an unaccountable delay in forwarding supplies. We want shoes and blankets and overcoats—indeed, almost everything."[1]

Although the War Department was addressing the shortages, many of the supplies were not getting where they needed to be, or in a timely manner, as some was not being sent to the proper address. Quartermaster General Montgomery Meigs claimed that supplies McClellan wanted were being sent. McClellan retorted they may have been sent, but they had not yet arrived and the army was suffering for it. The supplies, he said, "might as well remain in New York or Philadelphia so far as this Army is concerned."[2]

Washington's discontent over McClellan's delay, despite the logistics mix-up, was matched by the public's, who craved a forward movement as urgently as Lincoln did. And Lincoln was sensitive to public opinion. Not only did McClellan think this pressure was unreasonable, but so did many of his soldiers. They believed, as their general did, that the disenchantment with him was absurd and unfair. Many of them suspected, as he did, that Stanton and the Radicals in Washington were deliberately undercutting McClellan.

"The old cry as to McClellan's slowness is again being raised," Colonel Charles S. Wainwright wrote in his diary in mid-October. "I was much surprised at first myself that we did not cross the river at once, but the more I know of the condition of the army, and other matters, the less certain does it appear that we could have done so to advantage. This corps as yet has received next to no supplies.... the men are very badly off for shoes and blankets. It seems almost as if they purposefully kept them back at Washington."[3]

Whatever was happening, McClellan was not getting what he thought his army needed and he was not going to move until it did. "I am using every possible exertion to get this army ready to move," he protested to Halleck on October 15. "It was only yesterday that a part of our supplies and clothing arrived at Hagerstown. It is being issued to the troops as rapidly as possible."[4]

Halleck was not convinced. He told Governor Hamilton R. Gamble of Missouri, "With all my efforts I can get nothing done. There is an immobility here that exceeds all that any man can conceive of. It requires the lever of Archimedes to move this inert mass. I have tried my best, but without success." He was not giving up, however: "I do not yet despair, and shall continue my efforts."[5]

In the midst of these logistical wars, Lincoln wrote McClellan a long letter, again reasoning with him.

"You remember my speaking to you of what I called your over-cautiousness," Lincoln wrote. "Are you not over-cautious when you assume that you can not do what the enemy is constantly doing? Should you not claim to be at least his equal in prowess, and act upon the claim?"

Lincoln continued: "One of the standard maxims of war, as you know, is 'to operate upon the enemy's communications as much as possible without exposing your own.' You seem to act as if this applies *against* you, but can not apply in your *favor*. Change positions with the enemy, and think you not he would break your communication with Richmond within the next twenty four hours?"

"You," Lincoln wrote, "are now nearer Richmond than the enemy is by the route that you *can,* and he *must* take. Why can you not reach there before him, unless you admit that he is more than your equal on a march. His route is the arc of a circle, while yours is the chord. The roads are as good on yours as on his."

Lincoln reminded McClellan that he had desired that the general cross the Potomac below, instead of above, the Shenandoah and Blue Ridge Mountains, but did not order him to do so. Lincoln's idea was that this would at once menace the enemy's communications, which McClellan might then seize. If Lee should move northward, McClellan could follow him closely, holding his communications. If Lee should prevent McClellan from seizing his communications and move toward Richmond, the Union army could press him closely and fight him if a favorable opportunity should present—or at least try to beat him to Richmond on the inside track. Lincoln urged McClellan to "try: if we never try, we shall never succeed."

"We should not so operate as to merely drive him away," the president went on. "As we must beat him somewhere, or fail finally, we can do it, if at all, easier near to us, than far away. If we can not beat the enemy where he now is, we never can, he again being within the entrenchments of Richmond."

By this strategy Lincoln believed that as Lee moved, McClellan could strike him through the gaps of the Blue Ridge if the opportunity presented itself. For a great part of the way, McClellan would be practically between the enemy and both Washington and Richmond. This would permit Lincoln to spare him the greatest number of troops from Washington. If McClellan, running for Richmond ahead of Lee, caused the Confederates to veer toward Washington, McClellan could turn and attack them in rear. But Lincoln believed Lee should be engaged long before that point was reached. "It is all easy," Lincoln wrote, "if our troops march as well as the enemy; and it is unmanly to say they can not do it."

Lincoln closed, giving McClellan an out, by writing that this is "in no sense an order."[6]

This unsolicited tactical advice from this amateur military strategist depressed McClellan. He viewed Lincoln's letter as the harbinger of an out of a different sort: his own departure. Darius Couch, a West Point classmate and now a corps commander in McClellan's army, was surprised when, on October 16, the general reined up at Couch's corps headquarters at Harpers Ferry, which was again in Union hands. After briefly reviewing a map and discussing strategy, McClellan said,

"But I may not have command of the army much longer. Lincoln is down on me."

He fished the letter from his pocket and read it aloud to Couch, who was taken aback. "This brief conversation opened a new world for me," Couch later wrote. "I had never before been to any extent his confidant." Hearing the letter, Couch tried to reassure McClellan, saying he saw no ill feeling in the tone of it.

"Yes, Couch," McClellan said, "I expect to be relieved from the Army of the Potomac, and to have a command in the West."[7]

McClellan was not alone in thinking along these lines. Meade was writing home: "Every one who returns to camp says that McClellan's position is most precarious, and that if he does not advance soon and do something brilliant, he will be superseded. At the same time they do not, or will not, send from Washington the supplies absolutely necessary for us to have before we can move."[8]

Lincoln was continuing to press his general to act. On October 21, Halleck wrote McClellan, "[The President] directs me to say that he has no change to make in his order of the 6th instant. If you have not been and are not now in condition to obey it, you will be able to show such want of ability. The President does not expect impossibilities, but he is very anxious that all this good weather should not be wasted in inactivity. Telegraph when you will move, and on what lines you propose to march."[9]

What McClellan was not doing, Lee's plume-hatted cavalry commander J. E. B. Stuart had been doing. For the second time in the war—he had first done it on the Peninsula—Stuart rode entirely around McClellan's army, beginning on October 10 when he crossed the Potomac into Maryland and returning on October 12 when he recrossed the river into Virginia.

The first time Stuart circumnavigated the Union army was on a reconnaissance mission from June 12 to 15, before the Seven Days battles. That daring four-day reconnaissance in force by Stuart and his 1,200 cavalrymen had thrilled and energized the South and startled and chagrined the North. It had also brought Lee valuable information about Federal dispositions.

This second ride around McClellan's army shook everyone from the Antietam to Washington. It was embarrassing, and a blow to morale that no one needed. Welles in his diary called it "additional evidence of [McClellan's] alleged inertness and military imbecility."[10]

It further eroded Lincoln's confidence in McClellan. John Nicolay wrote his fiancée, Therena Bates, that the second ride around the army was "a little thing, accomplishing not much actual harm, and yet infinitely vexatious and mischievous. The President well-nigh lost his temper over it."[11]

Shortly after Stuart's second ride, Lincoln was speaking to a group of officers, who asked, "Mr. President, what about McClellan?"

"When I was a boy," Lincoln answered, "we used to play a game three times around, and out. Stuart has been around him twice; if he goes around him once more, gentlemen, McClellan will be out."[12]

McClellan had a problem with horses that wasn't related directly to the steeds of Stuart's cavalry. His army was in short supply of horseflesh, compounded the last week of October by an outbreak of hoof-and-mouth disease that put nearly 4,000 horses permanently out of service. And many of the rest were in poor condition.[13]

Without more cavalry horses in good condition, he warned Lincoln on October 21, "our communications from the moment we march would be at the mercy of. . . the enemy, and it would not be possible to cover our flanks properly or to obtain the necessary information of the position & movements of the enemy in such a way as to insure success." He had relayed to Washington a report from one of his cavalry commanders describing most of his horses as sore-tongued, sore-backed, and "broken down from fatigue and want of flesh."

This report detonated Lincoln's temper as much as Stuart's ride had. He shot back a wire: "I have just read your dispatch about sore-tongued and fatigued horses. Will you pardon me for asking what the horses of your army have done since the battle of Antietam that fatigues anything?"[14]

McClellan answered this thrust with a rundown on what his horses had been doing since September 7: constantly employed in reconnaissance, scouting, and picketing; six regiments marching 200 miles in pursuit of Stuart's cavalry, including 55 miles in one day; and constantly scouting 150 miles of riverfront since the battle of Antietam. On top of that, many of those same horses had been hard-driven on the Peninsula. "If any instance can be found where overworked cavalry has performed more labor than mine since the battle of Antietam," he told the president, "I am not conscious of it."[15]

To Nelly, McClellan vented his true reaction. He was "mad as a 'march hare'" over Lincoln's sharp wire, calling it "one of those

dirty little flings that I can't get used to when they are not mer-
ited." In another outburst he wrote, "If you could know the mean &
dirty character of the dispatches I receive you would boil over with
anger—when it is possible to misunderstand, & when it is not possible, whenever there is a chance of a wretched innuendo—there it
comes. But the good of the country requires me to submit to all this
from men whom I know to be greatly my inferiors socially, intellectually & morally! There never was a truer epithet applied to a
certain individual than that of the 'Gorilla.' "[16] Since McClellan had
borrowed the epithet from Stanton, who had coined it in his pre–
secretary of war days, it was at least something he could give the
hated secretary credit for.

Angry, but pushed to begin acting on Lincoln's October 6 and October
13 dispatches, McClellan on October 26 at last began crossing the
Potomac with his 100,000 troops in pursuit of Lee. As his army was
marching, Pinkerton sent him a final estimate of Lee's strength, peg-
ging it at 130,000 men. Meanwhile Lee, waiting in Virginia, was
counting only 70,000 present for duty.[17]
    On October 30, McClellan wrote Lincoln that the crossing contin-
ued and "All the Army is in motion to follow the general movement."[18]
But an unhappier general had never crossed a river. He was still convinced that, for logistical and tactical reasons, this fight should be
moved to the Peninsula where it had started six months ago—back to
the true line of operations, where the operational and tactical factors
were in his favor.[19]
    In his letter, McClellan launched into a condemnation and a dis-
claimer. "No greater mistake has been made," he wrote Lincoln, "than
the total failure to reinforce the old regiments. Please remember that I
have clearly stated what troops I leave behind & that I regard the number insufficient to prevent a raid & that while the responsibility has
been thrown upon me by Genl Halleck he has given me only limited
means to accomplish the object.
    "I write this," he continued, "only to place the responsibility where
it belongs & wish you to show this to Genl Halleck. I also wish before
entering upon this important campaign again to inform you that I am
most ill provided with cavalry & artillery horses...that it is not until
today that I have clothing enough in hand to supply the pressing wants
of my men."[20]

In his note to Nelly the next day, McClellan's bitterness was still brimming and vengeance was on his mind. "If I am successful in this campaign I think it will end in driving Stanton out—as he was good enough to say that he held office only for the purpose of crushing me, it will afford me great pleasure if I can in any honorable & open way be instrumental in consigning the rascal to the infamous fate he deserves. If I can crush him I will—relentlessly & without remorse."[21]

Lincoln was happy McClellan was moving, for whatever reason. As the army began to cross the Potomac, the president wired him: "I am so rejoiced to learn from your dispatch to Gen. Halleck, that you begin crossing the river this morning."[22]

CHAPTER 22

SACKED

Although Lincoln was gratified that McClellan was at last crossing the river, the president soon believed it was taking him too long to do it. The general was still delaying "on little pretexts of wanting this and that." Beginning to fear that McClellan "was playing false—that he did not want to hurt the enemy," Lincoln decided on a final litmus test.

"I saw how he could intercept the enemy on the way to Richmond," Lincoln later told John Hay. "I determined to make that the test. If he let him get away I would remove him."[1]

"General McClellan," he told members of the U.S. Sanitary Commission, "thinks he is going to whip the rebels by strategy; and the army has got the same notion. They have no idea that the war is to be carried on and put through by hard, tough fighting, that will hurt somebody, and no headway is going to be made while this delusion lasts."[2]

Lincoln had stood with the general far longer than any of his advisers had wished. He believed McClellan had many admirable qualities as a man and a commander. The battles of South Mountain and Antietam, he believed, "were fought with ability—as well as any Genl could have fought them." But since then McClellan had again been "too slow in his movements. He could and ought to have prevented the loss of Harpers Ferry, but was six days marching 40 miles, and it was surrendered. He did not follow up his advantages after Antietam. The army of the enemy should have been annihilated, but it was permitted to recross the Potomac without the loss of a man, and McClellan would not follow."

Lincoln had "coaxed, urged & ordered him, but all would not do." Now "at the expiration of two weeks after a peremptory order to that effect," he had only three quarters of his army across the river, and had been six days doing that, "whereas the rebel army had effected a crossing on one day."[3]

Lincoln's stoic patience was at an end. He was raising the ax, ready to let it fall.

Not knowing the sword of Damocles was thus hanging so close over his head, McClellan, now over the Potomac, was marching his army southward—but not swiftly—along the chord of the circle Lincoln had recommended in his October 13 letter. In eleven days he had covered but thirty-five miles.

His army, however, was upbeat. "I never saw the army so full of enthusiasm as it now is," one of his soldiers wrote in his diary, "everyone is anxious to meet the enemy and terminate the war by one grand battle. McClellan seems to have the final termination of the issue well in hand, and when we again meet Genl. Lee's army, they will suffer a defeat that will end their existence. We feel confident of this, and should I be correct...McClellan will be, as he really is today, the greatest military chieftain of the age."[4]

By November 5, the potentially greatest military chieftain of the age had reached Rectortown, Virginia. "After a considerable amount of marching & skirmishing," he wrote Nelly that night, "we have worked our way thus far down into rebeldom. We have had delightful weather for marching & a beautiful country to travel through." The next day he assured her, "The army still advances, but the machine is so huge & complicated that it is slow in its motions."[5]

Too slow to stay the ax. On November 4, Lee, by anticipating McClellan's movements, had put his army between him and Richmond, as Lincoln feared he would. For the president, it was "the last grain of sand which broke the camel's back."[6] Even as McClellan was writing his dear Nelly, the ax was falling. On November 5, learning that Lee was at Culpepper Court House, his army between McClellan and Richmond, Lincoln, true to his vow, wrote the order removing him from command of the Army of the Potomac.

McClellan's few allies in Washington had seen it coming, and one had tried to forestall it. Francis Preston Blair had been traveling in high circles in Washington since Andrew Jackson's time. He had a son, Francis, Jr.—"Frank"—who was sometimes a general in Lincoln's army and sometimes a congressman. Another son, Montgomery, was Lincoln's postmaster general.

Knowing Lincoln was considering sacking McClellan, Blair was worried for him. At Montgomery's urging, he drove out to the cottage at the Old Soldiers' Home for veterans on the outskirts of Washington, where Lincoln was staying for a few days, as he often did, particularly in the summer season, to see what he could do to save McClellan and keep him in command.

Lincoln listened respectfully to the old man, as he always did. When Blair had made his pitch, the president stood, stretched his long arms almost to the ceiling, and said: "I said I would remove him if he let Lee's army get away from him, and I must do so. He has got the 'slows,' Mr. Blair." He had tried long enough, Lincoln told Blair, "to bore with an auger too dull to take hold."[7] Nicolay wrote of McClellan, "He is constitutionally *too slow,* and has fitly been dubbed the great American tortoise."[8]

Brigadier General Catharinus P. Buckingham, on special duty at the War Department, was in his office adjoining Secretary Stanton's private room, and it was late—10 P.M. on November 6. Stanton was also in the building. Buckingham was finding out firsthand what a workaholic the secretary was.[9]

Buckingham hadn't been at this desk job very long, but desk jobs were what he did in this war. It is what he had done in the volunteer army in Ohio before coming to Washington, and it was what he was doing now on special assignment to the secretary's office.

Buckingham was fifty-five years old, white-bearded, smart, studious, and scholarly—an instructor at West Point for a time, then a professor of mathematics and natural philosophy at Kenyon College. But iron had been his thing. Before the war he had owned and run the Kokosing Iron Works in Knox County, Ohio. Robert E. Lee was one of his best friends; they had graduated from West Point in the same class in 1829, Buckingham only four pegs below him in graduating order.[10]

And here it was, two hours before midnight, and the secretary wanted to see him. When Buckingham stepped into Stanton's office, Halleck was also there. The secretary said he wanted Buckingham for a special errand—to go by train to McClellan's headquarters and take two unsealed envelopes. Buckingham was first to read them, then seal them, then take them to army headquarters.

In the quiet of his office, Buckingham opened the two envelopes and was thunderstruck. One envelope was addressed to McClellan. It contained two letters, an order from Lincoln relieving him from command of the army and another from Halleck ordering him to repair to his home in Trenton, New Jersey—"an American way of sending him to Coventry," as one soldier later wrote—and from there report by letter to the War Department.[11] The contents of the second envelope were no less surprising—two orders for Ambrose Burnside, one from Lincoln appointing him to command of the army succeeding McClellan, and the other from Halleck directing him to report his plans.

Buckingham's first thought was: Why me? Why did he have to be the one to deliver these two explosive sets of orders? McClellan was his friend. The next morning before leaving, the perplexed general saw Stanton at his house, and the secretary explained. He was sending Buckingham—an officer of his rank—because he feared Burnside would refuse the command, and Buckingham, if necessary, must use the strongest arguments possible to persuade him to accept. Second, Stanton explained, not only did he have no confidence in McClellan's military skill, but he very much doubted his patriotism and even his loyalty. He was afraid that McClellan might not give up the command, and he wished, therefore, that the order should be delivered by an officer of high rank, direct from the War Department, so it would carry the full weight of the president's authority.

Stanton's orders were for Buckingham to find Burnside first and get his decision. If he agreed to accept the command—whatever persuasion that might take—Buckingham was then to confront McClellan. However, if Burnside would not accept, despite Buckingham's persuasions, he was to return to Washington at once without seeing McClellan. This was a very delicate and precise assignment, even for a mathematician of Buckingham's talents. Under the circumstances, it might have been better if he had been a diplomat before the war rather than an iron manufacturer.

The weather complicated Buckingham's assignment. Northern Virginia was being battered by one of the worst snowstorms for that time of year on record. Buckingham's special train chugged from Washington toward Salem, near where Burnside's corps headquarters was believed to be, through driving snow and bitter cold.

Buckingham knew the universal feeling in the army about Burnside, and surely shared it. No sweeter, kinder, or truer-hearted man lived— loving, lovable, dashing, romantic—picturesque, with that spectacular growth of beard and sideburns that circled his face like a halo. But he was not a good fit for the command of an army. Burnside himself knew he was not. He had publicly said he was not when offered high command twice before—briefly after McClellan's failure on the Peninsula and again after Pope's defeat at Second Manassas—and no one had the least reason to believe otherwise, except perhaps Lincoln, Stanton, and Halleck, who were desperate.[12]

On the night of November 7 Buckingham found Burnside camped about thirteen miles south of Salem. He rode from the train by horseback, entered the general's chambers, closed the door, and made his loathsome errand known. Burnside declined the promotion at once; he wanted nothing to do with superseding his dearest friend.

Whatever his own private opinion might be, Buckingham now needed somehow to persuade Burnside to change his mind. Knowing Lincoln was set on removing McClellan, Buckingham argued that Burnside must accept. Burnside argued his want of confidence in himself and his particularly close friendship with McClellan, to whom he felt under the strongest personal obligations. Buckingham countered that McClellan's removal was foregone and that if Burnside did not accept the command, it would be given to Fighting Joe Hooker, whom Burnside thought an even less worthy successor to McClellan. Such a bleak prospect finally eroded Burnside's opposition, and at length, after much arguing, and with a heavy heart, he gave in.

Buckingham then asked the new commander of the Army of the Potomac to accompany him to deliver the news to the old one. So they rode together back through the snowstorm to Buckingham's train and took it up the line to McClellan's headquarters near Rectortown.

About an hour before midnight they found McClellan's quarters and knocked on his tent-pole. The general was there, writing his nightly letter to Nelly. He was not surprised to see them, despite the late hour and the weather. He had heard that a special train carrying

Buckingham from Washington had arrived near his camp earlier in the day. He also knew that Buckingham had left the train and, without coming to see him first, had proceeded on horseback through the driving snowstorm to Burnside's camp near Waterloo Bridge on the upper Rappahannock. McClellan at once suspected the truth, but he had kept his own counsel. Now here they were, both looking very solemn.

McClellan was nothing if not gracious. He received them in his usual cordial manner. Buckingham found this part of his task the most painful and distasteful. He had always entertained very friendly feelings for McClellan. But if the blow had to come, he had persuaded himself it was better not to be delivered by an unsympathetic hand in a mortifying way.

McClellan opened the conversation on general subjects, as if visitors arriving in a heavy snowstorm in the middle of the night were an everyday occurrence. After a few preliminary exchanges, Buckingham turned to Burnside.

"Well, general," he said, "I think we had better tell Gen. McClellan the object of our visit."

"I should be glad to learn it," McClellan said pleasantly.

Buckingham handed him the envelope with the orders from Lincoln and Halleck.

As McClellan opened the envelope, he saw that both men, especially Buckingham, watched him intently. While he read silently, not a muscle quivered nor did he show any emotion. They shall not have that triumph, he thought.

After a moment he turned with a smile to the miserable and mortified Burnside.

"Well, Burnside," he said, "I turn the command over to you."[13]

"I then assumed command," the unhappy Burnside recounted later, "in the midst of a violent snow-storm, with the army in a position that I knew but little of. . . . I probably knew less than any other corps commander of the positions and relative strength of the several corps of the army."[14]

"They have made a great mistake," McClellan wrote, picking up his pen again when his visitors had left and continuing his letter to Nelly, "alas for my poor country—I know in my innermost heart she never had a truer servant. . . . Our consolation must be that we have tried to do what was right—if we have failed it was not our fault."[15]

Darius Couch, commander of McClellan's Second Corps, with whom he had earlier shared Lincoln's October 13 letter on strategy, knew nothing of this dramatic change of command as he dismounted at nearly dark the next evening to oversee camp arrangements for his corps. As he stood there in the snow, McClellan rode up with his staff, accompanied by Burnside.

McClellan reined in and said immediately, "Couch, I am relieved from the command of the army, and Burnside is my successor."

Couch stepped up to him and took hold of his hand. "General McClellan," he said, "I am sorry for it."

He then strode around the head of McClellan's horse to Burnside. "General Burnside," he said, "I congratulate you."

Burnside made a dismissive gesture. "Couch, don't say a word about it." His manner told Couch he didn't wish to talk of it, that he thought it neither the time nor the place.[16]

By nightfall the entire army knew. McClellan told them in a special order dated November 7. "In parting from you," he wrote, "I cannot express the love and gratitude I bear to you. As an army, you have grown up under my care. In you I have never found doubt or coldness. The battles you have fought under my command will proudly live in our nation's history. The glory you have achieved, our mutual perils and fatigues, the graves of our comrades fallen in battle and by disease, the broken forms of those whom wounds and sickness have disabled— the strongest association which can exist among men—unite us still by an indissoluble tie."[17]

The army was staggered—"*thunderstruck*," John Gibbon, McClellan's former West Point classmate, graduating a year behind him in 1847, described it. "There is but one opinion upon this subject among the troops, and that is the Government has gone mad. It is the worst possible thing that could have been done and will be worth to the south as much as a victory. Everyone feels gloomy and sad that a man who has done so much for his country, should be treated in this manner."[18]

The soldiers were appalled. "Our George" was being taken from them again—this time apparently for good. A spasm of anger, outrage, chagrin, and gloom swept from top to bottom. It was "all as cold as Charity & dark as Egypt..." wrote the army's provost marshal general, Marsena R. Patrick, in his diary on November 8. "The Army is in mourning & this is a blue day for us all." The next night, Sunday, the ninth, he wrote in his diary of the feeling in the army—"a feeling as deep as I have ever seen." He reported the regulars "uproarious," demanding that if McClellan be removed at all, it be to the command of all the armies.[19]

There was wild talk, particularly among McClellan's staff, of defying the president's order, marching on Washington, and taking possession of the government, wresting it from the hands of the politicians. It was not a new idea. Several times in the past, as early as 1861, McClellan had been approached on the subject of setting up a dictatorship. He had seemed at first fascinated by the idea.[20]

On one occasion, when riding with another officer, McClellan had said, "I understand there is a good deal of talk of making a dictatorship."

"Ah," replied the other, "Mr. Lincoln, I suppose?"

"Oh, no," said McClellan, "it's me they're talking of."[21]

And riding through his army, as he so often did, listening to their huzzahs, he told Colonel Thomas Key, a member of his staff: "How these brave fellows love me, and what a power that love places in my hands! What is there to prevent my taking the government in my own hands?" Alarmed, Key said, "General, don't mistake those men. So long as you lead them against the enemy, they will adore you and die for you; but attempt to run them against their Government, and you will be the first to suffer."[22]

What prevented any such thing was McClellan's ultimate good sense. He was a soldier, and such disloyalty would be the supreme act of insubordination and rebellion. Not even against the administration he despised, would he do that. Now, having been fired, he recognized this sentiment rising again and moved quickly to quash it. He had tacked a precautionary word to the end of his message to his soldiers and officers announcing the change in command. "We shall ever be comrades in supporting the Constitution of our country and the nationality of its people," he wrote.[23] On the day he left for good, November 11, he would tell them, "I wish you to stand by Burnside as you have stood by me, and all will be well." [24]

McClellan's soldiers demanded to see him one more time. So on the morning of November 10, he rode out to say good-bye, passing by his entire army. As he rode past Patrick's troops in this last farewell, they cheered him, but it was too "irregular" to suit Patrick. Just as McClellan passed the front, Patrick gave his horse its reins and swung his hat over his head, shouting "Once More & All Together!"

There was an explosion of cheers that Patrick found "splendid" and "magical."

Other shouts, splendid and magical, rose from thousands of other throats as McClellan continued to ride through the army, past division after division and corps after corps, past troops drawn up in ranks on either side of the road for miles. Patrick marveled: "Such waving of tattered banners & shouts of Soldiery!"[25]

Gibbon called it "an impressive sight, a painful and in some respects an alarming sight." And as long as McClellan himself was in view, Gibbon heard loud shouts on all sides, "Send him back, send him back." One general whose revolutionary sentiment had not been quashed—shouted, "Lead us to Washington, General. We will follow you there."[26]

"Such a sight I shall never see again," Colonel Charles Wainwright wrote in his journal. He saw tears; there was hardly a dry eye in the ranks. "Very many of the men wept like children, while others could be seen gazing after him in mute grief, one may almost say despair, as a mourner looks down into the grave of a dearly loved friend."[27]

At 2 P.M., McClellan paused to share this bittersweet good-bye with Nelly. "I am very well & taking leave of the men," he wrote her. "I did not know before how much they loved me nor how dear they were to me. Gray haired men came to me with tears streaming down their cheeks. I never before had to exercise so much self control. The scenes of today repay me for all that I have endured."[28]

Whatever they may have thought of McClellan as a general, Wainwright believed that no one who saw him on this day "could help pronouncing him a good and great man: great in soul if not in mind." And when McClellan rode past the Second Corps and galloped out of their sight for the last time, Francis A. Walker, its assistant adjutant general, wrote. "Every heart...was filled with love and grief; every voice was raised in shouts expressive of devotion and indignation; and when the chief had passed out of sight, the romance of war was over for the Army of the Potomac."[29]

Not every soldier in the army shared this sense of the lost romance. Not everyone was bereaved by the departure of a beloved commander. Some—albeit a minority—were overjoyed. Some saw it as "the harbinger of victory." "That's good news," one of these deviants exclaimed. "I am mighty glad to hear that," said another. "This war will soon be ended," predicted a third.[30] An officer among the dissenters had been saying of McClellan since the debacle on the Peninsula, "The papers lie; they lie horribly. They are trying hard to make McClellan a great man; whereas I sometimes fear he is a great donkey."[31]

The few men who were thinking this way remembered how "his indecision or proneness to delay had made [his army's] campaigns the laughing-stock of the world." With them still were "the memories of a winter's inactivity at Manassas, the delay at Yorktown, the blunders on the Chickahominy, or the disgrace of the day after Antietam."[32]

McClellan left on November 11, believing Lincoln had relieved him from command "when the game was in my hands." John Gibbon agreed, writing that the effect "was that of applying brakes to a lightning express"—throwing "the engine off the track for the purpose of changing conductors," another officer put it.[33]

The Confederates, who knew McClellan so well, were glad to see him go. "We seemed to understand his limitations and defects of military character," Henry Kyd Douglas, of Jackson's staff, said of him, "and yet we were invariably relieved when he was relieved, for we unquestionably always believed him to be a stronger and more dangerous man than anyone who might be his successor."[34] A Confederate soldier said, "We liked him because he made war like a gentleman; *and we loved him for the enemies he had made!*"[35] Lee said he regretted parting with McClellan "for we always understood each other so well. I fear they may continue to make these changes till they find some one whom I don't understand."[36]

Lincoln had at last given up on the augur too dull to dig. It was a pity; he had tried. But the Young Napoleon had been a victim, in large part, of his own hubris and paranoia. He had failed to understand the rebel commanders in his front, who were his enemies. Perhaps worse, for the country and his own career, he had failed to understand Lincoln in his rear, who had tried for so long to be his friend and support. These failures had brought him down, his hope of military glory blasted.

McClellan left his army, passed through Washington, changing trains without stopping—bound for Trenton, to whatever future lay ahead.

CHAPTER 23

THE UNPOLITICAL POLITICIAN

The day he was fired, McClellan became, in the mind of many Democrats, their front-running candidate to unseat the man in the White House who had fired him.

He had become the darling of the most powerful and influential Democrats in the country, a high-powered coterie centered in New York City, a steaming Democratic hotbed, the largest party stronghold in the North. McClellan was a Democrat and still a popular figure with much of the public. McClellan was a good fit with these men. He was comfortable with them ideologically, socially, culturally, and intellectually. They felt as he did about the war. Most important, his enemies—Lincoln, his administration, and the Republican Radicals in the Congress—were also their enemies.

As early as 1862, thinking and planning ahead, many of the Democrats had been contemplating McClellan as their party's presidential candidate in the national election of 1864. One of them, Samuel L. M. Barlow, was a longtime friend and confidant who often exchanged telegraphed messages with McClellan. Next to Nelly, Barlow, a young Wall Street lawyer in his thirties and a power in the party, had been McClellan's most sympathetic correspondent during the stressful times in Washington and on the battlefield. The general had often turned to him for advice and support.

Indeed, many of these Democrats had sent telegraphed messages to the general in the past year and a half.[1] They considered him one of their own, and they were ready and waiting.

The American electorate gravitated to high-visibility hero-generals. It had elected George Washington, Andrew Jackson, William Henry Harrison, Zachary Taylor, and Franklin Pierce to the presidency. Winfield Scott had run, unsuccessfully, in 1852 against Pierce. Even the president of the Confederacy, Jefferson Davis, was a West Pointer and a hero-colonel in the Mexican War. His military reputation, in large part, had made him first a U. S. senator from Mississippi, then the Confederate president.

More often than not these hero-soldiers were candidates despite themselves. McClellan fell into this category. He was not a natively endowed politician. He had been trained as a soldier and an engineer, and he thought like a soldier and an engineer. He viewed the presidency through a nonpolitician's lens—which was not to actively seek that office, at least not publicly, but also not refuse it if it was offered and he was satisfied that it was his duty to accept it.

Soon after McClellan returned as ordered to New Jersey, he moved from Trenton to nearby New York City and began writing a report vindicating his fifteen months as commander of the Army of the Potomac. There he fell immediately into the hands of the waiting Democratic luminaries, among the most powerful and vicious of Lincoln's enemies.

Greeting him in New York when he moved there, besides Barlow, were the Democratic governor of New York himself, Horatio Seymour; the chairman of the Democratic National Committee, August Belmont, a rich and powerful financier; John Van Buren, son of the former Democratic president and now the New York state party chairman; Dean Richmond, a leading party strategist; and William Aspinwall, John Jacob Astor, and William B. Duncan—rich, intellectual, cultured friends and leading Democratic lights all. And all had been waiting for him.

Also waiting were the editors of two of the most powerful, influential, opinionated, anti-Lincoln Democratic newspapers in the country: Manton Marble of the *New York World,* who was wont to lash out daily against Lincoln's war, and William C. Prime of the *Journal of Commerce.*

When McClellan arrived in New York City to take up residence in the Fifth Avenue Hotel, Barlow and several of these men with deep pockets bought him a handsome, fully furnished, fully paid-for four-story brick house on West Thirty-first Street, in one of Manhattan's most upscale neighborhoods.[2]

For a time, McClellan believed he was going to be reassigned to some other command in the army, perhaps in the West. He was still the senior general on the army's active list. But the silence from Washington was deafening. It became obvious over the next year that he had been put on the shelf permanently by the Lincoln administration.

Since late 1862 the Army of the Potomac had been commanded by three successors to McClellan—Ambrose Burnside, Joe Hooker, and Gordon Meade. It had suffered back-to-back Union defeats in Virginia—at Fredericksburg under Burnside, and Chancellorsville under Hooker. But in July 1863 it had won the battle of Gettysburg in Pennsylvania under Meade. In the summer of 1863, after the disasters at Fredericksburg and Chancellorsville and before Gettysburg, there had been a groundswell of longing to bring McClellan back to again save the Union.

When Lee was again invading the North in the early summer of 1863, leading to the battle of Gettysburg in early July, Pennsylvania Governor Andrew Curtin was apprehensive again, as he was during the first Confederate incursion into Maryland the year before, that his state was seriously threatened. He sent Colonel Alexander McClure, a Pennsylvanian friendly with both Lincoln and McClellan, to Philadelphia to sound out leaders there about bringing McClellan back. Finding that they favored McClellan's return, McClure wrote Lincoln urging him to restore the deposed general to command of the army.

Lincoln quickly quelled that notion. "Do we gain anything by opening one leak to stop another?" he asked McClure. "Do we gain anything by quieting one clamor merely to open another and probably a larger one?"[3]

By the end of 1863, on the eve of the coming election year, McClellan had moved out of the $20,000 gift house in Manhattan and settled with his wife and daughter in a home he purchased in the quiet Orange Mountain region of New Jersey. Although he still professed no overt ambition for the presidency, McClellan was not without ambition, and ambition's ultimate prize, the presidency, was theoretically within his reach. The "taste was in his mouth a little," as Lincoln would say,[4] and what a perfect way to get back at that crowd in Washington. The pity of it was that to get it, he would have to work with politicians, a species he basically detested. Despite this animosity, he would allow himself to be courted by the men in New York. He would lie low publicly, denying he was a candidate, all the while privately welcoming and massaging the prospect.

From Philadelphia, his mother wrote McClellan on December 3, 1863, "The Democrats say, the *War Democrats,* that George B. McClellan, is to be the next president." Still trying not to appear a candidate, McClellan replied, "I feel very indifferent about the White House—for very many reasons I do not wish it—I shall do nothing to get it & trust that Providence will decide the matter as is best for the country."[5]

In short, he was still trying to be true to his political credo—not to seek that high office but to wait for something spontaneous to happen so he could not refuse it.[6]

By 1864, Lincoln's Republican Party was schism rent. The Radicals in his party wanted him out of the presidency in favor of a man who was more anti-South, antislavery, hard-nosed and less forgiving and benign, who would fight the war by their lights. They were actively seeking someone—anyone, Senator Wade might say—to run against Lincoln.

The Democracy, as the Democratic Party was known, was even more seriously schizophrenic, divided, and crippled. When the war came, many of its war-minded adherents had bailed out of the party, moving over to the new Union Party, as the Republican Party was rechristened by Lincoln to fight the war and attract bipartisan support. Jumping their traditional moorings into the arms of a longtime political enemy was not easy for many of these longtime Democrats. But even harder for them was to live with the smack of treason that had been attaching itself to their own party—a common peril for a party out of power when a war is raging. It is difficult to oppose the party waging it without being charged with being unpatriotic, even treasonous.

The Democrats who stayed with the parent party fell into either of two wings. One, the war wing, was composed of men such as these New Yorkers, who supported the cause—a total prosecution of the war, defeat of the Confederacy, and the immediate reestablishment of the Union as it had been. They were called War Democrats and had remained in the party to fight the rebellion from there—uneasy allies of Lincoln in the common cause. The other wing was the so-called Peace Democrats, who deplored the cause and wanted to end the war immediately and sue for peace at any price. They were willing, if necessary, to let the Southern states form a new independent nation—to let the sisters go in peace, as *New York Tribune* editor Horace Greeley had once put it in a weak moment.[7]

The seat of the War Democrats was New York, with McClellan their desired candidate for the 1864 election. The Peace Democrats were centered principally in the Midwest and along the border states, in Ohio and Indiana in particular. They had no clear candidate, and they considered McClellan an anathema. Their slogan was "the Constitution as it is, the Union as it was, and the Negroes where they are." Their idea of reform was to throw out the tyrant currently in the White House, end the war at once, and call a convention to restore the old Union, on its old footing—by compromise.[8]

These Peace Democrats were popularly called "copperheads," an epithet coined in 1861 to evoke the image of serpents of conspiracy. They were "like copperheads and rattlesnakes in winter," the *Cincinnati Daily Commercial* described them, "cold in their stiff and silent coils," the "blind and venomous enemies of our government found in our midst."[9]

McClellan, a firm War Democrat, despised them, considering them fools who saw the war—hence his part in it—as a failure. To his thinking, they were no better than the blackguard politicians in the administration who had kept him from winning the war.[10]

James Gordon Bennett, the acerbic, vigorously cross-eyed editor of the *New York Herald,* was unhappy with both McClellan and Lincoln, seeing both as candidates fit only for the political trash bin. But what really furrowed his brow were the Peace Democrats. "Of all the small, insignificant, contemptible cliques that have ever disgraced the politics of this country," he editorialized, "the peace clique is the worst. It is equally despised by honest Union men and honest rebels."[11]

Bennett also had something to say about this titanic split in the Democracy. "They have a peace leg and a war leg," he grumbled, "but, like a stork by a frog pond, they are as yet undecided which to rest upon."[12]

But this stork by the political frog pond needed both of its legs. Divided, it had no hope of wresting the White House from Lincoln—with McClellan or anybody else. Together they might stand a good chance, because many in the North were unhappy with the way the war was going—were desperately war weary—and might be ready to throw Lincoln out.

The two wings of this disgruntled party still had things in common. Both abhorred the way Lincoln had broadened the war into an abolition crusade with his Emancipation Proclamation. Both believed that in waging the war he had laid waste to civil liberties and had become a tyrant. Both believed the despised Republican Radicals were promoting partisan ends with a view to destroying both the South and the Democratic Party. And they believed alike that these Radicals in Washington were calling the shots, not Lincoln.[13]

It was still doubtful, however, that these two halves of the Democracy could work together in the crunch. A tremendous obstacle had to be hurdled—effectively to oppose Lincoln and the Republicans without seeming also to oppose the war and open themselves to the charge of treason. How could it avoid being lumped with the rebels in the Confederacy? The Republicans were already gleefully dumping all Democrats, whether for the war or against it, into that category—calling them all "copperheads," "secesh," "semisecesh," "disloyalists," and "Assistant Rebels." John Hay, Lincoln's young private secretary, was calling them all "foul birds...croaking treason...flapping their unclean wings about holy places and trying to roost under the National Aegis."[14]

The War Democrats believed McClellan the perfect antidote for this. He was ideal, a hero of the war, the only man who could legitimize Democratic opposition to the administration without having its loyalty questioned. He could challenge the Lincoln administration on its execution of policy without casting doubt on the party's patriotism.

The problem for the War Democrats was how to get McClellan nominated. Many Peace Democrats considered him no better than the Radicals and Lincoln. When he was commanding the Union army,

McClellan had suppressed civil liberties in Maryland in the name of national security, and the Peace Democrats had neither forgotten nor forgiven. They said they would support his nomination on a peace platform only and no other. On the eve of the election year, the party was in a fix, between the rock and the hard place.[15]

CHAPTER 24

TWO STORKS BY A FROG POND

The election year, 1864, came in with a rebellion in Lincoln's own party—another stork by a frog pond—followed by an unquiet spring and a howling summer. The year was unique in politics by its very nature: a democratic election in the midst of a civil war. Such a feat had never been pulled off before anywhere in the world. But Lincoln, with the most to lose, insisted on holding the election. He was to say in November, after the election, "We can not have free government without elections; and if the rebellion could force us to forego, or postpone a national election it might fairly claim to have already conquered and ruined us."[1]

The election year started with one of Lincoln's own cabinet members, Salmon Portland Chase, his secretary of the treasury, covertly running to unseat him. Chase had been working at it with Radical support for a number of months. He was a strong antislavery man, who as a lawyer in Ohio, before becoming a governor and then a U.S. Senator, had argued a series of famous court cases that built him a reputation as the "attorney-general for runaway slaves."[2] A man with a high-profile superiority complex, Chase believed he, and not this former frontier hick Lincoln, ought to be president.

His candidacy, which Chase ardently denied existed but which everyone, including Lincoln, knew did, collapsed when one of his supporters issued a blatantly mistimed "strictly private" circular that became sensationally public on February 20, saying Lincoln was unfit for the presidency and Chase ought to be nominated instead. A mortified Chase immediately shot Lincoln a disclaimer, denying having known anything about it until he read it in the newspapers like everybody else and offering his resignation. Lincoln declined the resignation, but Chase's candidacy, such as it was, expired.

After that first inside threat misfired, another unseat-Lincoln drive came in late May, when a loosely-knit group of Radical misfits from the president's own party met in Cleveland and nominated John Charles Fremont, a disgruntled general who had been the Republican Party's first—unsuccessful—candidate for president in 1856. Fremont was another general Lincoln had sacked—for incompetence—and neither he nor his Radical supporters had yet forgiven.

As these early-year and springtime political developments were unfolding, Lincoln crafted a sea change in the military hierarchy. In March, Congress created the new supreme rank of lieutenant general and the president filled it with Ulysses S. Grant, who had won stirring victories in the West at Vicksburg and Chattanooga in 1863. He was the first general lifted to that lofty rank since George Washington. As the new general-in-chief, Grant had retained Halleck as chief of staff in Washington and Meade as commander of the Army of the Potomac in the field.

Grant had moved east to oversee this new arrangement, leaving Major General William Tecumseh Sherman in command in the West, and in May launched an invasion of Virginia. With Lee countering his every move, but Grant pushing on relentlessly, the two armies fought first to a draw in the Wilderness and a bloody standoff at Spotsylvania Court House. Grant then threw his army against Lee's in an appallingly bloody charge at Cold Harbor at the gates of Richmond, then in mid-June settled into an ongoing energy-draining siege of Petersburg, at Richmond's back door.

In June, while the fighting was raging in Virginia, the Republican national convention convened in Baltimore and handily nominated Lincoln after all, despite Radical opposition. To broaden the ticket, the delegates nominated Andrew Johnson, a staunch Union-loving War Democrat from Tennessee, as his vice presidential running mate, replacing Hannibal Hamlin of Maine. In July, a Confederate raid on

Washington sent by Lee and commanded by Jubal Early was turned back only at the capital's doorstep.

The inconclusive events on the battlefield, lacking a clear and expected victory, made for an increasingly depressing summer in the North. Dead and wounded men were returning from the front in droves, and war weariness was setting in with a vengeance. The North was plunged into such despair over the endless and winless war that almost no one believed Lincoln could now possibly be reelected. The Democrats, delighted with the way things were going politically, had put off their nominating convention until August to see if things would get even worse and buy time for them to reconcile their internal differences.

The other party happy over Republican angst was the Confederacy, which also wanted Lincoln defeated. It now appeared to be their only hope for independence. "The fact...begins to shine out clear," the *Richmond Examiner* exulted, "that Abraham Lincoln is lost; and he will never be President again.... The obscene ape of Illinois is about to be deposed from the Washington purple, and the White House will echo to his little jokes no more."[3]

By early August, the pessimism in Lincoln's party was virtually universal, hanging on with a bulldog grip. Union Major General Benjamin Butler's chief of staff, on an assignment in New York to test the waters for his always politically motivated chief, wrote him, "I have seen and talked with nearly all the leading men in the city, and they all are of one opinion in regard to Lincoln. They consider him defeated."[4]

Thurlow Weed, New York's cagey behind-the-scenes Republican wire-puller, was telling Lincoln that his reelection was now an impossibility. "Nobody here doubts it," he told the president, "nor do I see anybody from other States who authorises the slightest hope of success."

Even Henry Raymond, the Republican national chairman who was also the editor of the *New York Times,* and who was supposed to stay upbeat and optimistic about campaigns he was running—that is what chairmen are supposed to do—was downcast. "I am in active correspondence with your staunchest friends in every state," he wrote Lincoln, "and from them all I hear is but one report, the tide is setting strongly against us."[5]

Horace Greeley, the erratic and eccentric editor of the *New York Tribune* who was given to wild emotional swings of opinion, was also wildly swinging into pessimism, "Mr. Lincoln is already beaten," he grumbled on August 18. "He cannot be elected. And we must have another ticket to save us from utter overthrow." He proposed three generals and an admiral as possible fallback candidates for the new ticket.[6] The cantankerous James Gordon Bennett at the rival *New York Herald* incessantly beat the drum for General Grant, who incessantly denied that he was a candidate.

Lincoln's closest friends were no less pessimistic. Illinois attorney Leonard Swett, in Washington working for Lincoln's reelection, wrote his wife, "Unless material changes can be wrought, Lincoln's election is beyond any possible hope. It is probably clean gone now."[7]

All this negative feeling disgusted Lincoln's personal secretaries, John Nicolay and John Hay, perhaps the only two men who were not predicting disaster. Looking at the wild pessimistic howl raging all about him, Nicolay wrote his fiancée of the "disastrous panic—a sort of political Bull Run." Nicolay tried to explain it. "The want of any decided military successes thus far, and the necessity of the new draft in the coming month," he wrote her in August, "has materially discouraged many of our good friends, who are inclined to be a little weak-kneed." Croakers, he told her, were talking everywhere about the impossibility of reelecting Lincoln "unless something is done."

Nicolay chalked all this talk up mainly to "anxiety and discouragement," and predicted "they will recover from it, after the Democrats shall have made their nominations at Chicago, and after the active fighting of the political campaign begins. The Democrats are growing bold and confident, and will be very unscrupulous, but I still [do] not think they can defeat Mr. Lincoln in any event."[8]

"I lose my temper sometimes talking with growling Republicans," Hay in turn wrote to Nicolay on August 26. "There is a diseased restlessness about men in these times that unfits them for the steady support of an administration.... If the dumb cattle are not worthy of another term of Lincoln then let the will of God be done & the murrain of McClellan fall on them." Hay wrote, "Most of our people are talking like damned fools."[9]

Lincoln was not so sure about that. Indeed, by late August, he had come to agree with all the damned fools. He wanted to be reelected—for the good of the country. He had said, "I don't think it is personal vanity, or ambition—but I cannot but feel that the weal or woe of this great nation will be decided in the approaching canvass. My own experience has proven to me, that there is no program intended by the

Democratic party but that will result in the dismemberment of the Union." He figured he had to run to prevent that.[10]

But by now he was seeing little hope of preventing it. "You think I don't know I am going to be beaten," he confessed to one visitor, "*but I do* and unless some great change takes place *badly beaten*."[11]

The gloom of the summer had clearly affected even him, so much so that on August 23, he wrote a memo to himself, folded it, sealed it, and asked his cabinet members not to read it but only sign it.[12]

The memo read:

This morning, as for some days past, it seems exceedingly probable that this Administration will not be re-elected. Then it will be my duty to so co-operate with the President elect as to save the Union between the election and the inauguration; as he will have secured his election on such ground that he can not possibly save it afterwards.[13]

By the time Lincoln wrote this memo, it was generally conceded by Democrats and Republicans alike that the Democratic candidate would be George McClellan.

Lincoln was conceding the election and hedging his bets for the country.

As their convention neared, the Democrats were loving all of this Republican pessimism and misery. Cyrus H. McCormick, the inventor of the reaper and an unrepentant Democrat, was looking forward to threshing the hated Republicans. "Old Abe is quite in trouble just now," he exulted. "I think he is already pretty well played out. The Democracy must defeat themselves if now defeated."[14]

The Democratic convention was to convene in Chicago on August 29. It would be the party's ninth national nominating convention and the latest that any of them had ever been held. The War Democrats, led by the New Yorkers, had their sights and hearts fixed firmly on going and seeing George McClellan nominated. They could only hope something reasonable in the way of a platform could be built for him to stand on.

To rev up enthusiasm, the War Democrats staged a monster pro-McClellan meeting in New York on August 10. It was one of the largest political rallies ever held in the city—30,000 to 100,000 in attendance, depending on the reporting newspaper's political bias. It was chaos. Music roared, cannon boomed, fireworks flamed. Pro-McClellan rhetoric exploded simultaneously from four different platforms in Union Square. Cheers erupted for McClellan and groans for Lincoln.[15]

The *New York World* reprinted songs that were sung, including the chorus to the tune of "Viva l'Amour":

> *He'll win the race—to the White House he'll go,*
> *Whether Lincoln and Chase are willing or no.*
> *Hurrah for the man, hurrah for the man, hurrah for the man we love.*

But the man they love didn't attend. McClellan was still acting as if he weren't a candidate. Indeed, he was getting tired of the necessity of dealing with politicians, an essential condition if one wished to be in politics. "I don't expect to see you before the 29th unless you come to Orange," he had written Barlow in early August. "I shan't come again to N. Y. & don't send me any d---d politicians." He had repeated that sentiment to William C. Prime, the editor of the *Journal of Commerce*. "Don't send any politicians out here—I'll snub them if they come—confound them!"[16]

McClellan agreed with a friend who had written him from Newport, Rhode Island: "If there is any one thing I should wish more than another, it would be, you avoid *all* politicians and never listen to them or put your pen to paper on politics."[17] That, however, was not the best strategy for a candidate for president.

Lincoln could hardly view the Democratic problem without some amusement. As jubilant and hopeful Democrats were swarming on Chicago-bound trains, Lincoln was telling his reporter friend, Noah Brooks, "They must nominate a Peace Democrat on a war platform, or a War Democrat on a peace platform; and I personally can't say that I care much which they do."[18]

Other Republicans were looking on the Democrats at the end of this dreary August with contempt and scorn. On the day the convention convened, August 29, one of Lincoln's friends called them "that collection of Public vagrants."[19] John Hay was also dismissive. He wrote John Nicolay from Warsaw, Illinois, saying that he was waiting, with the greatest interest, "the hatching of the big peace Snakes at Chicago."[20]

The War Democrats from New York had their weapons ready. They were carrying with them not only hope but copies of an oration McClellan had delivered at West Point in July and his Harrison's Landing letter to Lincoln written on the Peninsula in July 1862. They had stitched the two together into a single document called "McClellan's Platform." They would hand it out to every delegate along with the wire pulling and arm twisting they intended to do on the general's behalf.

The convention opened to a city in a tizzy. The ardently Democratic *Chicago Times* had predicted that the convention would be "the largest and most enthusiastic gathering ever held upon American soil.'[21] The far less sympathetic *Chicago Tribune* called it the "National Copperhead Convention" and compared it to a plague of locusts, "like an army of grasshoppers," swarming around the entrances of Chicago's hotels "like bees around a hive in midsummer." The *Tribune* complained that the leading thoroughfares were clogged, "black with humanity in broadcloth... eating up every green thing."[22]

The trouble for the pro–McClellan contingent from New York began immediately. On hand as a delegate from Ohio was the most venomous copperhead in the country, ex–Congressman Clement L. Vallandigham, the darling of the Peace Democrats, whom Lincoln's friend, the humorist Petroleum Nasby, persisted in calling "Vallandigum." He wandered the hallways and caucus rooms, an unmuzzled center of attention. Worse—indeed, the worst thing that could happen—he had maneuvered himself onto the resolutions committee.[23]

The committee reported a short platform of six resolutions, five of which were relatively harmless. But the second one was a killer, making many pro-McClellanites, particularly the New Yorkers, cringe. Authored and rammed through the committee by the notorious Vallandigum, it flat-out declared the war—which McClellan had so ardently fought—a failure. It charged that the Lincoln administration had failed to restore the Union by "the experiment of war" and that "justice, humanity, liberty, and public welfare demand that immediate efforts be made for a cessation of hostilities, with a view to an ultimate convention of States, or other peaceable means, to the end that at the earliest practicable moment peace may be restored on the basis of the Federal Union of States."[24]

The delegates, eager to get on with the nominations, impatiently approved the platform, with its "war failure" plank. You can't fight momentum. The New Yorkers might have defeated it on the floor, but many of them were too anxious to get their man nominated, whatever the platform said.[25]

This potential rough patch successfully negotiated, the nominations for president got much rougher. Two Peace Democrats caused an uproar and an outbreak of shouting and flying fists when they attacked McClellan on the floor as a tyrant, an enemy of civil rights, and an out-and-out failure as a general—no better than the detested Lincoln. The upheaval finally subsided—but before any voting occurred—on account of darkness in the hall, which had no lighting.

The next morning delegates came ready not to fight but to vote, and George McClellan was nominated on the first ballot. To mollify the unhappy Peace Democrats, the convention nominated one of theirs, Congressman George H. Pendleton of Ohio, as his vice presidential running mate.[26]

So the election was to be even more mixed up than Lincoln predicted—a War Democrat running as president with a Peace Democrat as a running mate, and both astride a peace platform—that is, if McClellan would agree to the arrangement. No one yet knew how he would react to either the running mate or the platform.

As the vast exodus from Chicago began, one of the unhappy Peace men was overheard mumbling that "the nominee for president was a nobody and the candidate for vice president a putty head."[27] More than one Democrat must have wondered whether what Cyrus McCormick had feared—that the Democracy might defeat itself—had just happened.

Lincoln believed that was indeed just what had happened. On reading the Chicago platform, he reportedly said, "The danger is past...after the expenditure of blood and treasure that had been poured out for the maintenance of the government and the preservation of the Union, the American people were not prepared to vote the war a failure."[28]

So the lines were drawn. Now the war for votes would begin.

CHAPTER 25

SOUND AND FURY

J ust as the future of the Union was being decided by fire on land and sea, by the middle of September it appeared that this election would be decided in that fashion as well.

The first suggestion that this might be so had played out on August 5 in an epic sea battle in Mobile Bay. On that day, sixty-three-year-old Union Admiral David Glasgow Farragut, who seemed to have no fear, climbed into the rigging of his flagship, the USS *Hartford,* shouted "Damn the torpedoes, full speed ahead!" and led his fleet of fourteen men-of-war through fire and smoke past the roaring guns of Fort Morgan that guarded the entrance to the bay. Inside, firing incessant broadsides and ramming and re-ramming, his ships subdued a powerful Confederate ironclad, the CSS *Tennessee,* and took the bay by force.

Of itself, that epic Union victory wasn't enough to turn an election around, but it was a burst of light from a battleground in the darkest of all summers for Abraham Lincoln. Emphatic victories had been hard to come by. Grant had cornered Lee in Petersburg Virginia, but had not been able to defeat him. The country was weary of it all. Farragut's dramatic triumph at Mobile would not reelect the president, but it was something.

Less than a month later, just hours after the Democrats were leaving Chicago with the repugnant war failure plank weighing heavily on some of their minds, another ordeal by fire shook the Confederacy and buoyed the Union. After four months of grueling, mile-by-mile advance from Chattanooga, Sherman took Atlanta, the queen city of the Confederacy, and wired Lincoln through Halleck, "Atlanta is ours, and fairly won."[1]

This dramatic turn of events could have been just enough by itself to turn the dark prospect of defeat for Lincoln into an election victory. By itself it might be the "some great change" Lincoln needed to take place lest he be "*badly beaten.*"[2]

Two weeks later, on September 19 in the Shenandoah Valley, thirty-three-year-old, bandy-legged Union Major General Phil Sheridan made a third dramatic statement by fire, defeating the Confederate force under General Jubal Early that had briefly threatened Washington in July.

These three trials by fire, Union victories all, probably constituted the three most eloquent stump speeches that would be delivered on Lincoln's behalf in the entire election canvass.

As these three statements from bay and battlefield were being delivered, George McClellan was undergoing a figurative trial by fire of his own. For seven days after his nomination in Chicago, while Atlanta was falling, nothing was heard from the nominee. There was only silence. Would he accept the nomination? Could he abide a plank that called not only the war a failure but, by inference, his career as a general?

Suddenly everything in the Democracy depended on him and what he would say and do. The convention had shaped a political oddity—a warrior-general standing on a peace platform. The party and the country knew that until it heard from McClellan, the other shoe had not yet dropped.

But McClellan was having trouble finding his voice. Few others were. Voices were pouring in to him on his mountaintop in Orange suggesting what he must do. And they were voices of Babel.

McClellan's New York allies knew that he must somehow find a way to undo the platform damage done at Chicago. He must paper over the division in the party and make everything right. For the sake of unity, he must somehow appear to repudiate the spirit of the Vallandigham plank without seriously alienating the Peace men and the copperheads. In short, he must work a political miracle—no easier, but perhaps no less crucial, than working a military miracle on a battlefield. McClellan had not been able to work the military miracle. Could he now work the political one?

As the letters pulling him both ways—urging acceptance and urging refusal—flooded in, McClellan sat down to agonize. For six days, time ticked by and the country waited. A cavalry colonel, defending him, said, "People think 'Mac' is d---d slow, if he don't eat 1,000 rebels every morning for breakfast."[3] It isn't that easy working great miracles.

Lincoln, asked what might be the delay, said, "Oh, he's intrenching." Also asked about rumors that McClellan might decline the nomination entirely, the president said, "Well, he doesn't know yet whether he will accept or decline. And he never will know. Somebody must do it for him. For, of all the men I have had to deal with in my life, indecision is most strongly marked in General McClellan."[4]

By September 6, McClellan was into his sixth draft of a letter. Scattered about him were scraps of paper written on, scratched out, written on again—tortured signs of wrestling with language. But now he was reasonably satisfied that he had nailed it.

That night he wrote Nelly, "I think I have it now in an admirable shape & am not afraid to go down to posterity on it." He assured her, that from the avalanche of letters he had received, "There can be no doubt as to the feeling of the people in this part of the world—they are with me." That same day he wrote William H. Aspinwall, one of his wealthy New York supporters, "My letter of acceptance is ready— you need have no fears on the subject—It is true to the country & to myself & in entire consistency with my record. I will either accept on my own terms . . . or I will decline the whole affair."[5]

The letter, addressed to the members of the committee from Chicago who had notified him of his nomination, became known to the country on September 8.

It began: "It is unnecessary for me to say to you that the nomination comes to me unsought." McClellan wanted to make that perfectly clear. The sentiment was not far removed from what he had said about his military responsibilities in the war. "The existence of more than one government over the region which once owned our flag," the letter continued, "is incompatible with the peace, the power, and the happiness of the people. The preservation of our Union was the sole avowed object for which the war was commenced. It should have been conducted for that object only. . . . The reestablishment of the Union in all its integrity is, and must continue to be, the indispensable condition in any settlement."

Within that one indispensable condition, McClellan said, every resource of statesmanship must be bent to secure peace. "The Union is the one condition of peace—" he reiterated, "we ask no more." The end of slavery was not a requirement.

McClellan then forswore the war-failure plank. "I could not look in the face of my gallant comrades of the army and navy who have survived so many bloody battles, and tell them that their labors and the sacrifices of so many of our slain and wounded brethren had been in vain; that we had abandoned that Union for which we have so often periled our lives."

With that clearly understood, McClellan wrote, "I accept the nomination."[6]

So there it was—a ringing call for union and an outright repudiation by the candidate of the platform on which he was expected to run. It was an act unprecedented in American politics.

Then the speechmaking began. Both sides unleashed the great orators of their party, rolling both their heavy and light cannon into line. The Republican Radicals were not particularly happy that Lincoln was still their candidate. But they were far less happy with the prospect of any Democrat, particularly McClellan, in the White House, so they started stumping with enthusiasm. The Peace Democrats, angered by McClellan's rejection of their war-failure plank but having nowhere else to go, emerged from their sulking tents to campaign halfheartedly for McClellan.

A young Republican, Abram J. Dittenhoefer, stumping for Lincoln and union summed up the political hellfire that followed: "Night and day, without cessation, young men like myself, in halls, upon street corners, and from cart-tails, were haranguing, pleading, sermonizing, orating, arguing, extolling our cause and our candidate, and denouncing our opponents. A deal of oratory, elocution, rhetoric, declamation, and eloquence was hurled into the trouble air by speakers on both sides."[7]

The campaigning was just as frantic in the Democracy. "The unnatural situation of four years exclusion from office," one Republican observed, "seems to have produced in them a 'sacra fames [great hunger],' and they are entering into this contest like a pack of ravenous wolves."[8]

Among the prominent men who rallied to McClellan's colors were a small coterie who could not be considered wolves, ravenous, or Democrats. They were prominent former Whigs: George Ticknor Curtis, an intimate of the late great Whig Daniel Webster; Robert C. Winthrop, longtime Massachusetts Whig and former Speaker of the House; and Edward Everett, the country's preeminent orator, second only to the great Webster in the hearts of New England Whigdom. Also flying the McClellan flag were a band of conservative Unionists who, like McClellan, had been alienated by Lincoln's Emancipation Proclamation, believing it had disastrously changed the nature of the war and complicated the aim of restoring the country to the Union as it had been.[9]

Rallies of unprecedented size by both parties shook the political firmament, buttressed by an outpouring of political pamphlets unmatched in any campaign before. The country was inundated by the sound and fury.[10]

Despite the millions of words, not much was being said. There were life-and-death issues to be argued: how to reconstruct the South when the war was won, emancipation, and postwar adjustment to the trauma of battle—questions for the ages. None of them was discussed. None was successfully brought to the stump. The Democrats tried. They repeatedly threw down the reconstruction gauntlet, an issue that was splitting the Republican conservatives and Radicals, hoping to sever the delicate webbing that held them together. But the Republicans were not biting. They had shelved the issue for the campaign.

Some Democrats for a time raised the issue of miscegenation—the amalgamation of the races, intermarriage of blacks and whites, which they charged that all Republicans and abolitionist alike believed in.

Those were the issues the Democrats were raising or trying to raise. None of them was sticking.

The Republicans, for their part, were hammering incessantly with one argument over and over: that specter of treason, trying to make the country believe that all Democrats, copperheads and moderates, Vallandighams and McClellans alike, were by definition traitorous. It was sticking.

None of the arguments smacked of substance. The campaign had come down to mud-slinging, trading insult for insult. Both sides were hurling charges of election fraud. The Democrats accused the Republicans of substituting Republican ballots for Democratic ones to skew the important soldier vote to Lincoln. The Republicans were outraged to discover several thousand dry-goods boxes full of fraudulent ballots for McClellan. So it went.[11]

The only two men in the country who stood above all this turmoil were the candidates themselves. Neither was campaigning. No one expected them to. At the time, it was not considered seemly for candidates for president to campaign for themselves. It was a tradition, this noncampaigning. So the candidates were saying nothing and going nowhere. Only three times in the entire canvass was the politics-hating McClellan drawn out into public. The first time was early, when his neighbors in Orange held a demonstration of support. Crowds from as far away as New York City thronged into town. Some 10,000 serenaded the candidate, and he briefly responded. In September, he showed himself at a rally in Newark but did not speak. He was then not seen or heard of publicly for nearly two months, until at a giant McClellan march in the streets of New York City near the eve of the election, he silently reviewed his political army from the balcony of the Fifth Avenue Hotel for two and a half hours.[12]

Lincoln was lying equally low publicly, not talking issues and making no appeals for public support. But he had not been a politician for thirty years—one of the shrewdest in the country—for nothing. Unlike McClellan, he had well-honed political instincts. He knew where all the political levers were, and there were few he was not skillfully pulling.

He took a hand in the affairs of the Republican speakers' bureau and told state committees what to do. Lincoln expected government workers who owed their jobs to him to pitch in with both volunteer time and money, and he let them off work on election day to return to their home states to vote. Most of his cabinet, Stanton in particular, pulled levers too, and pitched in with substantial money donations. No opportunity for election gain was overlooked.[13]

A sure test of how the campaign was tending came on October 11, when three key states—Ohio, Indiana, and Pennsylvania—held elections for state offices. Between them, those three, called the October states, held enough electoral votes to elect a president. Therefore, these early state elections were invariably a bellwether in presidential election years, generally a certain sign of how the vote would go in the more important race in November. In a burst of good fortune for Lincoln, all three went Union in October: Ohio by a whopping 54,000 votes, Indiana by 20,000, Pennsylvania by 13,000. The auguries for a Republican victory in November were loud and clear.

It was generally believed that a vote that was going to make a huge difference would be cast by men carrying guns—the soldiers in the Union armies. McClellan, perhaps the most popular general ever to command an American army, remembered their loving huzzahs and was counting on them.

Their vote was a new thing—new to this war. In no election before had the soldiers' vote mattered. It hadn't existed. Before, when a soldier went off to war, he in effect lost his franchise, for the only place a man could legally vote was in person at his home polling place. But in this war, many states had changed their laws to allow soldiers to vote in the field.

However, the day McClellan was nominated in Chicago, he began losing traction with his beloved soldiers. Although they loved him, they could not abide the company he was keeping—a party with a platform resolution calling their war a failure and seeking to negotiate with the enemy. A political cartoon pictured a soldier saying "I would vote for you General, if you were not tied to a Peace Copperhead." His companion in the cartoon added, "Good bye, 'little Mac'—if thats your company, Uncle Abe gets my vote." Not even McClellan's forswearing the detested plank seemed to blunt this feeling.[14]

Uncle Abe saw all this and believed the soldiers now intended to vote overwhelmingly for him. He and Stanton saw to it that those who could not vote in the field would be furloughed to go home and vote, as long as it did not weaken the army.

All the fury and damnation finally came to an end on November 8. All that was left was to vote. Henry Raymond wrote in the *New York Times*, "The day has come—the day of fate. Before the morning's sun sets, the destinies of this republic, so far as it depends on human agency, are to be settled for weal or for woe. . . . We are making this decision not for ourselves simply. We are settling the lot of the generations that shall come after us. If the people err, *'The child will rue, that is unborn/ The voting of this day.'* "[15]

Noah Brooks wrote that day of Washington's "quadrennial hegira." Virtually all of the capital had gone home to vote; scarcely a government bureau was left with enough personnel to conduct business. Much of the Army of the Potomac was once more on the march— toward the ballot box. And, as had happened so often in this war, a drenching rain was falling.

Out of the storm, late in the night, the votes began coming in. By midnight, Lincoln knew he was carrying all of New England, Maryland, Ohio, Indiana, Michigan, Wisconsin, and possibly Delaware. By one o'clock the next morning a 20,000-vote bulge in his favor was reported in Illinois. Pennsylvania was looking safe. There were signs New York was tipping to Lincoln. The voting in the Far West—Kansas, California, Oregon, Nevada—would not be known for two days or more, but when it was, it was solid for him.

As expected, Lincoln was carrying the agricultural areas inhabited, for the most part, by the native-born. He was winning the vote of skilled urban workers and professionals. He was winning the abolition vote. McClellan was drawing his heaviest backing from the immigrant proletariat in the big cities and in some rural areas with strong foreign majorities, populations that were ardently anti-abolitionist and anti-black.

Most devastating of all for McClellan was the fact that he was losing the soldier vote, which he had so counted on. It had turned against him nearly en masse—by seven votes of every ten in his own Army of the Potomac, by eight to two in the armies of the West. Of the 150,635 soldier votes counted separately—those cast on the field—he would win but 33,748 to Lincoln's 116,887.

When all the results were finally in, Lincoln had won by 2,213,665 votes to 1,802,237, a relatively slim margin of 411,428. But in the vote that counted, the Electoral College, he won by a landslide—212 to McClellan's 21. The general had carried only three states: New Jersey, Kentucky, and Delaware.

On election day, George McClellan resigned his commission. His military career, so full of promise since his days at West Point and so blighted and disappointing in the end, was over. Two days later, on November 10, knowing he had lost the election, he wrote his friend Barlow that he wanted nothing further to do with politics, which he had hated in the first place. He told Barlow that he was through with public life forever: I can imagine no combination of circumstances that can ever induce me to enter it again—I say this in no spirit of pique or mortification—it is simply the result of cool judgment."[16]

Over as well was his troubled Civil War relationship with Abraham Lincoln.

EPITAPH FOR A SOLDIER

In six months, the war would be over.

Grant, in early April 1865, broke through the Confederate lines in Petersburg, Richmond fell, and Lee retreated, seeking to save his army and unite with Joe Johnston's in the Carolinas. Johnston had long since recovered from his wound at Fair Oaks and was leading the Confederate army in attempting to stem William Sherman's march through South and North Carolina. After the fall of Atlanta, Sherman had stormed to Savannah in late 1864 and was marching inexorably north through the Carolinas.

At the small Virginia village of Appomattox Court House, Grant cornered Lee and forced his old enemy to surrender on April 9. Johnston surrendered his army to Sherman nine days later at Durham Station, North Carolina.

When Grant took Lee's surrender at Appomattox, Lincoln had less than a week to live. On the night of April 14, almost four years exactly from the day the war began, he was shot in the head in Ford's Theater in Washington by John Wilkes Booth, an actor with strong Southern sentiments, as he watched a performance of the comedy *Our American Cousin*. The next day, April 15, Lincoln died in a bed in a house across the street, victim of the assassin's bullet, the last of 620,000 casualties, Union and Confederate, in that terrible war.

McClellan would still have his beloved Nelly, his young daughter, May, a son soon to be born, a promising future as a famous and talented man—and life.

On January 25, 1865, still believing he had twice saved his country—first securing Washington after the chaos of First Manassas and again at Antietam—with little thanks for it, McClellan and his family left for Europe.

The general remained abroad for three years, returning to America in September 1868. He took up residence again in New Jersey and lived as an icon of the war. Although he had vowed after the 1864 election never to be lured into public life again, McClellan ran for governor of the Garden State in 1878. There were mitigating circumstances for this cave-in. He had, again, not sought the office but basically been drafted, nominated unanimously at the state Democratic convention in 1878. He won the election by a comfortable 12,753 votes and served one term with a solid if not distinguished record.

Not eligible for reelection, he left the office, happy to have it behind him. Over the years, however, he acquired a more benign and tolerant attitude toward politics, even becoming an active participant. In 1880, he stumped for the Democratic presidential ticket in New York, Pennsylvania, New Jersey, and Connecticut. He campaigned for Grover Cleveland in the 1884 election and for a time was considered for the cabinet—as secretary of war.

It was not his spirit but his heart that finally gave out. McClellan died of a heart attack at home on October 29, 1885, and nobody could believe it. Indeed, that the general could die at all rather defied rational belief. A friend said, "His physical bearing was such that of all men he was the very last with whom those who knew him could connect any thought of death."[1]

But he did die on that day, and his last words were for his beloved Nelly. "Tell her," he whispered weakly to his physician, "that I am better now." Then, resting his head on his chair-back, he peacefully passed away. He was fifty-eight years old.[2]

Following simple services in the Madison Square Presbyterian Church in New York City, McClellan was buried in the Riverview Cemetery in Trenton, in his private plot on a hill overlooking the Delaware River. He had once spoke of death as crossing "that great valley," going to "Him who waits for us on the other side," to "live ever in that bright light where there is no need of sun or moon or stars, and where the weary can rest without pain"—the "land where it is always afternoon"[3]—and where there is probably no need of reinforcements.

McClellan was mourned North and South. Confederate General Joe Johnston, his old enemy on the Peninsula, stood by his graveside and called him "a dear friend whom I have so long loved and admired." His classmate Confederate Major General Dabney Herndon Maury said, "A brighter, kindlier, more genial gentleman did not live than he." Another Confederate classmate said, "I was one of his intimates at the academy, and I still cherish a tender memory of him."[4]

Nelly, who cherished him above all others, spent most of the rest of her life in Europe and never remarried. She died in 1915 in Nice, France, and was buried by her husband's side in Riverview Cemetery.

McClellan had failed to fulfill his shining promise of military greatness. Many, then and long since, have speculated why this was so.

McClellan has defenders who believed as he did—that his failure was not his fault. One of them was Helmuth von Moltke, the chief of staff of the Prussian army in the nineteenth century. After the war, Moltke had a conversation with an American who said, "Some of us in America do not estimate McClellan so highly as we do some of our other generals." Moltke replied, "It may be so, but let me tell you that, if your Government had supported General McClellan in the field as they should have done, your war would have been ended two years sooner than it was."[5] One of McClellan's inner circle called this perceived lack of support "the first great crime of the war."[6]

This young, untried general, thrust so brutally so early into such great responsibility, carried more than the average load of emotional, cultural, and intellectual baggage. But tempering this negative baggage was a host of positive traits.

McClellan organized a great army, the greatest on the planet, as perhaps no other man could have. He "took hold of the green and awkward Army of the Potomac with intelligence and skill," one of his soldiers later wrote, "and soon put new life and vigor into it. Our demoralized regiments and brigades were reorganized and divisioned; our disorganized batteries were rehorsed and equipped and put to drill; our forts were overhauled and our line of defenses extended and strengthened."[7]

Few men were more charming or better liked personally. He radiated, one of his officers said, "personal magnetism which was a potent, if not an irresistible force."[8] His protective love of his men was angelic. His ability to stir the love of his army was astounding. One of his officers said of him, "No other commander ever aroused the same enthusiasm in the troops, whether in degree or in kind. The soldiers fairly loved to look upon him; the sight of him brought cheers spontaneously from every lip; his voice was music to every ear.... [H]e...could so move upon the hearts of a great army, as the wind sways long rows of standing corn."[9]

The tragedy was that McClellan could not convert this great charisma and hold over them into victory on the battlefield. In this, the instinct of a great general—imagination—failed him. He did not have a mind-set that was flexible and conditioned to change instantly if necessary. When he set his mind on a course, he tended to blank out facts that argued against it. He could always see how he could improve his army, make it better, more prepared, if given time. And he took the time, often at the expense of lost opportunity. He made promises, if properly supplied and reinforced, that he failed to fulfill. In time, as one of his soldiers later wrote, "he finally acquired the sobriquet of McClellan the Unready."[10]

"He created an army," one of his aides at Antietam wrote, "which he failed to handle, and conceived plans which he failed to carry out."[11] Lincoln, assessing the general, said, "He is well versed in military matters and has had opportunities of experience and observation. Still, there must be something wrong somewhere, and I'll tell you what it is. He never embraces his opportunities. That's where the trouble is. He always puts off the hour for embracing his opportunities."[12]

McClellan's military idol, the role model of most generals in his age, was Napoleon—a paradigm of adaptability, celerity, and instinct for strategic advantage and for the jugular. Admiring Napoleon in theory, McClellan never emulated him in practice. He had a defensive, not an offensive, mind-set. "He habitually magnified obstacles into impossibilities," one critic wrote, "and deferred great deeds to a future that had no possibility. A brave soldier, he made a timid general."[13]

Perhaps the Polish immigrant Count Adam Gurowski was right about him. Gurowski was both a gadfly and a military analyst with entrée to high levels of the government in Washington. He kept a detailed, passionate, and incendiary diary, which, to the despair of many, he published. In an entry in late 1861, he wrote: "McClellan's speciality is engineering. It is a speciality which does not form captains and generals for the field—at least such instances are very rare.... The intellectual powers of an engineer are modeled, drilled, turned towards the defensive—the engineer's brains concentrate upon selecting defensive positions, and combine how to strengthen them by art." So an engineer "is rather disabled from embracing a whole battle-field, with its endless casualties and space. Engineers are the incarnation of a defensive warfare."[14]

Whatever the reason, McClellan was not a bold attacker, which in the end a great general must be. In him, boldness always gave ground to caution. He seemed a paradigm for the kind of general Auguste de Marmont, Marshal of France, described in the early 1800s: "They prepare for battle with intelligence and skill; but then hesitation commences." A battle, Marmont said, "is such a chance medley, success depends on so many chances, that the general doubts and hesitates till the favorable moment is lost before he makes up his mind to give the word."[15]

It was said of Stonewall Jackson, McClellan's classmate at West Point, that he handed his soldiers a musket, a hundred rounds of ammunition each, a blanket, and then "druv us so like hell."[16]

That was never McClellan's approach to war. He was not the type of general to "druv" them like hell. He was a military pessimist, generally imagining the worst that might happen, not imagining that it could also be happening to the enemy as well. He was constantly preparing, to the point of painful overcaution. And always the enemy outnumbered him in his imagination.

Finally, he made the grievous mistake of misjudging—indeed, ignoring—the will of the people of the North, impatient for action, for victory, for a quick end of the war. He marched instead to his own drum, set to a more measured beat and unmindful of the more urgent pounding. It was a fatal fault.

But perhaps McClellan's greatest mistake of all was not bonding with Abraham Lincoln, his president and commander in chief, as Lincoln had early urged him to do. The general had not drawn on him for all the sense and information that he had.[17]

Lincoln always thought well of McClellan personally. He liked him as a man. Even as the Radicals castigated the general and demanded he be replaced, Lincoln stood by him, protected him as best he could as long as he could. But the president was under intense public and political pressure to win the war, and McClellan was not doing it. He finally had to sack him. The two men were never close. McClellan never reciprocated Lincoln's personal regard for him. It was unlikely that they ever could have been fast friends, their backgrounds were so dissimilar—Lincoln the rough-hewn man of the frontier, McClellan the descendent of eastern gentility.

McClellan's genteel upbringing, indeed, got seriously in the way. Being born to culture sometimes breeds hubris. What had seemed so fortunate to him—his upper-class upbringing—was in the end a fatal liability. Believing Lincoln below him in class, a cultural, intellectual, and social inferior, blinded him to the president's brilliance. He could not bring himself to consider that a man born so low, so common, could have a mind for the ages. A brilliant man himself, he could not see true brilliance in others. He was nearsighted. He could not see greatness.

McClellan's inability to see Lincoln's greatness, as Grant later could, in effect destroyed McClellan's career and made Grant's. Lincoln had held out his hand to McClellan, but McClellan refused to grasp it, refused to confide in the president, refused to make him his partner. Above everything else, that failure had been his Achilles' heel.

That, and his personal failings—among them paranoia, misjudgments, and overcaution—in the end contributed to his failure and kept him from the pantheon of great generals. In contrast, Lincoln, his erstwhile partner, is firmly enshrined in the pantheon of great presidents—in the mind of many, the greatest.

NOTES

PROLOGUE

1. McClellan, *McClellan's Own Story*, p. 162.
2. Hawthorne's words, from his description of Lincoln in Holzer, *The Lincoln Anthology*, p. 36.
3. McClellan, *McClellan's Own Story*, p. 162.
4. Heintzelman, Journal, 12 November 1861.
5. McClellan, *Civil War Papers*, p. 515.
6. This background on the Illinois Central is an amalgam from Corliss, *Main Line of Mid-America*, pp. 16–20, 90–91; Stover, *History of the Illinois Central Railroad*, pp. 15–21; Brownson, *History of the Illinois Central Railroad*, pp. 25, 31, 157, 159, 161; Sunderland, *Abraham Lincoln and the Illinois Central Railroad*, pp. 9, 12.
7. Rafuse, *McClellan's War*, p. 51.
8. Ibid., p. 72.
9. Newton, *Lincoln and Herndon*, p. 182; Stover, *History of the Illinois Central Railroad*, p. 90.
10. Sears, *George B. McClellan*, p. 59.

CHAPTER 1

1. Lincoln, *Collected Works*, vol. 1, p. 386.
2. Donald, *Lincoln*, p. 25.
3. Barton, *The Paternity of Abraham Lincoln*, p. 273.
4. Wilson, *Lincoln among His Friends*, p. 24.
5. Wilson and Davis, *Herndon's Informants*, p. 85. Also see Waugh, *One Man Great Enough*, p. 13.
6. Wilson, *Lincoln among His Friends*, p. 29.
7. Wilson and Davis, *Herndon's Informants*, pp. 106–7.
8. Wilson, *Lincoln among His Friends*, p. 26.
9. Lincoln, *Collected Works*, vol. 3, p. 511.
10. Michie, *General McClellan*, p. 1; Rafuse, *McClellan's War*, p. 26.
11. Michie, *General McClellan*, p. 6.
12. Rafuse, *McClellan's War*, pp. 13–14; Sears, *George B. McClellan*, pp. 2–3.
13. Rafuse, *McClellan's War*, p. 14.
14. Sears, *George B. McClellan*, p. 2; Myers, *General George Brinton McClellan*, p. 5.
15. Rafuse, *McClellan's War*, p. 14.

16. Michie, *General McClellan*, pp. 1, 2–3.

17. Sears, *George B. McClellan*, p. 3.

18. *Illinois State Register*, 24 June 1842; Herndon and Weik, *Herndon's Life of Lincoln*, pp. 207–8; Miers, *Lincoln Day by Day*, vol. 1, p. 186.

19. Martineau, *Retrospect of Western Travel*, vol. 1, pp. 57–58.

20. McClellan to Frederica English, 28 June 1842, George B. McClellan Papers.

21. Maury, "General T. J. (Stonewall) Jackson," p. 311.

22. Ibid.

23. Quoted in Michie, *General McClellan*, p. 12.

24. Keyes, *Fifty Years' Observation of Men and Events*, p. 197.

25. Gardner, "Memoirs," p. 8; Maury, *Recollections of a Virginian*, p. 59.

26. Gardner, "Memoirs," p. 8. I used the same quotes in much the same way in *The Class of 1846*, pp. 67, 66.

27. Morrison, "Getting through West Point," p. 308.

28. McClellan to John McClellan, 21 January 1843, McClellan Papers.

29. McClellan to Frederica English, 13 May 1846, McClellan Papers.

30. George Horatio Derby to Mary Townsend Derby, 14 May 1846, Derby Papers.

31. Smith, *Company "A,"* p. 10.

32. McClellan to Elizabeth McClellan, 4 February 1847, McClellan Papers.

33. Smith, *Company "A,"* p. 56.

34. Lincoln, *Collected Works*, vol. 1, p. 433. The full text of his speech is on pp. 431–42.

CHAPTER 2

1. Nicolay, *Personal Traits of Abraham Lincoln*, p. 80; Current, "Lincoln and the Eighth Circuit," p. 11; Wilson, *Lincoln among His Friends*, pp. 105, 114, 122; Weik, *The Real Lincoln*, p. 188; Lufkin, "Mr. Lincoln's Light from Under a Bushel—1850," p. 5.

2. Waugh, *One Man Great Enough*, pp. 175–76, 177.

3. Herndon and Weik, *Herndon's Life of Lincoln*, pp. 271–72.

4. Angle, *Abraham Lincoln by Some Men Who Knew Him*, p. 39.

5. Hertz, *Lincoln Talks*, p. 22.

6. Whitney, *Lincoln the Citizen*, pp. 189, 191. In these descriptions of Lincoln on the circuit I have also drawn on my own *One Man Great Enough*, pp. 171–79.

7. My description of this contentious time for McClellan draws on Sears, *George B. McClellan*, pp. 28–30.

8. Quoted in Myers, *General George Brinton McClellan*, p. 80.

9. McClellan, Pacific railroad diary, 9 November 1853, McClellan Papers. A detailed account of McClellan's role in the Pacific railroad survey is in Sears, *George B. McClellan*, pp. 36–41.

10. Davis, *Jefferson Davis*, vol. 1, p. 536.

11. Quoted in Myers, *General George B. McClellan*, pp. 88, 94.

12. Michie, *General McClellan*, pp. 41, 47, 51–52.

13. Nevins, *Abram S. Hewitt*, p. 158.

14. Corliss, *Main Line of Mid-America*, p. 90; Sears, *George B. McClellan*, p. 51.

15. Quoted in Macartney, *Little Mac*, p. 34.

16. Lincoln, *Collected Works*, p. 462. Italics are Lincoln's.

17. Wilson, *Intimate Memories of Lincoln*, p. 165; *Illinois Daily Journal*, 2 September 1854 in Lincoln, *Collected Works*, vol. 2, p. 227.

18. Myers, *General George Brinton McClellan*, p. 107.

19. Ibid., p. 109.

20. Ibid., p. 112.
21. Shakespeare, *Troilus and Cressida*, act 1, sc.1, line 101.
22. Robertson, *General A. P. Hill*, p. 12.
23. McClellan, *Civil War Papers*, p. 82.

CHAPTER 3

1. Fehrenbacher and Fehrenbacher, *Recollected Words of Abraham Lincoln*, p. 241.
2. Fehrenbacher, *Prelude to Greatness*, p. 48.
3. Lincoln, *Collected Works*, vol. 2, p. 461.
4. McClellan, *McClellan's Own Story*, p. 29.
5. McClellan, *Civil War Papers*, p. 5.
6. Cox's description of McClellan and Dennison's recruitment of him is from, "War Preparations in the North," pp. 89–90.
7. McClellan, *Civil War Papers*, p. 32.
8. Nicolay and Hay, *Abraham Lincoln,* vol. 4, p. 337.
9. The quotes here are from Sears, *George B. McClellan*, pp. 85, 101.
10. Cox, "McClellan in West Virginia," p. 135.
11. Official Records., ser. 1, vol. 2, p. 753. These will be cited henceforth in the notes and in Sources Cited as O. R.
12. McCulloch, *Men and Measures of Half a Century*, pp. 297–98.
13. I owe the substance of this paragraph to Sears, *George B. McClellan*, p. 95.
14. Rafuse, *McClellan's War*, p. 118.
15. McClellan, *Civil War Papers*, p. 71.

CHAPTER 4

1. Riddle, *Recollections of War Times*, p. 63.
2. Maurois, "A Princely Service," p. 58.
3. Sears, *George B. McClellan*, p. 64.
4. Ibid., p. 30.
5. McClellan to Mary Marcy, 14 May 1854, McClellan Papers.
6. I enjoyed considerable help with these thoughts from Rafuse, *McClellan's War*, pp. 15–16.
7. McClellan, *McClellan's Own Story*, p. 34.
8. McClellan, *Civil War Papers*, p. 132.
9. Rafuse makes many of these comparisons of Lincoln and McClellan in *McClellan's War*, pp. 75–89.
10. Ibid., p. 123.
11. See Sears, *George B. McClellan*, p. 17, 25, for the origins of this belief.
12. Ibid., p. 56.
13. Rafuse, *McClellan's War*, pp. 49, 123.
14. Russell, *My Diary North and South*, p. 288.
15. Beatty, *Memoirs of a Volunteer*, p. 27.
16. These McClellan military traits are taken in part from Michie, *General McClellan*, pp. 33, 41, 51.
17. McClellan, *Civil War Papers*, p. 46.
18. Quoted in Michie, *General McClellan*, p. 45. This analysis of McClellan's strengths and weaknesses owes much to Michie's work, the oldest and still one of the best McClellan biographies.

19. McClellan, *Civil War Papers*, p. 45.
20. McClellan's appreciation of Saxe is discussed in Rafuse, *McClellan's War*, p. 50.
21. Biddle, "Recollections of McClellan," pp. 464–65.

CHAPTER 5

1. Borrett, "An Englishman in Washington in 1864," p. 7.
2. Sandburg, "The Face of Lincoln," p. 2.
3. Russell, *My Diary North and South*, p. 288.
4. Ibid.
5. Lowell, "General McClellan's Report," pp. 551–52.
6. McClellan, *Civil War Papers*, p. 70.
7. Ibid., p. 71.
8. Nicolay and Hay, *Abraham Lincoln*, vol. 4, p. 444.
9. McClellan, *Civil War Papers*, p. 71.
10. McClellan's memorandum to Lincoln was written on August 2, 1861, and is in ibid., pp. 71–75.
11. These figures are from McClellan, *Report on the Organization and Campaigns of the Army of the Potomac*, p. 50.
12. McClellan, *McClellan's Own Story*, p. 67; Hassler, *General George B. McClellan*, p. 23.
13. Swinton, *Campaigns of the Army of the Potomac*, p. 62.
14. Russell, *My Diary North and South*, p. 288.
15. McClellan, *Civil War Papers*, p. 70.
16. Sears, *George B. McClellan*, p. 71.
17. Rusling, *Men and Things I Saw in Civil War Days*, p. 25.
18. McClellan, *McClellan's Own Story*, pp. 327–28.
19. Ibid., p. 141.
20. McClellan, *Civil War Papers*, p. 95.
21. Russell, *My Diary North and South*, pp. 318, 290, 301.
22. Sears, *George B. McClellan*, pp. 97–98.
23. Hawthorne, "Chiefly about War Matters," pp. 323–24.

CHAPTER 6

1. McClellan, *Civil War Papers*, p. 61.
2. Ibid., p. 44.
3. Rowland, *George B. McClellan and Civil War History*, p. 140.
4. Ibid., p. 82.
5. Myers, *General George Brinton McClellan*, pp. 101–2, 202.
6. Russell, *My Diary North and South*, pp. 306, 314.
7. McClellan, *Civil War Papers*, p. 81.
8. O.R., ser 1, vol. 11, pt. 3, p. 3.
9. McClellan, *Civil War Papers*, p. 87.
10. O. R., ser. 1, vol. 11, pt. 3, p. 4.
11. Michie, *General McClellan*, pp. 121–27.
12. Nicolay, *With Lincoln in the White House*, p. 56.
13. These various railings against Scott are in letters to Nelly in McClellan, *Civil War Papers*, pp. 81, 84, 85–86.
14. Ibid., pp. 107, 135, 136n.

15. Ibid., pp. 91, 92.
16. Ibid., pp. 106–7.
17. Ibid., pp. 113–14.
18. Ibid., pp. 107, 113. Calling his superiors "imbeciles" and "incapables" is on p. 114.
19. Ibid., p. 111.
20. Ibid., pp. 113, 114.
21. Michie, *General McClellan*, pp. 139–40.

CHAPTER 7

1. Rafuse, *McClellan's War*, p. 132; Myers, *General George Brinton McClellan*, p. 166.
2. Waugh, *One Man Great Enough*, p. 391; Boatner, *The Civil War Dictionary*, p. 654; Faust, *Historical Times Illustrated Encyclopedia of the Civil War*, p. 586.
3. Myers, *General George Brinton McClellan*, p. 210; Sears, *George B. McClellan*, pp. 108–9.
4. Sears, *George B. McClellan*, p. 129.
5. McClellan, *McClellan's Own Story*, pp. 136–37.
6. O. R., ser. 1, vol. 11, pt. 3, p. 4.
7. Ibid., pp. 4, 5–6.
8. McClellan, *McClellan's Own Story*, p. 113; Michie, *General McClellan*, p. 112.
9. O. R., ser. 1, vol. 51, pp. 491–93.
10. McClellan, *Civil War Papers*, p. 114.
11. Lincoln, *Collected Works*, vol. 5, pp. 9–10.
12. O. R., ser 3, vol. 1, p. 614.
13. McClellan, *Civil War Papers*, pp. 123–24.
14. Hay, *Inside Lincoln's White House*, p. 30.
15. All this is astutely discussed in Michie, *General McClellan*, pp. 146–48, 151–52.
16. McClellan, *Civil War Papers*, p. 128.
17. Rice, *Reminiscences of Abraham Lincoln*, p. 74.
18. Nicolay and Hay, *Abraham Lincoln*, vol. 4, pp. 442, 443.
19. Sears, *George B. McClellan*, pp. 134–36; Nicolay's opinion is from *With Lincoln in the White House*, p. 63.
20. McClellan, *McClellan's Own Story*, pp. 97–98.
21. Biddle, "Recollections of McClellan," p. 461.
22. Wade and Chandler quotes are from Rafuse, *McClellan's War*, pp. 137–38.
23. These viewpoints are admirably covered by Rafuse in ibid., pp. 163–64.
24. Ibid., p. 142.
25. U.S. Congress, *Report of the Joint Committee on the Conduct of the War*, vol. 1, p. 128.
26. Hay, *Inside Lincoln's White House*, p. 25.
27. Ibid., p. 32.
28. McClellan, *Civil War Papers*, p. 143.
29. Michie, *General McClellan,* pp. 155–56, 170–71.
30. Paris, *History of the Civil War in America*, vol. 1, p. 416.
31. Paris, "McClellan Organizing the Grand Army," p. 114.

CHAPTER 8

1. Hay, *Inside Lincoln's White House*, p. 30.
2. McClure, *Lincoln's Yarns and Stories*, p. 31.
3. Meigs, "General M. C. Meigs on the Conduct of the Civil War," p. 292.

4. This account of the meetings is from McDowell's "Manuscript Meetings of Council of War" in Swinton, *Campaigns of the Army of the Potomac*, pp. 79–84. See also Franklin, "The First Great Crime of the War," pp. 76–79.

5. McClellan's account is in *McClellan's Own Story*, pp. 156–58.

6. McDowell, "Manuscript Minutes of Council of War," p. 84.

7. Meigs, "General M. C. Meigs on the Conduct of the Civil War," pp. 292–93.

8. McDowell, "Manuscript Minutes of Council of War," p. 85; McClellan, *McClellan's Own Story*, p. 158.

9. Rafuse, *McClellan's War*, p. 172.

10. The McClellan-Ives connection is described in Sears, *George B. McClellan*, pp. 142–43.

11. Ibid., p. 142.

12. The case and the Stanton-Lincoln relationship in it is ably discussed in Thomas and Hyman, *Stanton*, pp. 63–66.

13. McClellan, *Civil War Papers*, p. 113.

14. This description is distilled from Doster, *Lincoln and Episodes of the Civil War*, pp. 114–15, 116.

15. Doyle, *In Memoriam, Edwin McMasters Stanton*, p. 42.

16. Doster, *Lincoln and Episodes of the Civil War*, p. 52.

17. Nevins, *War for the Union*, vol. 2, p. 35.

18. Gilmore, *Personal Recollections of Abraham Lincoln and the Civil War*, pp. 155, 156.

19. Fehrenbacher and Fehrenbacher, *Recollected Words of Abraham Lincoln*, p. 350.

20. Doyle, *In Memoriam, Edwin McMasters Stanton*. p. 248.

21. Hassler, *General George B. McClellan*, pp. 51–52; Sears, *George B. McClellan*, p. 149; Rafuse, *McClellan's War*, p. 177; Michie, *General McClellan*, p. 167.

22. Lincoln, *Collected Works*, vol. 5, pp. 111, 115.

23. McClellan, *Civil War Papers*, p. 143.

24. Sears, *George B. McClellan*, pp. 130–31.

25. Barnard, *The Peninsular Campaign and Its Antecedents*, p. 54.

26. Lincoln, *Collected Works*, vol. 5, pp. 118–19.

CHAPTER 9

1. McClellan's memo to the president is in his *Civil War Papers*, pp. 162–70. Also in O. R., ser. 1, vol. 5, pp. 42–45.

2. Michie, *General McClellan*, pp. 198–99.

3. McClellan, *Civil War Papers*, p. 155.

4. McClellan's letter of condolence is in ibid., p. 187.

5. The bridge incident is stitched from accounts in Sears, *George B. McClellan*, pp. 156–57, 158; and Michie, *General McClellan*, pp. 200–1. Stanton and Lincoln's outbursts are from a memorandum by Nicolay in *With Lincoln in the White House*, p. 72.

6. Fehrenbacher and Fehrenbacher, *Recollected Words of Abraham Lincoln*, p. 76.

7. McClellan, *McClellan's Own Story*, p. 196.

8. This encounter is described in Sears, *George B. McClellan*, pp. 157, 158–59. McClellan's take on the meeting, and his anger, is in McClellan, *McClellan's Own Story*, pp. 195–96.

9. Barnard, *The Peninsular Campaign and Its Antecedents*, pp. 51–52.

10. Lincoln, *Collected Works*, vol. 5, pp. 149–50.

11. Ibid., p. 151.

12. Swinton, *Campaigns of the Army of the Potomac*, p. 90.

13. Lincoln, *Collected Works*, vol. 5, p. 155.

14. McClellan, *Civil War Papers*, p. 202.

15. Hawthorne, *Hawthorne and His Wife*, vol. 2, p. 310; Sears, *George B. McClellan*, pp. 168–69.
16. Browning, *Diary of Orville Hickman Browning*, vol. 1, pp. 537–38.
17. Quoted in Sears, *George B. McClellan*, p. 169.

CHAPTER 10

1. Swinton, *Campaigns of the Army of the Potomac*, p. 100.
2. McClellan, *McClellan's Own Story*, p. 238.
3. Frobel, *The Civil War Diary of Anne S. Frobel*, p. 82
4. Bird and Bird, *The Granite Farm Letters*, p. 83.
5. Manarin, *Richmond at War*, p. 194n.
6. Cook, *The Siege of Richmond*, p. 104.
7. This plan of campaign is outlined by McClellan in O.R., ser. 1, vol. 5, pp. 57–58.
8. Hassler, *General George B. McClellan*, pp. 84–85.
9. O. R., ser. 1, vol. 5, p. 58.
10. McClellan, *Civil War Papers*, p. 223.
11. It is difficult to cite a specific source or sources for this summary of McClellan's political objectives. It is an account stitched from my reading of many sources, synthesized within my own thinking and set down in my own words. It mirrors in some degree other accounts.
12. Hassler, *General George B. McClellan*, pp. 91–92.
13. These figures are from ibid., pp. 78–80.
14. McClellan, *McClellan's Own Story*, p. 241.
15. McClellan, *Civil War Papers*, p. 220.
16. This fear for Washington's safety is succinctly discussed in Sears, *George B. McClellan*, pp. 171–72; also in Hassler, *General George B. McClellan*, pp. 78–81.
17. Hassler, *General George B. McClellan*, p. 74.
18. Julian, *Political Recollections*, p. 210.
19. Browning, *Diary of Orville Hickman Browning*, vol. 1, pp. 538–39; Hassler, *General George B. McClellan*, p. 82.
20. O. R., ser. 1, vol. 5, p. 58.

CHAPTER 11

1. McClellan, *McClellan's Own Story*, p. 254.
2. McClellan, *Civil War Papers*, p. 225.
3. O. R., ser. 1, vol. 11, pt. 3, p. 66.
4. Ibid., pp. 60–61.
5. McClellan, *McClellan's Own Story*, p. 10.
6. O. R., ser. 1. vol. 11, pt. 3, p. 71.
7. McClellan, *Civil War Papers*, pp. 229, 230.
8. O.R., ser. 1, vol. 11, pt. 3, p. 80. Also see "General McClellan," p. 548.
9. Hassler, *General George B. McClellan*, p. 91.
10. Goss, *Recollections of a Private*, p. 23.
11. Rafuse, *McClellan's War*, p. 212.
12. This train of events is ably discussed in Michie, *General McClellan*, pp. 241–42; and Sears, *George B. McClellan*, pp. 174–76. For McClellan's inflated estimate of Confederate strength around Yorktown, see O. R., ser 1, vol. 11, pt. 3, p. 76.
13. McClellan, *Report on the Organization and Campaigns of the Army of the Potomac*, p. 161.

14. McClellan, *Civil War Papers*, pp. 377, 361.
15. Ibid., p. 235.
16. The thinking in this assessment mirrors Sears, *George B. McClellan*, p. 176.
17. Welles, *Diary*, vol. 1, p. 124.
18. O. R., ser. 1, vol. 11, pt. 3, p. 79.
19. Hay, *At Lincoln's Side*, p. 19.
20. Lincoln, *Collected Works*, vol. 5, p. 182.
21. McClellan, *Civil War Papers*, p. 234.
22. Lincoln's letter is in *Collected Works*, vol. 5, pp. 184–85.
23. McClellan, *Civil War Papers*, pp. 251, 252.
24. Browning, *Diary*, vol. 1, p. 540.
25. Bates, *Diary*, p. 253.
26. Hay, *At Lincoln's Side*, p. 20.
27. O. R. ser. 1, vol. 11, pt. 3, p. 456.
28. McClellan, *Civil War Papers*, p. 232.
29. Sears, *George B. McClellan*, p. 181.
30. Lowell, "General McClellan's Report," p. 558.
31. Lincoln, *Collected Works*, vol. 5, p. 203.
32. McClellan, *Civil War Papers*, p. 252.
33. Quoted in Rafuse, *McClellan's War*, p. 219.
34. McClellan, *Civil War Papers*, p. 252.
35. Ibid., p. 253.
36. Sears, *George B. McClellan*, p. 182; Johnston, "Manassas to Seven Pines," p. 203.
37. Message to his friend Major General Ambrose E. Burnside, in O. R., ser. 1, vol. 9, p. 392.

CHAPTER 12

1. McClellan, *Civil War Papers*, pp. 255, 256.
2. O. R., ser. 1, vol. 9, p. 392.
3. McClellan, *Civil War Papers*, pp. 256, 258.
4. Macartney, *Little Mac*, pp. 167–68; McClellan, *McClellan's Own Story*, pp. 360–61.
5. Sears, *George B. McClellan*, p. 185.
6. O. R., ser. 1, vol. 9. p. 392.
7. Michie, *General McClellan*, pp. 281–82.
8. McClellan, *Civil War Papers*, pp. 260–61, 265.
9. O. R., ser. 1, vol. 2, p. 209.
10. McClellan, *Civil War Papers*, p. 261.
11. Lincoln, *Collected Works*, vol. 5, p. 216.
12. O.R., ser. 3, vol. 2, p. 2.
13. McClellan, *McClellan's Own Story*, p. 259.
14. Macartney, *Little Mac*, p. 198.
15. Browning, *Diary*, vol. 1, p. 563.
16. McClellan, *McClellan's Own Story*, p. 150.
17. Macartney, *Little Mac*, pp. 211. 213.
18. Sears, *George B. McClellan*, p. 190.
19. O. R., ser. 1, vol. 11, pt 3, pp. 176–77.
20. Lincoln, *Collected Works*, vol. 5, pp. 232, 236.
21. McClellan, *Civil War Papers*, p, 275.
22. Macartney, *Little Mac*, p. 167.

23. McClellan, *McClellan's Own Story*, pp. 362, 364.
24. O. R., ser. 1, vol. 11, pt. 3, pp. 191–92.
25. McClellan, *Civil War Papers*, p. 276.
26. Ibid., p. 278; O. R., ser. 1, vol.11, pt. 3, p. 193.
27. McClellan, *Civil War Papers*, p. 279.
28. Ibid., pp. 277, 278, 278n, 287; *McClellan's Own Story*, p. 365.
29. Macartney, *Little Mac*, p. 179.
30. Lincoln, *Collected Works*, vol. 5, p. 240.
31. McClellan, *Civil War Papers*, pp. 286–87.
32. Ibid., 291.

CHAPTER 13

1. Waugh, *Class of 1846*, pp. 75–76.
2. Davis and Hoffman, *Confederate General*, vol. 5, p. 175.
3. Ibid., vol. 4, p. 45; Warner, *Generals in Gray*, pp. 181–82.
4. McClellan, *Civil War Papers*, pp. 244–45.
5. Waugh, *Class of 1846*, p. 360.
6. McClellan, *Civil War Papers*, p. 286.
7. Ibid., pp. 286, 287.
8. Ibid., pp. 288–89.
9. McClellan, *McClellan's Own Story*, pp. 274–75.
10. McClellan, *Civil War Papers*, pp. 289, 290.
11. O. R., ser. 1, vol. 11, pt. 3, p. 220.
12. McClellan, *Civil War Papers*, pp. 294–95.
13. Meade, *Life and Letters*, vol. 1, pp. 277–78.
14. McClellan, *Civil War Papers*, pp. 295–96, 297–98, 299.
15. Lincoln, *Collected Works*, vol. 5, p. 276.
16. McClellan, *Civil War Papers*, pp. 302–3.
17. Goss, *Recollections of a Private*, p. 55.
18. These figures on enemy strength and McClellan's view of the consequences and the blame are in his *Civil War Papers*, pp. 309–10.
19. Lincoln, *Collected Works*, vol. 5, p. 286.
20. Rowland, *George B. McClellan and Civil War History*, p. 117; McClellan, *Civil War Papers*, p. 313.
21. Hassler, *General George B. McClellan*, p. 139.
22. Rowland, *George B. McClellan and Civil War History*, p. 212.
23. U.S. Congress, *Report of the Joint Committee on the Conduct of the War*, vol. 1, pp. 276–77.
24. Boatner, *Civil War Dictionary*, p. 659; Faust, *Historical Times Illustrated Encyclopedia of the Civil War*, p. 593.
25. Warner, *Generals in Blue*, pp. 376–77.
26. For Pope's rantings in Washington, see Cozzens, *General John Pope*, p. 78; U.S. Congress, *Report of the Joint Committee on the Conduct of the War*, vol. 1, pp 279–80; Tap, *Over Lincoln's Shoulder*, p. 127; Rafuse, *McClellan's War*, p. 237. The quote is from Chase, *Papers: Vol. 1. Journals*, p. 350.

CHAPTER 14

1. Dowdy and Manarin, *Wartime Papers of Robert E. Lee*, pp. 183–84. See also Rowland, *George B. McClellan and Civil War History*, p. 115.

2. Jones, *Personal Reminiscences...of Gen. Robert E. Lee*, p. 40. See also Rowland, *George B. McClellan and Civil War History*, pp. 203–4.
3. McClellan, *Civil War Papers*, pp. 322–23.
4. Bates, *Lincoln in the Telegraph Office*, pp. 109–10.
5. Lincoln, *Collected Works*, vol. 5, pp. 289–90.
6. McClellan, *Civil War Papers*, pp. 324–25.
7. Longstreet, "'The Seven Days,' Including Frayser's Farm," p. 403.
8. This rundown of McClellan's supply train draws from Sears, *George B. McClellan*, p. 217.
9. Ibid., pp. 221–22.
10. Shakespeare, *Love's Labor's Lost*, act 5. sc. 1. line 86.
11. Franklin, "Rear-Guard Fighting during the Change of Base," p. 382.
12. McClellan, *McClellan's Own Story*, p. 440.
13. Hassler, *General George B. McClellan*, p. 171.
14. Rafuse, *McClellan's War*, p. 231.
15. Seward, *Reminiscences of a War-Time Statesman and Diplomat*, p. 205.
16. McClellan, *McClellan's Own Story*, p. 439.
17. Fehrenbacher and Fehrenbacher, *Recollected Words of Abraham Lincoln*, p. 125.
18. Macartney, *Little Mac*, pp. 193–94; O. R., ser. 1, vol. 11, pt. 3, p. 299; McClellan, *Civil War Papers*, p. 339.
19. Macartney, *Little Mac*, p. 194.
20. McClellan, *Civil War Papers*, p. 286.
21. These two letters are in McClellan, *Civil War Papers*, pp. 374, 376–77.
22. Ibid., pp. 328, 327.
23. Lincoln, *Collected Works*, vol. 5, p. 301.
24. McClellan's letter is in O.R., vol. 11, pt. 1, pp. 73–74, and in McClellan, *Civil War Papers*, pp. 344–45.
25. Nicolay and Hay, *Abraham Lincoln*, vol. 5, p. 449.

CHAPTER 15

1. Welles, *Diary*, vol. 1, pp. 70–71.
2. Rafuse, *McClellan's War*, p. 234.
3. O. R., ser. 1, vol. 12, pt. 3, p. 474.
4. McClellan, *Civil War Papers*, pp. 374, 367.
5. Ambrose, *Halleck*, pp. 9–10; J. H. Wilson, *Under the Old Flag*, p. 99.
6. This biographical sketch is borrowed mainly from Warner, *Generals in Blue*, pp. 195–96.
7. McClellan, *Civil War Papers*, pp. 369, 367–68.
8. Browning, *Diary*, vol. 1, p. 563.
9. This thought is taken from Michie, *General McClellan*, pp. 242–43.
10. McClellan, *Civil War Papers*, p. 329; Macartney, *Little Mac*, p. 193.
11. McClellan, *Civil War Papers*, pp. 364–65.
12. O. R., ser. 1, vol. 12, pt. 2, p. 5; Sears, *George B. McClellan*, pp. 239–40.
13. O. R., ser. 1, vol. 11, pt. 3, pp. 337–38, 342.
14. Ibid., ser. 1, vol. 12, pt. 2, p. 5; ser. 1, vol. 11, pt. 3, p. 338.
15. Ibid., ser, 1, vol. 12, pt. 2, p. 5; ser. 1, vol. 11, pt. 1, pp. 80–81.
16. Heintzelman, *Journal*, 4 August 1862.
17. McClellan's wire to Halleck is in *Civil War Papers*, pp. 383–84, and O. R., ser. 1, vol. 12, pt. 2, pp. 8–9.
18. Halleck's response is in O. R., ser. 1, vol. 12, pt. 2, pp. 9–11.
19. McClellan, *Civil War Papers*, p. 391.
20. O. R., ser. 1, vol. 11, pt. 1, p. 89.

Chapter 16

1. McClellan, *Civil War Papers*, pp. 369, 382–83, 389.
2. Hassler, *General George B. McClellan*, p. 196.
3. Upton, *Military Policy of the United States*, p 324.
4. O. R. ser. 1, vol. 11, pt. 1, p. 88.
5. McClellan, *Civil War Papers*, p. 389.
6. Ibid., p. 201; Welles, *Diary*, vol. 1, p. 83.
7. McClellan, *McClellan's Own Story*, pp. 476–77.
8. Hassler, *General George B. McClellan*, p. 199; McClellan, *McClellan's Own Story*, p. 500.
9. McClellan, *McClellan's Own Story*, p. 505.
10. McClellan, *Civil War Papers*, pp. 399–400.
11. Ibid., pp. 411, 417.
12. Ibid., p. 416.
13. Hay, *Inside Lincoln's White House*, p. 37.
14. See Ropes, *Army under Pope*, p. 161, and Upton, *Military Policy of the United States*, p. 354.
15. McClellan, *Civil War Papers*, p. 419.
16. Ibid., p. 427.
17. Castleman, *Army of the Potomac*, p. 203.
18. Walker, *History of the Second Army Corps*, pp. 91–92.
19. Catton, *Army of the Potomac: Mr. Lincoln's Army*, p. 7; Haupt, *Reminiscences*, pp. 135, 135n.
20. Rafuse, *McClellan's War*, p. 266.
21. Ibid., pp. 404, 410, 417, 423; Michie, *General McClellan*, p. 384.
22. McClellan, *Civil War Papers*, p. 428.
23. McClellan, *McClellan's Own Story*, p. 535.
24. O. R., ser. 1, vol. 12, pt. 3, p. 807.
25. Wells, *Diary*, vol. 1, p. 102.
26. The letter is in Michie, *General McClellan*, pp. 393–94.
27. Chase, *Papers: Vol. 1. Journals*, p. 369; Welles, *Diary*, pp. 104–5.
28. Doyle, *In Memoriam, Edwin McMasters Stanton*, p. 149.
29. Hay, *Inside Lincoln's White House*, pp. 38–39.
30. For this chain of events and quotes, see Welles, *Lincoln and Seward*, pp. 196–98; also Welles, *Diary*, vol. 1, p. 113.
31. Nicolay, *Lincoln's Secretary*, p. 149.

Chapter 17

1. McClellan, "From the Peninsula to Antietam," pp. 550–51n.
2. Rafuse, *McClellan's War*, p. 271.
3. McClellan, *Civil War Papers*, p. 435; Macartney, *Little Mac*, pp. 231, 232.
4. I had help summarizing Lee's intentions from Harsh, *Sounding the Shallows*, pp. 132–35, 146–47.
5. Welles, *Diary*, vol. 1, p. 109.
6. This description of Lee's crossing into Maryland is synthesized from Moore, *Story of a Cannoner*, p. 132; Hotchkiss, *Make Me a Map of the Valley*, p. 78; and Douglas, "Stonewall Jackson in Maryland," p. 620.
7. Evans, *Intrepid Warrior*, p. 169.
8. Douglas, "Stonewall Jackson in Maryland," p. 621n.
9. Hunter, "A High Private's Account of the Battle of Sharpsburg," p. 509.
10. McClellan, *McClellan's Own Story*, p. 552.
11. For this thinking I borrowed in part from Rafuse, *McClellan's War*, p. 280.
12. Sears, *George B. McClellan*, p. 277; Michie, *General McClellan*, p. 405.

13. McClellan, *Civil War Papers*, pp. 437–38.
14. Welles, *Diary*, vol. 1, p. 111.
15. O. R., ser. 1, vol. 19, pt. 2, p. 201.
16. McClellan, *Civil War Papers*, pp. 444–45.
17. Lincoln, *Collected Works*, vol. 5, pp. 410, 412, 412n; McClellan, *Civil War Papers*, pp. 443–44.
18. McClellan, *Civil War Papers*, p. 446.
19. Ibid., p. 442.
20. Ibid., p. 449.
21. Lincoln, *Collected Works*, vol. 5, p. 418.
22. Dowdey and Manarin, *Wartime Papers of R. E. Lee*, p. 300.
23. Strother, "Personal Recollections of the War," p. 275.
24. Steiner, "Maryland Invaded," pp. 173–74.
25. McClellan, *Civil War Papers*, p. 458.
26. Special Orders No. 191 is in O. R., ser. 1, vol. 19, pt. 2, pp. 603–4.
27. Walker, "Jackson's Capture of Harper's Ferry," pp. 605–6.
28. McClellan, *Civil War Papers*, p. 453.
29. Gibbon, *Personal Recollections of the Civil War*, p. 73.
30. Part of this is synthesized from Rafuse, *McClellan's War*, pp. 291–92.
31. McClellan, *Civil War Papers*, p. 457.
32. Thompson, "In the Ranks to the Antietam," p. 558.
33. McClellan, "From the Peninsula to Antietam," p. 551n.
34. Walker, "Jackson's Capture of Harper's Ferry," p. 611.
35. Hill, "Battle of South Mountain, or Boonsboro," pp. 564–65, 577.
36. Faust, *Historical Times Illustrated Encyclopedia of the Civil War*, pp. 189–90.
37. Lincoln, *Collected Works*, vol. 5, pp. 426n, 426.
38. Rafuse, *McClellan's War*, pp. 303–4.
39. Hassler, *General George B. McClellan*, p. 259.
40. Rafuse, *McClellan's War*, pp. 307, 305; Swinton, *Campaigns of the Army of the Potomac*, pp. 208, 209; Hassler, *General George B. McClellan*, pp. 264, 266–67.
41. Rafuse, *McClellan's War*, p. 305.

CHAPTER 18

1. Paraphrased from Goss, *Recollections of a Private*, pp. 104–5.
2. McClellan, *Civil War Papers*, p. 465; O. R., ser. 1, vol. 19, pt. 1, p. 30.
3. McClellan's plan and disposition are in O. R., ser. 1, vol. 19, pt. 1, p. 30.
4. This description of the movement of the armies borrows from Waugh, *Class of 1846*, p. 372, and from [English Combatant], *Battle-Fields of the South*, vol. 2, p. 350.
5. Thompson, "With Burnside at Antietam," p. 660.
6. Coffin, "Antietam Scenes," p. 682; Macartney, *Little Mac*, pp. 258, 256.
7. [English Combatant], *Battle-Fields of the South*, vol. 2, p. 351.
8. Coffin, "Antietam Scenes," pp. 682–83. Also see Waugh, *Class of 1846*, p. 373, for attendant description.
9. This description owes much to Rafuse, *McClellan's War*, pp. 315, 317, and Waugh, *Class of 1846*, pp. 373–74.
10. Macartney, *Little Mac*, p. 255.
11. Alexander, *Fighting for the Confederacy*, p 159.
12. Douglas, *I Rode with Stonewall*, p. 169. The general description in this paragraph is borrowed from Waugh, *Class of 1846*, p. 374.

13. Longstreet, "The Invasion of Maryland," p. 669. This account of the fighting at Bloody Lane also had help from Sears, *George B. McClellan*, pp. 310–12.
14. Strother, "Personal Recollections of the War," p. 283.
15. McClellan, *Civil War Papers*, p. 468.
16. Waugh, *Class of 1846*, p. 386. The McClellan quote is from Strother, "Personal Recollections of the War," p. 284.
17. Biddle, "Recollections of McClellan," p. 468.
18. Douglas, "Stonewall Jackson in Maryland," p. 629.

CHAPTER 19

1. Much of this description of Hill's division racing toward Sharpsburg is borrowed from Waugh, *Class of 1846*, pp. 378, 383, 387.
2. This account of the first sighting of Lee's troops on the battlefield is from an account by the lieutenant in Clark, *Histories of the Several Regiments*, vol. 1, p. 575.
3. Hunter, "A High Private's Sketch of Sharpsburg," pp. 19–20; Coffin, "Antietam Scenes," p. 684.
4. Clark, *Histories of the Several Regiments*, vol. 2, p. 33.
5. McClellan, *McClellan's Own Story*, p. 606; Catton, *American Heritage New History of the Civil War*, p. 226.
6. McClellan, *Civil War Papers*, p. 470.
7. Rafuse, *McClellan's War*, pp. 329, 330.
8. McClellan, *Civil War Papers*, p. 470.
9. Ibid., pp. 469, 473.
10. Strother, "Personal Recollections of the War," p. 287.
11. Lamon, *Recollections of Abraham Lincoln*, p. 289.
12. For Lincoln's views about an enemy driven from Union soil as opposed to being destroyed, see a letter he wrote to General Gordon Meade, but did not send or sign, following the Union victory at Gettysburg in July, 1863, in Lincoln, *Collected Works*, vol. 6. pp. 327–28.
13. Swinton, *Campaigns of the Army of the Potomac*, p. 224.
14. Longstreet, *From Manassas to Appomattox*, p. 188.
15. Strother, "Personal Recollections of the War," p. 291.
16. Alexander, *Fighting for the Confederacy*, p. 146.
17. Strother, "Personal Recollections of the War," p. 568.
18. This brief discussion of the problem of pursuit after Antietam borrows from Rowland, *George B. McClellan and Civil War History*, pp. 210–11, 225.
19. Quoted in Mitchell, *Civil War Soldiers*, p. 67.
20. Lincoln, *Collected Works*, vol. 5, p. 426; Fehrenbacher and Fehrenbacher, *Recollected Words of Abraham Lincoln*, p. 153.
21. A nice discussion of this thinking is in Rafuse, *McClellan's War*, pp. 332–33, 355.

CHAPTER 20

1. The proclamation is in Lincoln, *Collected Works*, vol. 5, pp. 433–36.
2. McClellan, *Civil War Papers*, p. 481.
3. Macartney, *Little Mac*, pp. 303–4.
4. McClellan, *Civil War Papers*, p. 486.
5. Ibid., pp. 473, 476.
6. Ibid., p. 481.

7. McClellan, *McClellan's Own Story*, p. 137.
8. Goss, *Recollections of a Private*, p. 76.
9. Hay, *Inside Lincoln's White House*, p. 192.
10. Lyman, *Meade's Headquarters*, p. 193; Wallace, *Autobiography*, vol. 2, p. 783.
11. Welles, *Diary*, vol. 1, pp. 119, 320, 384, 121.
12. Halleck's fears are reflected in O. R., ser. 1, vol. 19, pt. 2, pp. 201, 280–81, 330, 360.
13. McClellan, *Civil War Papers*, p. 354.
14. Ibid., pp. 482–83.
15. O. R., ser. 1, vol. 19, pt. 2, pp. 342–43; McClellan, *Civil War Papers*, p. 483.
16. Hay, *Inside Lincoln's White House*, p. 232.
17. Rice, *Reminiscences of Abraham Lincoln*, p. xxxix.
18. Nicolay and Hay, *Abraham Lincoln*, vol. 6, p. 175.
19. Hay, *Inside Lincoln's White House*, p. 232; Fehrenbacher and Fehrenbacher, *Recollected Words of Abraham Lincoln*, p. 132.
20. O. R. ser 1, vol. 19, pt. 1, p. 10.

CHAPTER 21

1. Meade, *Life and Letters of George Gordon Meade*, vol. 1, p. 320; Williams, *From the Cannon's Mouth*, p. 140.
2. McClellan, *Civil War Papers*, p. 502.
3. Wainwright, *Diary of Battle*, pp. 114–15.
4. O. R., ser. 1 vol. 19, pt. 2, p. 429.
5. O. R., ser. 3, vol. 2, pp. 703–4.
6. Lincoln's letter is in *Collected Works*, vol. 5, pp. 460–61.
7. Couch, "Sumner's 'Right Grand Division,'" pp. 105–6. Much of the account in this McClellan-Couch exchange is from Waugh, *Class of 1846*, p. 396.
8. Meade, *Life and Letters*, vol. 1, p. 320.
9. O. R., ser. 1, vol. 19, pt.1, p. 81.
10. Welles, *Diary*, vol. 1, p. 169.
11. Nicolay, *With Lincoln in the White House*, p. 89. The information about the two rides is from Long, *Civil War Day by Day*, pp. 225–26, and 278.
12. Macartney, *Little Mac*, pp. 288–89.
13. Rafuse, *McClellan's War*, p. 362.
14. This wire exchange about fatigued horses is from McClellan, *Civil War Papers*, p. 504, and O. R., ser. 1, vol. 19, pt. 2, pp. 484–85.
15. O. R., ser. 1, vol. 19, pt. 2, p. 485.
16. McClellan, *Civil War Papers*, pp. 511, 515.
17. Sears, *George B. McClellan*, p. 337.
18. McClellan, *Civil War Papers*, p. 516.
19. This view of McClellan's is succinctly put by Rafuse, in *McClellan's War*, pp. 361–62.
20. McClellan, *Civil War Papers*, p. 516.
21. Ibid.
22. Lincoln, *Collected Works*, vol. 5, p. 477.

CHAPTER 22

1. Hay, *Inside Lincoln's White House*, p. 232.
2. Fehrenbacher and Fehrenbacker, *Recollected Words of Abraham Lincoln*, p. 300.
3. This thinking is taken from a conversation with Lincoln's Illinois friend Orville Browning, in Browning's *Diary*, vol. 1, pp. 589–90.

4. Donaldson, *Inside the Army of the Potomac*, p. 158.
5. McClellan, *Civil War Papers*, pp. 518–19.
6. Fehrenbacher and Fehrenbacher, *Recollected Words of Abraham Lincoln*, p. 381.
7. This description of Blair's pleading on behalf of McClellan is borrowed from Waugh, *Class of 1846*, p. 349. The quotes are from Curtis, *McClellan's Last Service to the Republic*, p. 96, and Smith, *Francis Preston Blair Family in Politics*, vol. 2, p. 144.
8. Nicolay, *With Lincoln in the White House*, p. 91.
9. The account that follows of the firing of McClellan is distilled mainly from a letter by Buckingham to the *Chicago Tribune*, 4 September 1875, in Paris, *History of the Civil War in America*, vol. 2, pp. 555–57n. It also draws heavily on my own *Class of 1846*, pp. 397–403.
10. Boatner, *Civil War Dictionary*, p. 95; Warner, *Generals in Blue*, pp. 49–50.
11. Morford, *Red-Tape and Pigeon-Hole Generals*, p. 184.
12. Burnside is described in Walker, *History of the Second Army Corps*, p. 137. While he was well liked, simply no one thought Burnside commander-of-an-army material. Parmenas Taylor Turnley, an acid-tongued member of McClellan's class of 1846, wrote: "All there ever was of him [was], to wit, *his whiskers!*" (Turnley, *Reminiscences*, p. 409).
13. McClellan's thoughts, actions, and reactions are from *McClellan's Own Story*, pp. 651–52; and his *Civil War Papers*, p. 520.
14. U. S. Congress, *Report of the Joint Committee on the Conduct of the War*, vol. 1, p. 650.
15. McClellan, *Civil War Papers*, p. 520.
16. Couch, "Sumner's 'Right Grand Division,'" p. 106.
17. O. R., ser. 1, vol. 19, pt. 2, p. 551.
18. Gibbon, *Recollections of the Civil War*, p. 96.
19. Patrick, *Inside Lincoln's Army*, pp. 173–74.
20. Macartney, *Little Mac*, p. 192.
21. Cox, *Military Reminiscences of the Civil War*, vol. 1, p. 364.
22. Piatt, *Memories of the Men Who Saved the Union*, p. 294.
23. O. R., ser. 1, vol. 19, pt. 2, p. 551; McClellan, *McClellan's Own Story*, pp. 652–53.
24. *New York World*, 12 November 1862.
25. Patrick, *Inside Lincoln's Army*, p. 174.
26. Gibbon, *Recollections of the Civil War*, pp. 97–98.
27. Wainwright, *Diary of Battle*, p. 125.
28. McClellan, *Civil War Papers*, p. 522.
29. Wainwright, *Diary of Battle*, p. 125; Walker, *History of the Second Army Corps*, pp. 137–38.
30. *New York Times*, 12 November 1862.
31. Rusling, *Men and Things I Saw in Civil War Days*, p. 258. For more on that minority point of view, see the *New York Times*, 12 November 1862, and Morford, *Red-Tape and Pigeon-Hole Generals*, pp. 178–92.
32. Morford, *Red-Tape and Pigeon-Hole Generals*, p. 188.
33. McClellan, *McClellan's Own Story*, p. 150; Gibbon, *Personal Recollections of the Civil War*, p. 97; Strother, "Personal Recollections of the War," p. 582.
34. Douglas, *I Rode with Stonewall*, p. 202.
35. Nisbet, *Four Years on the Firing Line*, p. 116.
36. Longstreet, "The Battle of Fredericksburg," p. 70.

CHAPTER 23

1. Bates, *Lincoln in the Telegraph Office*, pp. 103–4.
2. Sears in *George B. McClellan* names and discusses this coterie of Democrats, pp. 345–46. For details about the home they bought for the general see Myers, *General George Brinton McClellan*, p. 405.

3. McClure, *Recollections of Half a Century*, pp. 318–19.
4. Lincoln had said that about himself when he was emerging as a potential presidential candidate in 1860. See Lincoln, *Collected Works*, vol. 4, p. 45.
5. McClellan's exchange with his mother is in *Civil War Papers*, pp. 563n, 563.
6. Much of the tenor and wording of this early discussion of McClellan's career in presidential politics is borrowed from my own book, *Reelecting Lincoln*, pp. 23–31. I will be relying on it to some degree through this chapter and the next two.
7. *New York Tribune*, 9 November 1860.
8. Roseboom, *History of Presidential Elections*, pp. 191–92.
9. *Cincinnati Daily Commercial*, 4 September 1861, 15 May 1862.
10. Waugh, *Reelecting Lincoln*, p. 90.
11. *New York Herald*, 24 June 1864.
12. Fermer, *James Gordon Bennett and the New York Herald*, p. 266.
13. This summary of things in common is paraphrased from Waugh, *Reelecting Lincoln*, p. 91.
14. Brooks, *Mr. Lincoln's Washington*, pp. 13, 69; Hay, *Inside Lincoln's White House*, p. 120.
15. Waugh, *Reelecting Lincoln*, pp. 93–94.

CHAPTER 24

1. Lincoln, *Collected Works*, vol. 8, p. 101.
2. Chase, *Inside Lincoln's Cabinet*, p. 18.
3. *Richmond Examiner*, 12 August 1864, reprinted in the *New York World*, 16 August 1864.
4. Butler, *Private and Official Correspondence*, vol. 5, p. 67.
5. The Weed and Raymond quotes are in Lincoln, *Collected Works*, vol. 7, pp. 514n, 517–18n.
6. Greeley's view was included twenty-five years later in a long article detailing a call for a new convention in the summer to pick a new nominee replacing Lincoln. See the *New York Sun*, 30 June 1889.
7. Tarbell, *Life of Abraham Lincoln*, vol. 2, p. 201.
8. Nicolay, *With Lincoln in the White House*, pp. 153, 151.
9. Hay, *At Lincoln's Side*, p. 92.
10. Lincoln, *Collected Works*, vol. 7, p. 506.
11. Butler, *Private and Official Correspondence*, vol. 5, p. 35.
12. Waugh, *Reelecting Lincoln*, p. 360.
13. Lincoln, *Collected Works*, vol. 7, p. 514.
14. Cyrus H. McCormick to Manton Marble, 17 August 1864, Marble Papers.
15. *New York Times*, 11 August 1864.
16. McClellan, *Civil War Papers*, p. 586.
17. Sidney Brooks to George McClellan, 15 July 1864, McClellan Papers.
18. Brooks, *Washington in Lincoln's Time*, p. 164.
19. Lincoln, *Collected Works*, vol. 7, p. 524n.
20. Hay, *At Lincoln's Side*, p. 91.
21. *Chicago Times*, 25 August 1864.
22. *Chicago Tribune*, 27 August 1864.
23. Waugh, *Reelecting Lincoln*, pp. 280, 283.
24. *Official Proceedings of the Democratic National Convention*, p. 27.
25. Waugh, *Reelecting Lincoln*, p. 286.
26. A detailed account of the chaos on the floor and its outcome is in ibid., pp. 286–92.
27. Brooks, *Mr. Lincoln's Washington*, pp. 378–79.
28. Fehrenbacher and Fehrenbacher, *Recollected Words of Abraham Lincoln*, p. 355.

CHAPTER 25

1. O. R., ser. 1, vol. 38, pt. 5, p. 777.
2. Butler, *Private and Official Correspondence*, vol. 5, p. 35.
3. Unidentified letter from Philadelphia, 19 September 1864, Marble Papers.
4. Nicolay, *Personal Traits of Abraham Lincoln*, pp. 308–9; Fehrenbacher and Fehrenbacher, *Recollected Words of Abraham Lincoln*, p. 446.
5. McClellan, *Civil War Papers*, pp. 593–94.
6. The text of McClellan's letter is in *Official Proceedings of the Democratic National Convention*, 60–61, and McClellan, *Civil War Papers*, pp. 590–92.
7. Dittennoefer, *How We Elected Lincoln*, pp. 87–88.
8. E. W. Dennis to Joseph Holt, 24 October 1864, Holt Papers.
9. Rafuse discusses these deserters from Lincoln's side in *McClellan's War*, pp. 54–55.
10. Waugh, *Reelecting Lincoln*, p. 312.
11. A summary of the criminations and recriminations from both sides is in the *New York Herald*, 4 November 1864.
12. Waugh, *Reelecting Lincoln*, pp. 327–28.
13. For a detailed account of Lincoln's lever pulling see ibid., pp. 329–31. In their biography, *Stanton*, Thomas and Hyman devote a chapter to the behind-the-scenes maneuvering of the secretary of war on Lincoln's behalf, pp. 318–35.
14. Sears, *George B. McClellan*, p. 379.
15. *New York Times*, 8 November 1864.
16. McClellan, *Civil War Papers*, p. 618.

EPILOGUE

1. McClellan, *McClellan's Own Story*, p. 20.
2. Ibid., p. 17.
3. Myers, *General George Brinton McClellan*, pp. 512–13.
4. Sears, *George B. McClellan*, p. 401; Maury, *Recollections of a Virginian*, p. 60; Gardner, "Memoirs," p. 8.
5. Curtis, *McClellan's Last Service to the Republic*, p. 126.
6. Franklin, "First Great Crime of the War," p. 81.
7. Rusling, *Men and Things I Saw in Civil War Days*, p. 24.
8. Fry, "McClellan and his Mission," p. 932.
9. Walker, *History of the Second Army Corps*, p. 138.
10. Rusling, *Men and Things I Saw in the Civil War,* p. 37.
11. Strother, "Personal Recollections of the War," p. 581.
12. *Cincinnati Gazette*, August 11, 1862, in Fehrenbacher and Fehrenbacher, *Recollected Words of Abraham Lincoln*, p. 10.
13. Piatt, *Memories of the Men Who Saved the Union*, p. 290.
14. Gurowski, *Diary*, vol. 1, pp. 127–28.
15. Quoted in Meigs, "General M. C. Meigs on the Conduct of the Civil War," p. 292.
16. Sears, *George B. McClellan*, p. 253.
17. Hay, *Inside Lincoln's White House*, p. 30.

SOURCES CITED

Alexander, Edward Porter. *Fighting for the Confederacy: The Personal Recollections of General Edward Porter Alexander.* Edited by Gary W. Gallagher. Chapel Hill, NC: University of North Carolina Press, 1989.

Ambrose, Stephen E. Halleck. *Lincoln's Chief of Staff.* Baton Rouge, LA: Louisiana State University Press, 1996.

Angle, Paul M., ed. *Abraham Lincoln by Some Men Who Knew Him.* Chicago: Americana House Publishers, 1950.

Barnard, J. G. *The Peninsular Campaign and Its Antecedents, as Developed by the Report of Maj.-Gen Geo. B. McClellan, and other Published Documents.* New York: D. van Nostrand, 1864.

Barton, William E. *The Paternity of Abraham Lincoln: Was He the Son of Thomas Lincoln?* New York: George H. Doran Co., 1920.

Bates, Edward. *The Diary of Edward Bates, 1859–1866.* Edited by Howard K. Beale. Washington, DC: United States Government Printing Office, 1933.

Bates, David Homer. *Lincoln in the Telegraph Office: Recollections of the United States Military Telegraph Corps during the Civil War.* New York: Century Co., 1907.

Beatty, John. *Memoirs of a Volunteer, 1861–1863.* Edited by Harvey S. Ford. New York: W. W. Norton, 1946.

Biddle, William F. "Recollections of McClellan." *United Service: A Quarterly Review of Military and Naval Affairs* 11 (May 1894): 460–69.

Bird, Edgeworth, and Sallie Bird. *The Granite Farm Letters: The Civil War Correspondence of Edgeworth & Sallie Bird.* Edited by John Rozier. Athens, GA: University of Georgia Press, 1988.

Boatner, Mark Mayo III. *The Civil War Dictionary.* New York: David McKay Co., 1959.

Borrett, George. "An Englishman in Washington in 1864." *Magazine of History with Notes and Queries* 38 (1929): 5–15.

Brooks, Noah. *Mr. Lincoln's Washington: Selections from the Writings of Noah Brooks, Civil War Correspondent.* Edited by P. J. Staudenraus. South Brunswick, NJ: Thomas Yoseloff, 1967.

———. *Washington in Lincoln's Time.* Edited by Herbert Mitgang. New York: Rinehart & Co., 1958.

Browning, Orville Hickman. *The Diary of Orville Hickman Browning, 1850–1864.* Edited by Theodore Calvin Pease and James G. Randall. 2 vols. Springfield, IL: Illinois State Historical Library, 1925.

Brownson, Howard Gray. *History of the Illinois Central Railroad to 1870.* Urbana, IL: University of Illinois Press, 1915.

Butler, Benjamin F. *Private and Official Correspondence of Gen. Benjamin F. Butler during the Period of the Civil War.* Edited by Jessie A. Marshall. 5 vols. Norwood, MA: Plimpton Press, 1917.

Castleman, Alfred L. *The Army of the Potomac. Behind the Scenes. A Diary of Unwritten History; from the Organization of the Army by General George B. McClellan, to the Close of the Campaign in Virginia, about the First Day of January, 1863.* Milwaukee, WI: Strickland & Co., 1863.

Catton, Bruce. *The American Heritage New History of the Civil War.* Edited by James M. McPherson, New York: Viking, 1996.

——. *The Army of the Potomac: Mr. Lincoln's Army.* Garden City, NY: Doubleday & Co., 1962.

Chase, Salmon P. *Inside Lincoln's Cabinet: The Civil War Diaries of Salmon P. Chase.* Edited by David Donald. New York: Longmans, Green & Co., 1954.

——. *The Salmon P. Chase Papers: Vol. 1. Journals, 1829–1872.* Kent, OH: Kent State University Press, 1993.

Chicago Times.

Chicago Tribune.

Chittenden. L. E. *Recollections of President Lincoln and His Administration.* New York: Harper & Brothers, 1891.

Cincinnati Daily Commercial.

Cincinnati Gazette

Clark, Walter, ed. *Histories of the Several Regiments and Battalions from North Carolina in the Great War, 1861–65.* 5 vols. 1901. Reprint. Wilmington, NC: Broadfoot Publishing Co., 1991.

Coffin, Charles Carleton. "Antietam Scenes." In *Battles and Leaders of the Civil War,* vol. 2, edited by Robert U. Johnson and Clarence C. Buel. 1887. Reprint. Secaucus, NJ: Castle, n.d.

Cook, Joel. *The Siege of Richmond: A Narrative of Military Operations of Major-General George B. McClellan during the Months of May and June 1862.* Philadelphia: George W. Childs, 1862.

Corliss, Carlton J. *Main Line of Mid-America; The Story of the Illinois Central.* New York; Creative Age Press, 1950.

Couch, Darius N. "Sumner's 'Right Grand Division.'" In *Battles and Leaders of the Civil War,* Vol. 3, edited by Robert U. Johnson and Clarence C. Buel, 1887. Reprint, Secaucus, NJ: Castle, n.d.

Cox. Jacob D. *Military Reminiscences of the Civil War.* 2 vols. New York: Charles Scribner's Sons, 1900.

——. "McClellan in West Virginia." In *Battles and Leaders of the Civil War,* vol. 1, edited by Robert U. Johnson and Clarence C. Buel. 1887. Reprint. Secaucus, NJ: Castle, n.d.

——. "War Preparations in the North." In *Battles and Leaders of the Civil War,* vol. 1, edited by Robert U. Johnson and Clarence C. Buel. 1887. Reprint. Secaucus, NJ: Castle, n. d.

Cozzens, Peter. *General John Pope: A Life for the Nation.* Urbana, IL: University of Illinois Press, 2000.

Current, Richard N. "Lincoln and the Eighth Circuit." Paper delivered at the Lincoln Colloquium, 11 October 1987, Springfield, IL.

Curtis, George Ticknor. *McClellan's Last Service to the Republic, together with a Tribute to His Memory.* New York: D. Appleton & Co., 1886.

Davis, Varina H. *Jefferson Davis, Ex-President of the Confederate States of America: A Memoir by His Wife.* 2 vols. 1890. Reprint. Freeport, NY: Books for Libraries Press, 1971.

Davis, William C., and Julie Hoffman, eds. *The Confederate General.* 6 vols. n.p.: National Historical Society, 1991.

Derby, George Horatio. George Horatio Derby Papers. U. S. Military Academy Library, West Point, NY.

Dittenhoefer, Abram J. *How We Elected Lincoln: Personal Recollections of Lincoln and Men of His Time.* New York: Harper & Brothers, 1916.

Donald, David Herbert, *Lincoln.* New York: Simon & Schuster, 1995.

Donaldson, Francis Adams. *Inside the Army of the Potomac: The Civil War Experience of Captain Francis Adams Donaldson.* Edited by J. Gregory Acken. Mechanicsburg, PA: Stackpole Books, 1998.

Doster, William E. *Lincoln and Episodes of the Civil War.* New York: G. P. Putnam's Sons, 1915.

Douglas, Henry Kyd. *I Rode with Stonewall.* Chapel Hill, NC: University of North Carolina Press, 1968.

———. "Stonewall Jackson in Maryland." In *Battles and Leaders of the Civil War,* vol. 2, edited by Robert U. Johnson and Clarence C. Buel. 1887. Reprint. Secaucus, NJ. Castle, n. d.

Dowdey, Clifford, and Louis H. Manarin, eds. *The Wartime Paper of Robert E. Lee.* Boston: Little, Brown & Co., 1961.

Doyle, Joseph B. *In Memorium, Edwin McMasters Stanton: His Life and Work.* Steubenville, OH: Herald Printing Company, 1911.

[English Combatant.] *Battle-Fields of the South, from Bull Run to Fredericksburg; with Sketches of Confederate Commanders, and Gossip of the Camps.* 2 vols. London: Smith, Elder & Co.. 1863.

Evans, Clement Anselm. *Intrepid Warrior, Clement Anselm Evans, Confederate General from Georgia: Life, Letters, and Diaries of the War Years.* Compiled and edited by Robert Grier Stephens, Jr. Dayton, OH; Morningside, 1992.

Faust, Patricia L., ed. *Historical Times Illustrated Encyclopedia of the Civil War.* New York: Harper & Row, 1986.

Fehrenbacher, Don E. *Prelude to Greatness: Lincoln in the 1850s.* Stanford, CA: Stanford University Press, 1962.

Fehrenbacher, Don E. and Virginia Fehrenbacher, eds. *Recollected Words of Abraham Lincoln.* Stanford, CA: Stanford University Press, 1996.

Fermer, Douglas. *James Gordon Bennett and the New York Herald: A Study of Editorial Opinion in the Civil War Era, 1854–1867.* New York: St. Martin's Press, 1986.

Franklin, William B. "The First Great Crime of the War." In *The Annals of the War, Written by the Leading Participants North and South.* Dayton, OH: Morningside House, 1988.

———. "Rear-Guard Fighting during the Change of Base," In *Battles and Leaders of the Civil War,* vol. 2, edited by Robert U. Johnson and Clarence C. Buel. 1887. Reprint. Secaucus, NJ: Castle, n.d.

Frobel, Anne S. *The Civil War Diary of Anne S. Frobel.* Edited by Mary H. and Dallas M. Lancaster. 1986. Reprint. McLean, VA: EPM Publications, 1992.

Fry, James B. "McClellan and His Mission." *The Century Magazine* 48 (October 1894): 931–46.

Gardner, William Montgomery. "The Memoirs of Brigadier-General William Montgomery Gardner." Edited by Elizabeth McKinne Gardner. Typescript copy of a series of articles in the *Memphis Commercial Appeal,* 1912. U. S. Military Academy Library, West Point, NY.

"General McClellan," *Atlantic Monthly* 59 (April 1887): 546–59.

Gibbon, John. *Personal Recollections of the Civil War.* 1928. Reprint. Dayton, OH: Press of Morningside Bookshop, 1988.

Gilmore, James R. *Personal Recollections of Abraham Lincoln and the Civil War.* 1898. Reprint. Mechanicsburg, PA: Stackpole Books, 2007.

Goss, Warren Lee. *Recollections of a Private: A Story of the Army of the Potomac.* New York: Thomas Y. Crowell & Co., 1890.

Gurowski, Adam. *Diary. 3* vols. 1862–1866 .Reprint, New York: Burt Franklin, 1968.

Harwell, Richard B. *The Union Reader.* New York, Longmans, Green & Co., 1958.

Harsh, Joseph L. *Soundings the Shallows: A Confederate Companion for the Maryland Campaign of 1862.* Kent, OH: Kent State University Press, 2000.

Hassler, Warren W., Jr. *General George B. McClellan: Shield of the Union*. Baton Rouge, LA: Louisiana State University Press, 1957.

Haupt, Herman. *Reminiscences of General Herman Haupt*. Milwaukee, WI: Wright & Joys Co., 1901.

Hawthorne, Julian. *Hawthorne and His Wife: A Biography*. 2d ed. 2 vols. Boston: James R. Osgood & Co., 1885.

Hawthorne, Nathaniel. "Chiefly about War Matters." In *Tales, Sketches and Other Papers*. University Edition. New York: Sully and Kleinteich, 1883.

Hay, John. *Lincoln and the Civil War in the Diaries and Letters of John Hay*. Selected by Tyler Dennett. New York: Dodd, Mead & Co., 1939.

———. *At Lincoln's Side: John Hay's Civil War Correspondence and Selected Writings*. Edited by Michael Burlingame. Carbondale, IL: Southern Illinois University Press, 2000.

———. *Inside Lincoln's White House: The Complete Civil War Diary of John Hay*. Edited by Michael Burlingame and John R. Turner Ettlinger. Carbondale, IL: Southern Illinois University Press, 1997.

Heintzelman, Samuel P. *The Journal of Samuel P. Heintzelman*. Manuscript Division, Library of Congress, Washington, DC.

Herndon, William H., and Jesse W. Weik. *Herndon's Life of Lincoln*. Introduction and Notes by Paul M. Angle. Cleveland, OH: World Publishing Co., 1943.

Hill, D. H. "The Battle of South Mountain, or Boonsboro." In *Battles and Leaders of the Civil War*. Edited by Robert U. Johnson and Clarence C. Buel. 1887. Reprint. Secaucus, NJ: Castle, n.d.

Holt, Joseph. Papers. Manuscript Division, Library of Congress, Washington, DC.

Holzer, Harold, ed. *The Lincoln Anthology: Great Writers on His Life and Legacy from 1860 to Now*. New York: Library of America, 2009.

Hotchkiss, Jedediah. *Make Me a Map of the Valley: The Civil War Journal of Stonewall Jackson's Topographer*. Edited by Archie P. McDonald. Dallas, TX: Southern Methodist University Press, 1989.

Hunter, Alexander. "A High Private's Account of the Battle of Sharpsburg." Papers No. 1 and 2. *Southern Historical Society Papers* 10 (1882): 503–12; 11 (1883): 10–21.

Illinois State Journal.

Illinois State Register.

Johnston, Joseph E. "Manassas to Seven Pines." In *Battles and Leaders of the Civil War*, Vol. 2, edited by Robert U. Johnson and Clarence C. Buel. 1887. Reprint. Secaucus, NJ: Castle, n.d.

Jones, J. William. *Personal Reminiscences, Anecdotes, and Letters of Gen. Robert E. Lee*. New York; D. Appleton & Co., 1876.

Julian, George W. *Political Recollections, 1840–1872*. 1884. Reprint. Miami, FL: Mnemosyne Publishing Co., 1969.

Kelley, William D. *Lincoln and Stanton: A Study of the War Administration of 1861 and 1862, with Special Consideration of Some Recent Statements of Gen. Geo. B. McClellan*. New York: G. P. Putnam's Sons, 1885.

Keyes, Erasmus D. *Fifty Years' Observation of Men and Events Civil and Military*. New York: Charles Scribner's Sons, 1884.

Lamon, Ward Hill. *Recollections of Abraham Lincoln*. Edited by Dorothy Lamon Teillard. 1895. Reprint. Lincoln, NE: 1994.

Lincoln, Abraham. *The Collected Works of Abraham Lincoln*. Edited by Roy P. Basler. 8 vols. New Brunswick, NJ: Rutgers University Press, 1953.

Long, E. B., with Barbara Long. *The Civil War Day by Day: An Almanac, 1861–1865*. Garden City, NY: Doubleday & Co., 1971.

Longstreet, James. *From Manassas to Appomattox*. 1895. Reprint. New York: Great Commanders, 1994.

———. "The Battle of Fredericksburg." In *Battles and Leaders of the Civil War,* vol. 3, edited by Robert U. Johnson and Clarence C. Buel. 1887. Reprint Secaucus, NJ: Castle, n.d.

———. "The Invasion of Maryland." In *Battles and Leaders of the Civil War,* vol. 2, edited by Robert U. Johnson and Clarence C. Buel. 1887, Reprint. Secaucus, NJ: Castle, n.d.

———. "'The Seven Days,' Including Frayser's Farm." In *Battles and Leaders of the Civil War,* Vol. 2, edited by Robert U. Johnson and Clarence C. Buel. 1887. Reprint. Secaucus, NJ: Castle, n.d.

Lowell, James Russell. "General McClellan's Report," *North American Review* 98 (April 1864): 550–66.

Lufkin, Richard Friend. "Mr. Lincoln's Light from Under a Bushel—1850," *Lincoln Herald* 52 (December 1950): 2–20.

Lyman, Theodore. *Meade's Headquarters, 1863–1865*. Edited by George R. Agassiz. Boston: Atlantic Monthly Press, 1922.

Macartney, Clarence E. *Little Mac: The Life of General George B. McClellan*. Philadelphia: Dorrance & Co., 1940.

Manarin, Louis H., ed. *Richmond at War: The Minutes of the City Council, 1861–1865*. Chapel Hill, NC: University of North Carolina Press, 1966.

Marble, Manton M. Papers. Manuscript Division, Library of Congress, Washington, DC.

Martineau, Harriet. *Retrospect of Western Travel*. 3 vols. 1838. Reprint. New York: Greenwood Press, 1969.

Maurois, André. "A Princely Service," *American Heritage* 17 (April 1966): 52–63, 80–81.

Maury, Dabney Herndon. *Recollections of a Virginian in the Mexican, Indian, and Civil Wars*. 3d Ed. New York: Charles Scribner's Sons, 1894.

———. "General T. J. (Stonewall) Jackson: Incidents in a Remarkable Career of the Great Soldier," *Southern Historical Society Papers* 25 (1897): 309–16.

McClellan, George B. *The Civil War Papers of George B. McClellan: Selected Correspondence, 1860–1865*. Edited by Stephen W. Sears. New York: Ticknor & Fields, 1989.

———. *McClellan's Own Story: The War for the Union, the Soldiers Who Fought It, the Civilians Who Directed It, and His Relations to It and to Them*. Edited by William C. Prime. New York: Charles L. Webster & Co., 1887.

———. *The Mexican War Diary of George B. McClellan*. Edited by William Starr Myers. Princeton, NJ: Princeton University Press, 1917.

———. Papers. Manuscript Division, Library of Congress, Washington, DC.

———. *Report on the Organization and Campaigns of the Army of the Potomac, to Which Is Added an Account of the Campaign in Western Virginia, with Plans of Battle-Fields*. New York: Sheldon & Co, 1864.

———. "From the Peninsula to Antietam." In *Battles and Leaders of the Civil War*. Vol. 2, edited by Robert U. Johnson and Clarence C. Buel. 1887. Reprint. Secaucus, NJ: Castle, n. d.

McClure, Alexander K. *Abraham Lincoln and Men of War-Times: Some Personal Recollections of War and Politics during the Lincoln Administration*. 3d ed. Philadelphia: Times Publishing Co., 1892.

———. *Colonel Alexander K. McClure's Recollections of Half a Century*. Salem, MA: Salem Press Co., 1902.

———. *Lincoln's Yarns and Stories: A Complete Collection of the Funny and Witty Anecdotes that Made Abraham Lincoln Famous as America's Greatest Story Teller*. Chicago: John C. Winston Co., n. d.

McCulloch, Hugh. *Men and Measures of Half a Century: Sketches and Comments*. New York; Charles Scribner's Sons, 1889.

McDowell, Irvin. "Manuscript Minutes of Council of War." In William Swinton, *Campaigns of the Army of the Potomac*. 1866. Reprint. Secaucus, NJ: Blue & Grey Press, 1988.

Meade, George Gordon, ed. *Life and Letters of George Gordon Meade*. 2 vols. New York: Charles Scribner's Sons, 1913.

Meigs, Montgomery C. "General M. C. Meigs on the Conduct of the Civil War," *American Historical Review* 26 (January 1921): 285–303.

Michie, Peter S. *General McClellan*. New York: Appleton, 1901.

Miers, Earl Schenck, ed. *Lincoln Day By Day: A Chronology, 1809–1865*. 3 vols. Washington, DC: Lincoln Sesquicentennial Commission, 1960.

Mitchell, Reid. *Civil War Soldiers*. New York: Viking, 1988.

Moore, Edward A. *The Story of a Cannoneer under Stonewall Jackson*. Lynchburg, VA: J. P. Bell Co. 1910.

Morford, Henry. *Red-Tape and Pigeon-Hole Generals: As Seen from the Ranks during a Campaign in the Army of the Potomac*. New York: Carleton, 1864.

Morrison, James L., Jr., ed. "Getting through West Point: The Cadet Memoirs of John C. Tidball, Class of 1848," *Civil War History* 26 (December 1980): 304–25.

Myers. William Starr. *General George Brinton McClellan: A Study in Personality*. New York: D. Appleton, 1834.

Nevins, Allan. *Abram S. Hewitt, with Some Account of Peter Cooper*. New York: Harper & Brothers, 1935.

———. *The War for the Union: War becomes Revolution, 1862–1863*. New York: Charles Scribner's Sons, 1960.

Newton, Joseph Fort. *Lincoln and Herndon*. Cedar Rapids, IA: Torch Press, 1910.

New York Herald.

New York Sun.

New York Times.

New York Tribune.

New York World.

Nicolay, Helen. *Lincoln's Secretary: A Biography of John G. Nicolay*. New York: Longmans, Green & Co., 1949.

———. *Personal Traits of Abraham Lincoln*. New York: Century Co., 1912.

Nicolay, John G. *With Lincoln in the White House: Letters, Memoranda, and Other Writings of John G. Nicolay, 1860–1865*. Edited by Michael Burlingame. Carbondale, IL: Southern Illinois University Press, 2000.

Nicolay, John G., and John Hay. *Abraham Lincoln: A History*. 10 vols. New York: Century Co., 1890.

Nisbet, James Cooper. *Four Years on the Firing Line*. Edited by Bell Irvin Wiley. 1963. Reprint. Wilmington, NC: Broadfoot Publishing Co., 1987.

Official Proceedings of the Democratic National Convention Held in 1864 at Chicago. Chicago: Times Steam Book and Job Printing House, 1864.

O. R. (Official Records) U. S. War Department. *The War of the Rebellion: A Compilation of the Official Records of the Union and Confederate Armies*. 70 vols. in 128 parts. 1880–1901. Reprint. Harrisburg, PA: Historical Times, 1985.

Paris, Philippe Comte de. *History of the Civil War in America*. 4 vols. Edited by Henry Coppee. Philadelphia: J. H. Coates & Co., 1875.

———. "McClellan Organizing the Grand Army." In *Battles and Leaders of the Civil War*, vol. 2, edited by Robert U. Johnson and Clarence C. Buel. 1887. Reprint. Secaucus, NJ: Castle, n.d.

Patrick, Marsena R. *Inside Lincoln's Army: The Diary of Marsena Rudolph Patrick, Provost Marshal General, Army of the Potomac*. Edited by David S. Sparks. New York: Thomas Yoseloff, 1964.

Piatt, Donn. *Memories of the Men Who Saved the Union*. New York: Bedford, Clarke, & Co., 1887.

Rafuse, Ethan S. *McClellan's War: The Failure of Moderation in the Struggle for the Union*. Bloomington, IN: Indiana University Press, 2005.

Rice, Allen Thorndike, ed. *Reminiscences of Abraham Lincoln by Distinguished Men of His Time*. 1888. Reprint. New York: Haskell House Publishers, 1971.

Richmond Examiner.

Riddle, Albert Gallatin. *Recollections of War Times: Reminiscences of Men and Events in Washington, 1860–1865*. New York: G. P. Putnam's Sons, 1895.

Robertson, James I., Jr. *General A. P. Hill: The Story of a Confederate Warrior*. New York: Random House, 1987.

Ropes, John Codman. *The Army under Pope*. New York: Charles Scribner's Sons, 1905.

Roseboom, Eugene H. *A History of Presidential Elections: From George Washington to Richard M. Nixon*. 3d ed. New York: Macmillan, 1970.

Rowland, Thomas J. *George B. McClellan and Civil War History: In the Shadow of Grant and Sherman*. Kent, OH: Kent University Press, 1998.

Rusling, James F. *Men and Things I Saw in Civil War Days*. New York: Eaton & Mains, 1899.

Russell, William Howard. *My Diary North and South*. Edited by Eugene H. Berwanger. 1988. Reprint with new material. Baton Rouge, LA: Louisiana State University Press, 2001.

Sandburg, Carl. "The Face of Lincoln." In Frederick Hill Meserve and Carl Sandburg, *The Photographs of Abraham Lincoln*. New York: Harcourt, Brace, 1944.

Sears, Stephen W. *George B. McClellan: The Young Napoleon*. New York: Ticknor & Fields, 1988.

Seward, Frederick W. *Reminiscences of a War-Time Statesman and Diplomat, 1830–1915*. New York: G. P. Putnam's Sons, 1916.

Shakespeare, William. *Love's Labor's Lost*. In *The Yale Shakespeare*. Edited by Karl Young. New Haven, CT: Yale University Press, 1961.

———. *Troilus and Cressida*. In *The Yale Shakespeare*. Edited by Karl Young. New Haven, CT: Yale University Press, 1961.

Smith, Gustavus W. *Company "A," Corps of Engineers, U. S. A., 1846–'48, in the Mexican War*. N.p.: Battalion Press, 1896.

Smith, William Ernest. *The Francis Preston Blair Family in Politics*. 2 vols. New York: Macmillan, 1933.

Steiner, Lewis H. "Maryland Invaded." In *The Union Reader: As the North Saw the War*. Edited by Richard B. Harwell. New York: Longmans, Green & Co., 1958.

Stover, John F. *History of the Illinois Central Railroad*. New York: Macmillan, 1975.

Strother, David Hunter. "Personal Recollections of the War. By a Virginian." *Harper's New Monthly Magazine* 36 (February 1868): 273–91, (April 1868): 567–82.

Sunderland, Edwin S. S. *Abraham Lincoln and the Illinois Central Railroad, Main Line of Mid-America*. New York: Privately printed, 1955.

Swinton, William. *Campaigns of the Army of the Potomac*. 1866. Reprint. Secaucus, NJ: Blue & Grey Press, 1988.

Tap, Bruce. *Over Lincoln's Shoulder: The Committee on the Conduct of the War*. Lawrence, KS: University of Kansas Press, 1998.

Tarbell, Ida M. *The Life of Abraham Lincoln*. 2 vols. New York: Lincoln Memorial Association, 1900.

Thomas, Benjamin P., and Harold M. Hyman. *Stanton: The Life and Times of Lincoln's Secretary of War*. New York: Alfred A. Knopf, 1962.

Thompson, David L. "In the Ranks to the Antietam." In *Battles and Leaders of the Civil War,* Vol. 2, edited by Robert U. Johnson and Clarence C. Buel. 1887. Reprint. Secaucus, NJ: Castle, n.d.

———. "With Burnside at Antietam." In *Battles and Leaders of the Civil War,* vol. 2, edited by Robert U. Johnson and Clarence C. Buel. 1887. Reprint. Secaucus, NJ: Castle, n. d.

Turnley, Parmenas Taylor. *Reminiscences of Parmenas Taylor Turnley: From the Cradle to Three-Score and Ten.* Chicago: Donahue & Henneberry, 1892.

U. S. Congress. *Report of the Joint Committee on the Conduct of the War. Part 1: Army of the Potomac.* 6 vols. Washington, DC: Government Printing Office, 1863–1865.

Upton, Emory. *The Military Policy of the United States.* 4th Impression. Washington, DC: United States Government Printing Office, 1917.

Wainwright. Charles S. *A Diary of Battle: The Personal Journals of Colonel Charles S. Wainwright, 1861–1865.* Edited by Allan Nevins. New York: Harcourt, Brace & World, 1962.

Walker, Francis A. *History of the Second Army Corps in the Army of the Potomac.* New York: Charles Scribner's Sons, 1886.

Walker, John G. "Jackson's Capture of Harper's Ferry." In *Battles and Leaders of the Civil War,* Vol. 2, edited by Robert U. Johnson and Clarence C. Buel. 1887. Reprint. Secaucus, NJ: Castle, n. d.

Wallace, Lew. *Lew Wallace: An Autobiography.* 2 vols. New York: Harper & Brothers, 1906.

Warner, Ezra. *Generals in Blue: Lives of the Union Commanders.* Baton Rouge, LA: Louisiana State University Press, 1992.

———. *Generals in Gray: Lives of the Confederate Commanders.* Baton Rouge, LA: Louisiana State University Press, 1987.

Waugh, John C. *The Class of 1846: From West Point to Appomattox—Stonewall Jackson, George McClellan and Their Brothers.* New York Warner Books, 1994.

———. *One Man Great Enough: Abraham Lincoln's Road to Civil War.* New York: Harcourt, 2007.

———. *Reelecting Lincoln: The Battle for the 1864 Presidency.* New York: Crown Publishers, 1997.

Weik, Jesse W. *The Real Lincoln: A Portrait.* Boston: Houghton Mifflin Co., 1922.

Welles, Gideon. *Diary of Gideon Welles.* 3 vols. Houghton Mifflin Co., 1911.

———. *Lincoln and Seward.* 1874. Reprint. Freeport, NY: Books for Libraries Press, 1969.

Whitney, Henry C. *Lincoln the Citizen. Vol. 1 of Life of Lincoln.* New York: Current Literature Publishing Co., 1907.

Williams, Alpheus S. *From the Cannon's Mouth: The Civil War Letters of General Alpheus S. Williams.* Edited by Milo M. Quaife. Detroit, MI: Wayne State University Press, 1959.

Wilson, Douglas L., and Rodney O. Davis, eds. *Herndon's Informants: Letters, Interviews, and Statements about Abraham Lincoln.* Urbana, IL: University of Illinois Press, 1998.

Wilson, James Harrison. *Under the Old Flag: Recollections of Military Operations in the War for the Union.* 2 vols. New York: D. Appleton & Co., 1912.

Wilson, Rufus Rockwell. *Intimate Memories of Lincoln.* Elmira, NY: Primavera Press, 1984.

———. *Lincoln among His Friends: A Shelf of Intimate Memories.* Caldwell, ID: Caxton Printers, 1942.

INDEX

Lincoln, Mary Todd (wife), 26, 106
Lincoln, Nancy Hanks (mother), 5–6
Lincoln, Sarah (sister), 5
Lincoln, Sarah Johnston (stepmother), 6
Lincoln, Thomas (father), 5–8
Lincoln, Thomas ("Tad") (son), 63–4
Lincoln, William Wallace ("Willie")
    (son), 72
Lincoln-Douglas debates, 2, 28
Lincoln-McClellan relationship, 1–3, 33,
    36–8, 41, 50–1, 54–7, 59, 61–4,
    67, 72–4, 81–3, 86–92, 97–8, 103,
    110–11, 115–17, 120, 127, 133,
    166–74, 178, 183, 201, 217–18
  correspondence between, 72, 89–91, 98,
    103, 110–11, 115–17, 170–4,
    178, 183
  and Harpers Ferry engineering gaff, 73–4
  and Harrison's Landing letter, 116–17,
    127, 201
  and Henry Halleck, 120
  intellectual prowess, 2, 33, 37–8, 116–17
  and McClellan's losses, 110–11
  and meetings, 59, 73
  and military strategy, 61–4, 67, 74, 81–3,
    86–92, 97–8, 166–72
  and the railroad, 1–3
  and slavery, 36–7, 56–7
  and treason, 74
Linder, Usher F., 17
London Times, 38
Longstreet, James, 143, 145, 151, 159
Louisiana Purchase, 15, 21
Lowell, James Russell, 42, 91

Magruder, John B., 87–8
Malvern Hill, battle of, 112–14
Manassas, Virginia, 31, 48–9, 63, 66–7,
    70–1, 76, 82, 90, 92, 130–2, 138–9,
    181, 186, 214
  See First Manassas; Second Manassas
Mansfield, Joseph K. F., 41, 148, 150
Marcy, Randolph B., 18, 19, 23–4, 47,
    73, 123
Marmont, Auguste de (Marshal of
    France), 217
Maryland, 73, 109, 136–46, 150, 157–9,
    164, 166, 172, 189, 193, 210
Maryland campaign, 136–46
  map of, 136

Maury, Dabney Herndon, 10, 215
Mayo, Joseph, 79
McClellan, Elizabeth Brinton (mother),
    7–8, 190
McClellan, George (father), 7–8
McClellan, George Brinton ("Little Mac")
  academic success of, 10–11
  ancestry of, 8
  appearance of, 41
  birth of, 7
  boyhood, 2, 8
  character of, 7, 10–11
    See military character
  civilian pursuits, 1–3, 20, 22–3, 29–30
    See Illinois Central Railroad
  correspondence with wife, 24–5, 31, 33,
    37, 39, 42–5, 47–52, 55, 76, 87–92,
    98, 102–4, 115, 127–31, 137, 140,
    142, 157–8, 164–6, 173–5, 178,
    181–2, 185, 187, 205
  death of, 214–15
  education of, 8–10
    See United States Military Academy
    at West Point; University of
    Pennsylvania
  and the Emancipation Proclamation,
    163–4
  and faith, 35–6
  and fame, 31–3, 35, 44, 142
  and Halleck, 123–5, 128
  health of, 12, 60–1, 64, 99
    malaria, 12, 99
    typhoid, 60–1
  as innovator, 19–20
    See McClellan saddle
  marriage of, 23–5
    See Mary Ellen Marcy McClellan
  military education, 9–11
    See U.S. Military Academy at West
    Point
  and Philadelphia society, 2, 7–8, 36, 190
  and politics, *See* politics, and McClellan
  and Pope, 128
  refined character of, 1–2, 10–11, 19,
    24, 32, 36, 42–3, 218
  on slavery, 36–7, 56–7
  on Winfield Scott, 50, 54
  as writer, 18, 188
    See Lincoln-McClellan relationship;
    military appointments; military